Herbert Read

The Stream and the Source

Herbert Read
The Stream and the Source

GEORGE WOODCOCK

Montreal/New York/London

Black Rose Books No. MM364
National Library of Canada Cataloguing in Publication Data
Woodcock, George, 1912–1995
Herbert Read : the stream and the source / George Woodcock
Includes bibliographical references and index
ISBN 9781551643199 (bound) ISBN 9781551643182 (pbk.)

1. Read, Herbert, 1893–1968. 2. Poets, English–20th century–Biography.
3. Critics–Great Britain–Biography. I. Title. II. Title: Stream and the source.

PR6035.E24Z95 2008   828'.91209   C2008-902980-1

BLACK ROSE BOOKS

C.P. 1258   2250 Military Road   99 Wallis Road
Succ. Place du Parc Tonawanda, NY   London, E9 5LN
Montréal, H2X 4A7   14150   England
Canada   USA   UK

To order books:
In Canada: (phone) 18005659523 (fax) 18002219985
email: utpbooks@utpress.utoronto.ca
In the United States: (phone) 18002833572 (fax) 18003515073
In the UK & Europe: (phone) 44 (0)20 89864854 (fax) 44 (0)20 85335821
email: order@centralbooks.com
Our Web Site address: http://www.blackrosebooks.net
Printed in Canada

Contents

Herbert Read

The Stream and the Source

I

Introduction

I

This is not intended as a Life of Herbert Read. Read died only in 1968, and for many reasons it is not yet time for a definitive biography to be written. Furthermore, I was too close to Read in ideas and perhaps even in temperament to be able to take that stance in the middle distance which seems appropriate for the objective biographer.

I enjoyed for the last quarter of a century of his life the privilege of Read's friendship, and for a long time I was closely associated as a fellow anarchist in one facet of his many-sided life. I observed him also in many other contexts: in his role of publisher for example, for he was responsible for the appearance of several of my books; as a journalist, for he contributed to more than one journal in which I had an editorial hand; as an efficient administrator in the offices of the Industrial Design Unit where I would sometimes visit him; as a worker for civil liberties; as a private person entertaining one within the gloomy portals of the Reform Club or in more relaxed mood among his children and his friends—at his house in the Buckinghamshire countryside. And, while such occasions gave me memorable insights into Read's character, they also created a sense of personal closeness which, I know from experience, is detrimental to the biographer's proper detachment.

What I present, then, if it is a biography at all, must be described as an intellectual biography, an attempt to bring into a significant relationship all the many facets of Read's contribution to his time as an imaginative writer and a seminal thinker. The chart of a creative life that emerges will have a significance beyond its particular relevance as the study of a writer as personality, standing in the isolation that, in one way, is the destiny of us all. For few men, at least among writers in English, extended so far beyond themselves as Read did; few men reflected more sensitively and in a greater variety of ways the preoccupations of the age in which they lived, and it is hard to think of a writer who interpreted so thoroughly, in both creative and critical terms, what we now regard retrospectively as 'the modern movement'. 'Our poetic virtues must lie, if anywhere, in "the interpretation of the time",' he wrote in his last book, *The Cult of Sincerity*, 'and to interpret the time we must be part of it.'

But at no time was Read a lover of innovation for its own sake, and there was only a partial truth in remarks like that of Wyndham Lewis: 'Pundits such as my friend Read like to suggest that life is always just beginning and that they are in at the birth if not the actual midwife.' Read did indeed believe that life was always beginning, but every beginning, he realized, was in fact part of a process of becoming that sprang from primeval sources. Read as his anarchist writings declare was a revolutionary; he was also as his willingness to shock other anarchists by accepting a knighthood demonstrates— a conservative. His insistence on describing himself as a romantic and on finding romantic elements in modern painting and poetry, his deep interest in the art of children and primitive peoples, his attempt to discover through Jungian insights the origins in the prehistoric past of the symbols modern artists utilize, and his deep sense of personal origins that made him return to die in the valley where he was born: all these were signs of a view of existence and a view of art as existence's highest manifestation that in so far as it was not classical might justly be described as obstinately traditional.

Read himself was fully aware of the appearance of contradiction that on another occasion made Wyndham Lewis wonder at his bewildering duality, at the apparent divergence between the meticulous restraint of his own imaginative writing and 'what you so pertinaciously push in the visual arts'. Like Whitman and Proudhon, both of whom he admired, Read had no fear of appearing to contradict himself. He once remarked that 'it is perfectly possible, even normal, to live a life of contradictions'. He realized the complexity of the creative act, and he often claimed that the essential mutability of his own view of art and of life was adequately defined in the title of his first volume of criticism, *Reason and Romanticism*. 'Wisdom ...' he suggested in *Anarchy and Order*, 'is the needle which comes to rest between reason and romanticism (a word which comprises instinct, intuition, imagination, and fantasy).' To that paradoxical marriage of apparent opposites one might add other equally arresting and equally serious titles of Read's books: *Icon and Idea; Annals of Inno-*

cence and Experience; and—a title repeated in many contexts *The Contrary Experience.*

The deviation into the romantic, followed by the reconciliation with rationality, which Read described in the last paragraph of *The Contrary Experience* as 'the opposed terms of a progression', is a process that recurs constantly in his writings and in his life, and it leads him to the summingup of his intent and his achievement which forms the last paragraph of the same book:

> The very bases of reason, the perceptions of an unclouded intellect, are continually being contradicted by the creative fictions of the imagination, by a world of illusion no less real than the reality of our quick awareness. It is the function of art to reconcile the contradictions inherent to our experience; but obviously an art that keeps the canons of reason cannot make the necessary synthesis. Only an art that rises above conscious reality, only a transcendent or super-real art, is adequate. In this fact lies the final and inescapable justification of romantic art, and it is to the elucidation and illustration of this truth that I have devoted my intellectual energy in the years that are now spent.

But it would be far too drastic a simplification to chart Read's life and achievements by that rather relentless image of a pendulum swinging from side to side while ever moving forward which— thanks to Hegel and Marx the idea of the dialectic implants in one's mind. Read uses other images, and in particular that of the Heraclitean flux.

> That I can combine anarchism with order, a philosophy of strife with pacifism, an orderly life with romanticism and revolt in art and literature all this is inevitably scandalous to the conventional philosopher [he wrote in his eighth decade in *The Cult of Sincerity*]. This principle of flux, the Keatsian notion of 'negative capability', justifies everything I have written, every attack and defence. I hate all monolithic systems, all logical categories, all pretences to truth and inevitability. The sun is new every day.

And elsewhere in the same book he looks back and remarks, 'My life has been guided by chance, and that I accept as a natural condition.'

Yet one is aware and recurrent images in his work increase the awareness that Read's life had an underlying shape which is best evoked not by the conceptual metaphor of the dialectic, but rather by an image of archetypal nature: the mandala, the ancient symbol of the solar cycle, the shield of Achilles, the sacred circle that, apart from its uses in ritual and contemplation, unites within a single form the universe's many aspects, and parallels the karmic wheel of existence portrayed by Tibetan Buddhists. Read himself refers to the 'magic circle' of the mandala as 'the symbol of the self as a psychic unity', a symbol whose recognition in the art of infants was for him 'an apocalyptic experience'; he sees mandalas in general as 'images of wholeness and integration, inviting withdrawal from the chaotic distraction of daily perception, inducing contemplation and selfless meditation'.

Read's two most personal books, *The Green Child* and *The Contrary Experience*, can be seen as mandalas rendered in literary form, for their meanings are multiple, yet their designs are unified within circles of experience. In *The Green Child*, the fictional hero Olivero, and in *The Contrary Experience* that character's creator, Read himself, both leave the country of childhood and afterwards both return to seek regeneration. Olivero's earthly adventures end when he follows a stream that against all the laws of reason flows upward to its source in the Yorkshire moors; there he descends with the Green Child into the mysterious realm beneath the earth from which she has emerged. In his own return to Yorkshire, Read himself followed, metaphorically at least, a stream that ran towards its source, seeking in the place of his origin a renewal of that ecstatic contact with the natural world he had experienced in his childhood and recorded in *The Innocent Eye*. If I were to choose a passage from Read's writing as an epigraph to this book, it would probably be a paragraph from the last pages of *The Contrary Experience*, written at the age of seventy, after he had completed, by returning to a house a few miles away from the farm where he was born, the circle that began when he left the Vale of York at the age of ten.

> Spiritually the world is now one desert, and prophets are not honoured in it. But physically it still has a beautiful face, and if we could once learn to live with nature, if we could return like prodigal children to the contemplation of its beauty, there might be an end to our alienation and fear, a return to those virtues of delight which Blake called Mercy, Pity, Peace and Love.

In Read's poetry and criticism, in his theories of aesthetics and education and anarchism, this consciousness of the need for a return to the pristine and the natural is always present, balanced by a knowledge that the power we gain from such an Antaeuslike contact with earth is expressed nowhere more intensely than in the work of romantic art. For

> what we call romantic art passes beyond these laws and proclaims its freedom, its novelty, its uniqueness. This act of freedom cannot be justified, logically, any more than can an act of faith. It is an intuition, not merely of form and its plastic expression, but also of the paradox of a particular individual, a particular personality.

Obviously, not everything in Read's writings or in his career can be explained by reference to a single model like the mandala. One must allow, as Read insisted in the passage I have just quoted, that the act of freedom which produces a work of art is a leap outside any rationally conceived pattern. But so much of Read's work did in fact involve rational interpretation, explanation and argument, and so comparatively little was poetry, fiction or drama dependent on direct inspiration, that we may accept the mandala and the dialectic as complementary working patterns. The dialectic suggests the *mode* of progression by the interplay of reason and intuition. The mandala suggests the *direction* of progression, that of a circle returning on itself, like the world-encompassing snake, Uroboros.

The mandala also suggests Read's personal view of life in so far as it accepts a pattern and deviates from the general inclinations of our age. Most modern men have plotted their lives in the form of a trajectory of progress. The momentum may decline, the arc may fall, but when it reaches ground they are at least farther forward than they were in the beginning. They live by a concept of material advancement which Puritans share with Marxists. Read's concept, though he was in no ordinary sense a religious believer and claimed no mystical experience, was that of the spiritual man and also that of the anarchist who looks, not forward to some Utopia at the end of progress, but round a curve of intention that will lead men out of corruption into simplicity.

In planning this book I have adopted a loosely schematic pattern aimed at illuminating Read's works rather than narrating his life. But

I have been unable to depart entirely from the chronological mode, since Read, as he once admitted in a poem paraphrasing Krishna's advice to Arjuna before the mythical battle of Kurukshetra, lived in action. However strongly he may at times have desired it, he never followed the cloistered life of the artist dedicated solely to giving form to the products of his imagination, and it may be as many of his friends suspected that he was temperamentally unfitted for such an existence. In actuality he rarely gave himself time to write anything that was not occasional and in some way connected with the multifariously active life he had chosen as an impresario of the arts: museum worker, critic, teacher, lecturer, editor, publisher, journalist, organizer of institutes and societies. It was this life that gave him a position of importance in the artistic world of his time apart from the quality or influence of his writings. Towards the end of his life, in *The Contrary Experience*, Read noted sadly; 'The two experiences—to live in action and to live in meditation—are forever incompatible.' But the fact remains that Read did combine them, and to a great extent successfully, thereby giving a characteristic tone even to his most intimate writings. His poems were largely, in Roy Fuller's phrase, 'private images of public ills', many of them written in response to the two great wars that savaged the world in his lifetime, or to other political events that stirred his feelings, while *The Green Child*, though a complex novel, has another distinctive truth as a chart of its writer's inner journey.

Thus one cannot escape the image, mutable though it may be, of the man, in life and action, and I have no desire to do so. Nevertheless, since I have not assumed the duties of the biographer, I have not claimed his privileges. All I need to tell is what may elucidate the works I discuss, and therefore, in considering the more intimate aspects of Read's life, I have generally respected the reticences he observed in writing about himself. They are reticences I am personally inclined to share; there are similarities between Yorkshire taciturnity and Salopian pride.

It is because Read's actions cannot be neglected that I have presented as the second part of this opening chapter a brief biography as a kind of chart to assist those who read the remaining chapters; my own recollections of him I have included mainly in the chapter where they appear most illuminating that on his career as an anarchist. In arranging the major body of the book I have tried to bear in mind a cautionary remark Read once made regarding William Morris. 'It is customary to consider Morris in his threefold aspect as poet, craftsman and socialist. In this way we break down the fundamental unity of the man.' In considering Read I have followed a scheme that for me has been illuminating, treating first his imaginative writing as it proceeds by levels of indirection from autobiography to fiction to poetry; I have then considered him as the critic of poetry, the critic of visual arts, and the aesthetic philosopher, and this has led through his ethical conclusions to his anarchism and his theories of education, and so to the last integrating chapter. But I am conscious that these chapters, like Read's life, form a circle rather than a progression, related to a centre rather than a goal, and that it would have been equally valid to have begun with the criticism or the political writings and have ended with the poetry. And here, as I shall suggest, we may find the wisdom by which, given his peculiar patterns of thought, Read so carefully evaded a schematic philosophy and so rarely wrote books dominated by linear patterns of reasoning. There are many threads that unite Read's books in ways that are neither linear nor circular, and at the centre of every knot one finds the fact that his philosophy—aesthetic or libertarian according to its particular manifestation—sets its roots always in biological reality, in the 'natural conditions of existence' by means of which, as Read once remarked, a man 'can give an answer to most of the problems of life'. For behind all Read has to tell us of poetry and art there is the consciousness that this would be pointless if it did not arouse in man the sense of an inner goal which in the end Read can only state in moral terms; for the devious purpose of art, while it is certainly not to inculcate moral lessons, is nevertheless to foster a moral consciousness and a power to face and to nullify the apparent absurdity of existence. Therefore, as we study the variety of Read's life and achievement, of his creations and his thoughts, let us bear in mind always his simple statement of faith.

> When we cast out the fear of death and renounce any desire to dominate the least of our fellow-men, then we can live in peace and happiness. And that is the final aim: neither to believe, nor suffer, nor renounce; but to accept, to enjoy, to realize the anarchy of life in the midst of the order of being. (*Anarchy and Order*.)

2

In 1893 a few miles from Stonegrave, where he died, Herbert Read
was born in a modest stone farmhouse named Muscoates. It lies—for
it is still in existence and occupied in the flat alluvial land of the Vale
of York; the nearest towns, almost equally distant, are Kirkbymoor-
side and Helmsley. Topographically, this is border country, for only
a few miles to the north the land begins to rise and the lush narrow
dales, with their luxuriant woodland, strike—as Read described
them like green rays into the purple darkness of the Moors'. The
dales and the moors were the remoter background of Read's childhood. His father was a farmer of the plains who grew wheat, grazed
cattle and bred hunters, but the old Saxon church which the family
attended lay at the beginning of Kirkdale. Beside the becks that ran
down this and other dales from the moors above, his father's and
mother's families both owned water-mills which in his childhood
were still in full operation.

Even in the 1890's, it was for England a setting of unusual rustic-
ity. By car, on modern highways, Muscoates today is a mere hour's
drive from York; even the isolated mills of Bransdale, in Read's childhood accessible only by rough tracks over the moor, are served now
that they are deserted ruins by the network of asphalt highways. But
as boys Read and his brothers were hardly aware of that outside
world which has now turned the North Riding into a weekend play-
ground for the nearby cities; visitors from outside were rare, and the
children seldom went away from the farm in its basin of isolation
between the wolds and the moors. This was the last decade of the
nineteenth century and Read's early memories included the bonfires
lit to celebrate the relief of Ladysmith and Mafeking. He lived in a
pre-mechanical seclusion that had already become exceptional in an
England whose Industrial Revolution was already generations old,
for the only machine he remembered from those years of his childhood was the traction engine which every autumn brought the
threshing outfit into the stackyard. That lost idyllic countryside
which the Georgian poets vainly went out of the towns to rediscover,
Read saw with childhood's innocent eye, and in many ways the memory of it affected his writing to the end.

The Reads had been farmers and millers as far back as the records
show; so had the Strickland family to which his mother Eliza
belonged, and both families regarded themselves as superior to the

ordinary yeomen of the district. Rural memories are long, and when
I went to the district in 1970, nearly sixty years after Read's father,
who was also named Herbert Edward, had died and the family had
left Muscoates, I heard it said that 'the Reads were snobs'. They
employed a governess, they rode to hounds, and, like many better-off
farmers of the North, they shared the Scottish respect for education,
so that at least one son in each generation went to Cambridge. The
same tradition persisted among the Stricklands; on the stone walls of
one of the mills they owned in Bransdale one can still see the texts in
Greek and Hebrew which Emmanuel Strickland, a remote uncle of
Herbert Read, carved in 1837, after his return from Cambridge,
when he was serving as curate at the nearby village of Ingleby Green-
how. But Read's father, that hard-working farmer, was a lightly read
man, and the love of books, which came to Read when he was still a
child at Muscoates, was unfostered by any of his family; yet by the
time he was ten and his father died, it had become a passion beyond
life's curing.

That death in 1903 brought a traumatic break in Read's existence.
The farm was sold. He and his brothers were taken to an environment
as far removed from the rural setting as one could possibly imagine,
for they were admitted to Crossley's School, a kind of nonconformist
version of Christ's Hospital, half orphanage, half boarding-school,
which stood on the bare moors outside Halifax. There, in an immense
stone building, living in a crowd of boys under Spartanly strict conditions, Read spent the most unhappy five years of his life.

> From fields and hedges and the wide open spaces of the moors; from the
> natural companionship of animals and all the mutations of farm life, I
> had passed into a confined world of stone walls, smoky skies, and two
> hundred unknown and apparently unsympathetic strangers.

Since the boys were allowed out of the school grounds only on Sun-
days, when they marched in crocodile formation to one of the local
dissenting chapels, the regime in this Calvinist establishment was
obviously even stricter than that of ordinary English public schools;
it shared with them a fanatical emphasis on sports and a theory that
boys will develop character only if they are badly fed and uncomfort-
ably housed.

Read's sense of alienation from the idyllic life of Muscoates lasted his whole school career. He found consolation in omnivorous

reading and by the age of thirteen he was already writing for a sur-
reptitiously produced school magazine. The one benefit his teachers
conferred was to encourage him in writing essays ('the only subject
in which I displayed any exceptional talent'); to them, he later
acknowledged, he owed his first perceptions of literary form and
structure. Even when he became a writer, the essay remained his
favourite form; his very poems would often take on the shape of
compact, obliquely pointed essays.

Crossley's School sent its pupils out into the world at the age of
fifteen. Read then moved to Leeds, where his mother was living, and
became a clerk in the local Savings Bank. Here was the immediate
broadening of experience. Carrying the cash-bags on foot from
branch to branch he came to learn from day to day the life and scape
of an industrial city; the other face of England, turned away from the
rural remoteness of the Vale of York. Most of the bank's customers
were thrifty working people, and so he made his first acquaintance
with the classes, so different from the farmers and millers and
labourers of the North Riding, that industry had created. And the
bank's hours of business for work usually ended by four in the after-
noon gave him leisure for reading, now vastly extended by the avail-
ability of a public library, and led him to dream of a better career than
provincial banking. He thought of medicine, but a doctor cousin persuaded him that he was temperamentally unsuited; he then thought
of law. He became politically conscious, adopting his father's fervent
conservatism and devouring the novels of Disraeli, which opened the
way to authors more unsettling. This Tory interlude should be
remembered, for it reflected a strain of aristocratic feeling that was to
remain with Read throughout his life and to shape his personal
vision of anarchism. Most important, at the age of seventeen he
began to write poems, and he was encouraged in this activity by a
Quaker tailor with a passion for literature to whom his brother had
been apprenticed. This man, completely unrelated, bore the same
name as Read's brother, and it was to this William P. Read that in
1926 Herbert dedicated his first *Collected Poems;* the dedication was
deserved, for the older man not only read Read's verses with a kind
but sometimes critical eye, but also introduced him to many of the
English poets, classic and modern, and revealed to him the riches of
continental European literature, of writers like Ibsen and Chekhov,
like Turgenev and Dostoevsky.

Read's relatives wished him to remain a banker or to acquire some easily accessible profession like that of solicitor, but he was resolved as the eldest son to follow the family tradition of attending a university. Cambridge was financially beyond possibility, but by living at home and borrowing money from a dour sheep-farming uncle, Read was able to attend the recently founded University of Leeds. Rejecting the ordinary academic discipline to which his fellow undergraduates submitted in the hope of ensuring their careers, he extended the process of self-education he had already begun in childhood. For the books that influenced him most were not those in the curricula he followed or those discussed in the lectures he sporadically attended, but the works of writers like Nietzsche which he found in the university library and read to the detriment of the studies that might have led towards a degree. He never fitted easily into the undergraduate community, though he became an ardent member of the debating society, and he developed as an autodidactic rather than an academic scholar, a course continued to the end of his life thanks to an extraordinary ability to absorb quickly the essence of profound and difficult books. During the years between 1912 and 1914 Nietzsche influenced him more decisively than any other writer but Blake, and shortly after Nietzsche he came to Marx and Sorel, to Ruskin and Morris and Edward Carpenter, and to the libertarian writers who by 1917 had completed his conversion to anarchism.

By this time Read had already been in the army for three years. Before the war started he had considered himself a pacifist, but in those days before the great wars young men did not always work out carefully the active implications of such beliefs, and Read was at the same time a member of the Leeds University Officers' Training Corps. When the war broke out he was in camp and he automatically became an officer cadet. He accepted his situation with a Nietzschean sense of challenge and adventure. In January 1915 he was commissioned in the Green Howards, and shortly afterwards he left for France. For Read, as for many others, the war was a time of moral testing. He found himself more courageous, and more able to adapt to the hard and boring life of the trenches, than he had expected, and he did not allow military life to interfere with the literary vocation he had now decided he must follow. He always went into the trenches with a miniature library, and he went through his most harrowing experiences in the retreat from the Somme in 1918 with a copy of

Walden in his pocket. He had continued to write verse including two
vanished plays in North Riding dialect during his uncompleted period
at the University, and now, in the army, he was publishing his poems.
In 1915 his first small book of verse, *Songs of Chaos*, appeared, and
in the same year others of his poems were published in *The Egoist*, his
first step towards acceptance in modernist literary circles. Converted
temporarily to Guild Socialism, he wrote in the *New Age* and *The
Guildsman*. His interest in the visual arts began immediately before
the war, and through the Leeds Arts Club he gained the friendship of
artists like Frank Rutter and Jacob Kramer. Under their influence he
began to paint, and taking a sketchbook into the trenches with him,
he became temporarily a disciple of the Futurists, exhibiting some of
his drawings in 1917. He did not continue painting for long, but the
discussions on the nature of art which he conducted with Rutter and
Kramer were eventually to bear splendid fruit in his art criticism. In
1917 Rutter and Read started an avant-garde magazine, *Art and Letters*. Read had spent most of 1916 in England recovering from a
wound, but at this time he was in France and he did not return until
the middle of 1918 after the retreat from the Somme, when he joined
the Tees Garrison and encountered Ford Madox Ford. Then, in one
memorable week in October 1918, he visited London and found that
Art and Letters had established him as a young writer worth cultivating. One after the other in that short period he met the men who were
to become his friends and associates, as leaders of the post-war
movement in English literature. They included Ezra Pound and T. S.
Eliot, Wyndham Lewis and Richard Aldington, the Sitwell brothers
and F. S. Flint, the spokesman of imagism.

Read was one of the fortunate men of his generation in that he
survived a great deal of front-line fighting, and emerged from the war
strengthened as a writer, though the horror of the experience never
left him. As a theme, war recurred constantly in his poetry; it helped
to shape his political and social thought, and even his views on art
which, as he came to believe, held the lost secret of peace and sanity.

Rather surprisingly, Read had toyed with the idea of taking a regular commission in the army, but instead 'this naked warrior ...
became a civil servant,' a curious decision for one who thought himself an anarchist, and one he was soon to regret. In 1919 he joined the
Ministry of Labour, and some months later he was transferred to the
Treasury, where he rose rapidly to the demanding position of Private
Secretary. Read was an able organizer, as he showed in many direc-

tions later in life. 'The business of coordinating details, presenting summaries, writing minutes and memoranda, though I never saw it as an end in life, never seemed irksome or difficult for me; it was simply part of one's literary aptitude.' He might easily have made a distinguished career in the public service if he had not found his attention divided between the writing which he did conscientiously every night, and the mechanically bureaucratic work which he came to detest mainly because it exhausted his mental energies, and made writing more difficult.

His release came by the chance that so often looks like the intervention of destiny. Papers relating to a vacancy for an Assistant Keeper in the Victoria and Albert Museum passed through his hands at the Treasury. He asked for and gained the post, considerably impoverishing himself by the decision, but in compensation acquiring a congenial employment that determined his future career.

By the time he joined the Victoria and Albert, he was contributing to Wyndham Lewis's *Tyro*, and had begun the association as an essayist and reviewer with Eliot's *Criterion* that lasted through the journal's lifetime. In 1923 Read published his first collection of mature poems, *Mutations of the Phoenix*, and 1924 his first book in prose, which was also his first book on the visual arts: *English Pottery*, written jointly with Bernard Rackham. It reflected the work in which he specialized at the Museum, and was followed by books on *English Stained Glass* (1926) and *Staffordshire Pottery Figures* (1929).

By the later Twenties Read was emerging as a respected literary critic with works like *Reason and Romanticism* (1926), *Phases of English Poetry* (1928) and *The Sense of Glory* (1929). Partly as a result of such books and partly through T. S. Eliot's intervention—he attracted the attention of academic scholars, and during the winter of 1929–30 he delivered at Cambridge the Clark Lectures on Wordsworth.

In 1930 Read began to publish in *The Listener* the regular commentaries on art particularly modern and primitive art which he continued to contribute for many years, until they became an institution in the British art world. Out of his early *Listener* essays he compiled his first volume of art criticism beyond his special field of ceramics, *The Meaning of Art* (1930). It was followed rapidly by a series of works on specific aspects of the contemporary visual arts Art *Now* (1933), *Art and Industry* (1934), *Art and Society* (1937)—which became classics in their field and established Read in the place of

Roger Fry, who died in 1934, as the leading British authority on contemporary art.

Read's success as a critic led in 1931 to his appointment as Watson Gordon Professor of Fine Arts at Edinburgh University; in the following year Leeds University, where he had not remained long enough to gain an ordinary degree, made him an honorary Doctor of Letters. In 1933, Read resigned his Professorship at Edinburgh, and returned to London, where he assumed the editorship of the *Burlington Magazine*; to augment his scanty salary he settled into a life of literary journalism and reading for publishers, especially Faber and Faber, where Eliot was a director. He did not return immediately to Broom House, the home at Seer Green near Beaconsfield which he had designed and occupied In 1927,

> By an oak tree on an acre of wild land
> Its walls white against the beechwood
> Its roof of Norfolk reed and sedge.

Instead he went to live until 1938 in Parkhill Road on the southern side of Hampstead, whose studios played an important role in the modern movement in British art. Henry Moore, Barbara Hepworth, Ben Nicholson and Paul Nash were all working there in the 1930's, and Read was deeply associated with them. When they formed a *cénacle* with the title of Unit One, it was Read who edited and introduced their manifesto. His abiding interest in their work was later shown by the separate studies he wrote on three of them, Paul Nash, Ben Nicholson and Henry Moore. His links with these artists represented the essentially English aspect of his nature; he refused to consider himself British and had a healthy resentment of the Scots, whom he accused of stealing the ballad literature of the North country. He was closest of all to his fellow Yorkshireman, Henry Moore, finding in Moore's work a projection into sculptural form of intuitions which they shared as men of the dales and fells; he was to write three books on Moore, including a full-length biography.

Yet, throughout the 1930's, and thereafter, Read was alive to the significant movements in continental Europe. The constructivism of Gabo and Pevsner, Kandinsky's abstractionism and Klee's symbolic expressionism, all appealed to him, and he became especially involved with the successors to the Dadaists, both those who remained individual rebels like Hans Arp, and those who marched behind

André Breton in the flamboyant orthodoxy of the Surrealist movement. Read was actively involved in the Surrealist exhibition which caused a minor scandal in the London of 1936, and wrote, as an introduction to the volume of writings accompanying the show (entitled *Surrealism*), an essay which revealed a liaison in his own mind between surrealism and the romanticism to which he had always adhered. But he was as little amenable to organized surrealism as he would later be to organized anarchism: in 1939 he was declared a heretic and expelled from the British Surrealist Group. Nevertheless, under the name of *superrealism*, he incorporated into his general philosophy of art a strong element of surrealist thought, and particularly the surrealist stress on the spontaneous impulse.

In the 1930's the Surrealists were ideologically Marxist, though they were disowned by Stalinist orthodoxy. Read had read Marx with more sympathy than most anarchists, but he was unwilling to commit himself to so patently authoritarian a doctrine as the Leninist variety of Marxism. Yet as soon as his resignation from the Civil Service in 1931 allowed him to speak freely on political matters, he took up his position on the Left, manifesting once again the anarchist outlook which he had developed during the years up to 1917. In 1935 he published a pamphlet, *Essential Communism*, putting forward an attitude to the organization of society and of property virtually identical with that of Kropotkin. This was his first substantial literary venture into the field of political thought; it was followed by volumes which more explicitly declared his libertarian allegiances: *Poetry and Anarchism* (1938), *The Philosophy of Anarchism* (1940), *The Politics of the Unpolitical* (1943) and *Existentialism, Marxism and Anarchism* (1949). During and after the Spanish Civil War, Read became loosely associated with anarchist propaganda groups in Britain which ran papers like *Spain and the World*, *Revolt*, *War Commentary* and *Freedom*; he wrote sporadically for these periodicals, but more regularly for *Now*, which was nearer to his own point of view as an anarchist who was also an artist. Yet his only formal allegiance was to the Freedom Defence Committee, a civil-libertarian group composed of individuals from all groups of the independent Left. During the 1950's his interest in political change became passive, and his links with the orthodox anarchists lapsed after he accepted a knighthood in 1953. His collection of libertarian writings, *Anarchy and Order*, though it was published in 1954, consisted entirely of material written well before the end of the 1940's.

Read's broadening artistic interests during the 1930's, and the revival at the same time of his political interests, did not bring about a diminution of his concern for literature or of his urge to write imaginatively. To that decade indeed belong the finest of his prose works: his novel *The Green Child* (1935) and his first autobiographical sketch, *The Innocent Eye* (1933). By 1940 he had expanded *The Innocent Eye* beyond childhood into *Annals of Innocence and Experience*, the latter part of which is an apologia for his career as a writer, an art critic and an anarchist. He also wrote in this decade many of the poems collected in *Poems 1914–34* (1935), as well as *Thirty-five Poems* (1940) and the essays forming *In Defence of Shelley* (1936), which extended his reputation as one of the most perceptive critics of the Romantics.

Read had long been connected peripherally with the publishing world, as an adviser to Faber & Faber, Heinemann and Macmillan, and in 1939 he finally decided to abandon the ill-paying editorship of the *Burlington Magazine*, and to join Routledge & Kegan Paul as a director. He held the position—not always happily—for a quarter of a century. He was responsible for bringing out the early books of many younger poets, particularly, in the 1940's, those who could be classed as neo-Romantic; he persuaded his partners to become more daring in their choice of texts in the political and social sciences; he fostered and directed the massive project of translating into English and publishing the collected works of C. G. Jung.

The last was almost as a task of piety, for Read had long been impressed by the light which psychoanalytical theory had thrown on critical problems in literature and the visual arts. His interest was manifested as early as 1925 in the essay entitled 'Psychoanalysis and the Critic' which he published in *The Criterion*, and the theories of the psychoanalysts became an integral part of the intellectual apparatus with which he considered the work of a poet or painter. Until the later 1930's, he was most influenced by Freud, but later he found Jung's massive scholarship and his theories of the collective unconscious more stimulating and suggestive. His own role as general editor of the English translation of Jung's works brought him into a warm personal association with the Swiss psychoanalyst and mythologist that lasted until Jung's death.

World War II, whose inevitability Read accepted without abandoning his critical standpoint as an anarchist and a quasi- pacifist, did not interfere greatly with the variety or the intensiveness of his activities. The emotions aroused by the outbreak of a second great conflict in his lifetime were responsible for some of his best poetry, collected in *A World Within a War* (1943). In 1943 he became the first director of the Industrial Design Unit, which was based on ideas adumbrated in *Art and Industry*, and applied to its formation the organizational talents he had developed in the Civil Service. He became deeply interested in children's art, organizing a series of exhibitions which travelled under the auspices of the British Council first to the United States and later, after 1945, to the continent of Europe. Out of this interest emerged his most influential book, *Education Through Art* (1943), which expanded his reputation beyond the circles of art and literature into the far wider field of educational theory and practice. It led to the foundation, as a subsidiary UNESCO organization, of the International Society for Education through Art, through which Read's theories of aesthetic education became for a while the gospel of thousands of teachers in many countries. Read himself saw in *Education Through Art* an aspect most of his readers missed: he regarded the idea of awakening men to the sense of freedom by educational rather than by political means as his most original contribution to anarchist theory.

After the war, Read's life changed radically, and for almost two decades he dedicated much of his time to the role of the wandering teacher, lecturing on art, literature and education in all the five continents, and in countries as far apart and as different in culture as Germany and Australia, Argentina and Japan. Each year he took an active part in that gathering of the Jungian élite, the Eranos Tagung, at Ascona; he was always in Venice for the Biennale; he conducted seminars at Princeton and Wesleyan Universities, delivered the Charles Eliot Norton Lectures at Harvard, taught in the Kenyon School of English, held the Mellon Lectureship at the National Gallery of Art in Washington, and took part in the founding ceremonies of UNESCO in Paris. Often he complained that the time he should have devoted to poetry, or drama, or another novel, was consumed by such activities, and he lamented the fragmentation of his life, but he seems to have been driven by a compulsion to spread his ideas, a missionary urge that would not let him rest. This often led his friends to turn a sceptical ear to his lamentations. They felt that if he followed it so assiduously this must indeed be the life he desired. They were right; but so was Read, and the conflict between the two urges that warred within him—those of the teacher and the creator— was often excruciating.

Read's travels hardly diminished his activities in England. He still worked as a publisher; he gave radio talks and prepared radio documentaries; he still wrote for many periodicals, and during the 1950's he published several important books, largely composed of the edited scripts of the lectures he had given on his travels. They included, in the visual arts, *The Philosophy of Modern Art* (1952) and *The Art of Sculpture* (1956), in literature his final statements on romanticism embodied in *The True Voice of Feeling* (1952), and in the more general fields of aesthetic philosophy those crucial works, *Icon and Idea* (1953) and *The Forms of Things Unknown* (1960). To this period also belongs his fine poetic dialogue, *Moon's Farm* (1955). In 1947 he had become the chairman of the Institute of Contemporary Arts, which he was largely instrumental in organizing, and during the 1950's he was involved in setting up the British Society of Aesthetics.

Yet there was a balancing factor at work, for the period when Read went on his farthest travels was also the period when he prepared his final return to Yorkshire. In 1949 he bought Stonegrave House, from which he made his forays into London and his expeditions into the wider world. Yet it was not until 1964 that, by abandoning his work as a publisher, he was able finally to live most of his time in Yorkshire, and thus to complete the circle of his life.

During the 1950's Read was inactive politically largely because his acceptance of a knighthood led to ostracism by the orthodox anarchists. At the beginning of the 1960's, however, he found a cause in the Campaign for Nucleur Disarmament and for the first time in his life he took part in street demonstrations; he was also, until he disagreed on questions of tactics, a member of the radical pacifist Committee of 100. During his last years he wrote several essays reassessing his theories of anarchism, which were included in his final book, *The Cult of Sincerity* (1968).

In 1964 Read fought his first bout with the sickness that was to kill him, when he appeared to recover from cancer of the tongue. Freed of publishing and less inclined to travel, he worked in his eighth decade, with a strong sense of the shortness of time, on his last books. Some were final collections of essays and lectures: *The Origins of Form in Art* (1965) and *Art and Alienation* (1967). Others were individual studies, written out of love and empathy, of artists to whom he had long felt close; they were Henry Moore and Hans Arp. It is significant of Read's later interests that both were sculptors.

Like so much of his life, Read's last public act took the form of a quest. He was invited to take part in the Cultural Congress to be held in Havana in January 1968. 'I feel I want to be active again,' he told the poet Kathleen Raine when he received the invitation. 'I don't mean working any harder than I do, but just in the sense of accepting challenges. Cuba is a challenge—to see what kind of a new world they are making. It cannot be worse than ours and may be much better.' He had gone to China in 1959 with the same hope, and had come back with the thought that in the communes he had seen something near to anarchism in action. In Havana he delivered his last lecture. It dealt with a subject he had often discussed before, the relationship between the artist and his society, and it ended with a statement that summarized as effectively as any single sentence can do the guiding attitude of Read's career. 'There can be no great art in the future until we have achieved social unity and social justice, and until a free and joyous activity has replaced the devitalizing tyranny of the machine.'

He returned to face the renewed attacks of cancer. At first the treatment seemed successful; by the spring it was obvious that he was doomed. He died on the 12th June 1968, in his seventy-sixth year. He was buried near to his parents in the churchyard of Kirkdale where he had been baptized. The circle of existence was closed, the mandala completed.

2

The Innocent Eye

It was a book of criticism that Read entitled *The Sense of Glory*; if there is any quality that unites his work, in every field, it is this. The glory of the world perceived through a child's eye and later through the awakening mind of a creative artist permeates his autobiographical writings and gives a peculiar lambent quality to his poetry and his rare works of fiction. It extends into his critical writings, where he is seeking always that special fire of inspiration which liberates man from the mere imitation of the laws of nature, and it inspires his anarchism, that doctrine of man glorified by freedom. It even extends into his organizational efforts, into the centres and societies he created, into the great lecturing journeys, all intended to stir in men the aesthetic sense that would somehow preserve in them the visionary gleam which Read detected in the art of children as Wordsworth had detected it in the perceptions of childhood, the gleam Wordsworth too had associated with glory. The causes Read supported, the artists whose work he loved, his own work in all its variety, were emanations of that wonder at life of which he had been aware from the moment when he passed out of childhood, where it had been instinctive and therefore unperceived, into adolescence. Then, as he tells us, his active imagination stirred in great though indefinite ambitions, and 'threw upon the cloudy future an infinite ray in which there could always be seen, like a silver knight on a white steed, this unreal figure which was myself, riding to quixotic combats, attaining a blinding and indefinable glory'.

Life, which so ironically fulfils our ambitions, made sure that Read became a knight in actuality, and on the stone that was raised over his grave in the shadow of Kirkdale's fir-trees he is described as 'Knight, Poet, Anarchist'. If by knight we mean man imbued by the sense of glory, and by anarchist a man imbued by the sense of freedom, the description is true. But it is necessary also to observe the appropriateness of the centrality of the poet. For it was as a poet that Read saw himself always, and where the poetic sensibility continues through a whole lifetime, no matter how small the actual output of works that may technically be called poems, the consequent sense of vocation wields an incalculable influence on the rest of a man's work and even over his way of life. In the case of Read, one can be more precise than this, for the significant core of his work, the centre of the mandala, as it were, is contained in three of the many volumes he produced: the autobiographical fragments contained in *The Contrary Experience*, the final version (1966) of the *Collected Poems*, and *The Green Child*.

In those books one discovers the purest emanations of his sense of glory. His organizational activities, it already appears, have been ephemeral in their effects, and much of his critical writing—as distinct from his essays in aesthetic philosophy—was avowedly occasional in intent and temporary in impact, though even here one is aware that the nearer to poetry the work is, the more substantial and durable it appears. I shall suggest that Read's essays on the romantic poets combine a degree of intuitive apprehension with a quality of rational discourse which make them superior to most of his criticism of the visual arts, and that it is not accidental that the best of his writings on the politics of the unpolitical should have been *Poetry and Anarchism*. Again, the closer the link with the poetic function, the greater the illumination which the work appears to reflect.

It is because of this view of the centrality of Read's poetic works, using that term in its original Greek sense of creation and applying it to examples of imaginary prose as well as of verse, that I begin with the three volumes I have named, and proceed in a series determined by levels of indirection. First, in various small works embodied in *The Contrary Experience*, Read is presenting what is already an intensely subjective reconstruction of the events which I have narrated objectively in the last chapter. Such narratives as *The Innocent Eye*, *In Retreat* and 'The Raid' are not mere narratives, but experiences transformed into formal patterns that stir the imagination and begin to take on the autonomous life of artifacts. Still, in these experiences, the author is the recognizable centre, and they can be regarded as autobiographies modified by the poet's shaping sensibility.

The Green Child, on the other hand, is poetic fiction modified by autobiography. As I have suggested, it shows striking parallels in form and even in content with *The Contrary Experience*. Both are

cyclic narratives in which the hero discovers that the point of departure and the point of return are the same: in which, as Jung said to
Read after reading *The Green Child* with 'a rumbling in the depths
that kept me awake all night', 'you discover ... that the thing you
really meant had been left behind in your native village'. Jung had no
doubt at all that the unconscious autobiographical element in *The
Green Child* was even greater than the conscious, and he was probably right. Nevertheless, the relationship between *The Green Child*
and Read's own experience is substantially less direct than in the case
of *The Contrary Experience*. Similarly, there is a further stage in
unconscious transformation and in conscious shaping from *The
Green Child* to the poems, and it is this progression into formal
autonomy and emotional concentration that I shall observe in dealing with the three books. The present chapter will be concerned with
the prose works, and the next with the poems.

Before considering separately the autobiographies and the novel,
one should observe certain formal characteristics that mark Read's
approach in all these works. In *Annals of Innocence and Experience*
he describes how 'circumstances' dictated the forms he should choose
for his writings. He had originally, during World War I when he was
considering his career, thought of becoming a novelist in the manner
of Henry James, and was influenced in this ambition by Ford Madox
Ford. But while Ford was inclined to think of the novel as the only
viable literary form in our age, to which every other genre should be
approximated (as he tended to approximate even his professedly factual memoirs), Read showed a greater formal flexibility.

> My view was rather that the man, the person, came first; and that it was
> immaterial in what particular form he expressed himself—poem, novel,
> essay, metaphysics or criticism—as long as he remained true to himself
> and to aesthetic principles. The choice of form had to be determined by
> his circumstances. (*Annals of Innocence and Experience.*)

Read, in other words, was a true Man of Letters, in the sense understood in France and other European countries, of a writer who refuses to accept a hierarchy of forms, but is willing to turn his talents to
any use that does not compromise his integrity.

Read goes on at this point to say that his choice was determined
by his decision to join the civil service and by the fact that this would
leave him insufficient time for a form so elaborate as the novel. He

therefore made up his mind to limit himself to poetry and the critical essay.

> The poem, according to my belief and practice, would come when it would: its generation being a mystery of the unconscious, no precautions that I could take would increase my product by one line. ... The critical essay is different. One can accumulate notes and ideas over three or four weeks, in trains and buses no less than in the blessed evening hours; and then, when the moment is ripe, a week-end will suffice for the first draft—did suffice for me. Most of my books were built up in this manner essay by essay. An exception, like *The Green Child*, owes its existence to an unexpected break in the routine; this book I am writing now, to another. (*Annals of Innocence and Experience*.)

One may doubt whether the form which Read's writing took was so completely a matter of circumstance and choice as he has suggested. Determined novelists have managed to write under the most difficult conditions, without continuous time to spare or even moderate privacy, while it is unlikely, given the character of Read's actual writing, that he would ever have made a novelist in the Jamesian sense.

I suggest rather that in the discontinuous mosaic of the book of essays he had discovered a form that accorded with his temperament and with his romantic rejection of classic structuralism. When one considers Read's books in general, one realizes that he very rarely follows a linear pattern. Like the symbolists, like Joyce, he was inclined to juxtapose various treatments of an idea rather than to insist on a logical continuity. Only one of his works of literary criticism, *Wordsworth*, presents a truly linear form, and that is a special case, since Read is telling a literary detective story. Similarly, in the field of the visual arts, the only work that has a strong linear continuity, going on from argument to argument, is *Education Through Art*, written in great part with the intent of inspiring reforms in the educational system. Elsewhere, Read has preferred the group of essays that circle around a central point of interest, rather than the series of chapters that follow from one to the other.

As the most cursory examination shows, neither *The Green Child* nor *The Contrary Experience* falls outside this pattern. *Annals of Innocence and Experience*, the original core of *The Contrary Experience*, was a compilation, consisting of *The Innocent Eye*, originally published in 1933, the war narrative *In Retreat*, which had appeared in 1925, its companion piece 'The Raid', printed in *The Criterion* in 1927, and a number of other chapters written in 1939 to make the work into a comprehensive autobiographical record. When Read came to complete his autobiography as *The Contrary Experience* in 1962, he took this material originally published between 1925 and 1940, and added to it not only a group of discontinuous chapters written after his return to Stonegrave in 1949, but also a 'War Diary' which was actually a series of letters written between 1915 and 1918 to a girl who had been a fellow student at Leeds University.

The Green Child, admittedly, is not a compilation of materials published at various times. Yet, though Read claims to have written the novel during a six weeks' holiday in the summer of 1934, there is no doubt that the idea of writing something around the traditional story of the Green Children had been in his mind ever since he had included a version of the original tale as an example in *English Prose Style* in 1928. One can assume that he had thought about the various aspects of the story for some time, and that when he came to write it he linked together somewhat tenuously, by means of common characters, a group of originally unrelated plots. For the three sections into which *The Green Child* falls are not merely chronologically discontinuous; they are in fact works in three different genres.

More than twenty years ago, in Henry Treece's symposium entitled *Herbert Read*, Robert Melville presented an able critique of the first third of the book, considered as a complete work; this is the section dealing with the return of Olivero from distant lands to encounter the Green Child, Sally, whose arrival in the village had taken place on the very day of his departure and had haunted him since; it includes the fight between Olivero and Kneeshaw, the miller who had taken the Green Child in unconsummated marriage, and ends after Kneeshaw's death with Olivero and the Green Child ascending the reverse flow of the stream and stepping into the whirlpool where it disappears. As Melville points out, this can be interpreted as a self-contained work terminated by a voluntary drowning. It could, one might add, very easily stand on its own as a work in the genre of the sophisticated fairy tale used often in English fiction during the years between the wars; David Garnett's *Lady into Fox* and the novels of T. F. Powys immediately come to mind.

Melville's further comments assess the relationship of this part of *The Green Child* to the remaining sections of the book:

Strictly speaking, the title of the novel belongs only to this section. Sally, the Green Child, does not appear at all in the second part, which is the story of Olivero's life before their meeting, and in the third part her name is changed to Siloën and attached to one of the slightly nauseating inhabitants of a subterranean world: these two sections, the story of President Olivero and the study of the green people, are descriptions of Utopias— a patronizing Utopia for the masses and a puritanical, quasi-intellectual one for individuals. It seems probable that the two distinct Oliveros who appear in them are projections of that Silver Knight who figures in Read's adolescent day-dreams ... and represent two experimentally isolated aspects of the personality of their creator; so the stories in which they appear could be considered as parts of an uncentred composition (having a not too remote analogy in Paul Klee's Le Temps et les Plantes), as studies of coexistent aspects of Olivero artificially developed as successive sections, if only the story which gives the book its title were equally unqualified by complex emotional experience. As it is, although they have been attached to this story with admirable ingenuity, the attachment has no formal necessity.

What Melville correctly perceives is the structural discontinuity between the various parts of The Green Child, and the possibility of their separate origins in the novelist's imagination. However, I would disagree with him in assigning greater complexity or importance to the first part. The second part, which describes Olivero's journey to the republic of Roncador, the revolution there, and his subsequent rule as a benevolent dictator, is much more than 'a patronizing Utopia for the masses'; it is also an investigation of the relationship between freedom and organization, and a psychological study of the mentality of a benefactor. Similarly, the third section is much more than 'a puritanical, quasi-intellectual (Utopia) for intellectuals'. It is also a demonstration of the anti-vitalism that is implicit in the Utopian tradition, and a criticism of the aesthetics of classicism—and all this quite apart from its basic interest as a crystalline fantasy written in crystalline prose.

Thus the three parts of The Green Child are of roughly equal relevance, whether we consider them as projections of the central character or as philosophic romances, and together they form a symbolic cycle, in which their very discontinuity becomes part of a non-linear continuity, just as the segments of a Tibetan wheel-of-life have only

the most tenuous relationship with each other yet have equal importance when one considers them as juxtaposed facets of the total figure, which is existence itself. And while it is true that the structural
links between the parts of *The Green Child* are even more tenuous
than at first one is led to assume by the common presence of Olivero
with his romantic obsessions centred in the Green Child, a less visible web is actually created by analogies and correspondences. To give
for the present only one example, each part reaches its climax in a
kind of death. At the end of the first part Olivero dies to his life on
earth by descending into the pool; at the end of the second part he
dies to his life as a dictator by arranging a fake assassination; at the
end of the third part he dies in reality.

Thus, even the works which Read presents as less accidental in
structure than his books of essays, show in fact the same essential discontinuity, coupled with a unity of conception that is centripetal
rather than linear in its movement. This tendency to break away
from the time-bound structures adopted in classical writing is related to Read's preferences in the visual arts, and finds an obvious echo
in his adherence to anarchism as a form of unpolitical politics based
on a mosaic rather than a pyramidal type of social organization (the
federation rather than the state), rejecting the philosophy of linear
progress in favour of that of cyclic return.

But, if the structure of Read's works tends to be organic and cyclic
rather than linear and mechanical, and thus to reflect the romantic
rather than the classical form of structure, this is almost the only way
in which his prose can be described as in the accepted sense experimental. Indeed, I doubt very much if Read even regarded experimen-
talism as in itself as a valid criterion of art. Experiment is merely the
way in which the artist finds the appropriate form to express whatever within him calls for expression, or to reveal, if he is another kind
of artist, whatever calls for revelation. To the extent that Read
regarded form as the ultimate quality of works of art, the residuum
that would survive, it was not the element of experiment—of becoming—that justified them, but the final state of being in which they
lived on as autonomous artifacts, objects of contemplation.

Here we approach the reconciliation of those apparently con-
tradictory elements in Read's attitude which Wyndham Lewis was
to find so puzzling. The innovative works of art which he continued
to praise as long as they demonstrated a respect for the elements of
form and style, he defended not because they were experimental,

but because each in his view presented a valid and unique insight through symbolic means into the reality of collective human experience. And if his own prose did not appear, except in the most general structural sense, to be innovative in the same way as that of James Joyce, it was because Read was not moved to express himself in terms of extreme linguistic dislocation. His natural bent in prose writing was in fact complementary to his tastes in the visual arts. Any attempt by a painter to achieve literary effects or to express concepts by visual means introduced an impurity into that play of image, symbol and form which was in his view the only message of the work. On the other hand, if Read as a critic had not been adept in exposition, in transforming the achievements of the artist into conceptual form, he would not have been so convincing as an interpreter. He achieved, in fact, an unusual symbiosis between the aesthetic sensibility and the powers of rational expression (the paradox once again of Reason and Romanticism), and the median where these two aspects of his perception came together lay in his poetry. His prose, even at its most imaginative, was disciplined to a clear objectivity, but combined with that objectivity was a noticeable element of informality, expressed most strikingly in his already noted inclination towards discontinuity. The more organized the thought, it seemed, the less organized the form; the more organized the form, as in Read's poetry and the visual artists whom Read preferred, the less organized the thought.

All this has been expressed most admirably by Read himself in a passage of *Annals of Innocence and Experience* where he discusses the kind of prose whose 'shifting outlines' he most admires. He presents an interesting and curious list of works, some obviously romantic like *Undine* and *Carmen*, others not so clearly so, like *A Sentimental Journey* and *Candide*, and some so much alone in their departure into fantasy that, like Alain Fournier's *Le grand Meaulnes*, they seem isolated from all possible identification with literary movements. Describing the genre, Read also describes his own imaginative prose:

> It is short, it is deliberate; at once realistic and imaginative, objective and reflective. It avoids the psychological approach of the novel and is more than a short story. When it has a moral or satirical motive, like Voltaire's *Candide*, it is sometimes called the *conte philosophique*. The philosophy, however, is best left to the inference of the reader.

Such writings are not constructive art forms: they have neither the organization of the novel nor the simple unity of the short story. They are rather projections of an idea, of an incident, of a phantasy; intellectually conceived, but exhibiting the fresh texture of a personal style and the brightness of a concrete imagination. It is impossible to justify my preference for this genre on any theoretical grounds: I fancy that it is determined simply by the material conditions which make it the form most easily within my grasp, both as a reader and as a writer.

It is these characteristics of brevity and deliberation, of realism balanced by imagination, of objectivity combined with reflectiveness, that characterize Read's non-expository prose. Whether we are considering his autobiographical sketches or his prose fiction, like *The Green Child* and that curious unpublished novella for children, 'Penny Wise and Pound Foolish', this is the framework of qualities within which they must be viewed. Perhaps they are nearest to that short, simple and highly intellectual narrative which the French call a *récit*. *The Green Child* is a *récit* founded in fantasy; *The Innocent Eye* is a *récit* founded in fact.

2

The Contrary Experience is perhaps the most extraordinary example among Read's books of the kind of volume in which a group of superficially very different writings coagulate, as it were, by affinity. Neither in composition nor in conception is it a consecutive autobiography; it is a series of pieces written at various times and assembled into a collection which has its own unity—the unity of a single developing life recorded in the personal reflections and recollections of forty years. *The Innocent Eye is a* deliberately conceived jewel of memory: the bright images that remain to a man of forty from a rural childhood severed sharply by family tragedy. In the second part, 'A War Diary, 1915–18', the tone shifts from recollective deliberation to the urgency of an immediate present, as a young man appears with his artistic and intellectual powers developing and flourishing in the immediate shadow of death—the 'attempt to build a Heaven in Hell's despite' as Read calls it in his 1962 introduction to this collection of letters contemporary with the events he describes. The third part, 'The Falcon and the Dove', first appeared as the major part of

Annals of Innocence and Experience; Read looks back, at the beginning of the second great war of his life, over the years of development from adolescence that shaped his craft as a writer, his views of art, his anarchist philosophy. Within this reminiscent account are embedded the two more immediate war narratives *In Retreat* and 'The Raid'. Finally, in 'A Dearth of Wild Flowers', Read brings *The Contrary Experience* to a close with a series of rural essays inspired by his return, in his late fifties, to that very Yorkshire countryside which he had left as an orphan child almost half a century before.

Assembling the various parts of *The Contrary Experience* in the last decade of his life Read gave a roughly chronological form to the book. As a result, one's final impression is dominated by the mood of the last section, and what one sees in the mind's eye is no longer the contemporary critic looking confidently into the future, as at the end of *Annals of Innocence and Experience in* 194.0, but rather the aged poet walking the Yorkshire hills, looking back into the clear pool of childhood, and lamenting a past that for all its faults was better than the present; lamenting 'the end of a way of life out of which whatever poetry and intelligence we possess arose as naturally as poppies and cornflowers from the undisciplined earth'. We are losing touch, he tells us, with the organic processes, and we 'walk like blind animals in a darker age than history has ever known'. Only in the triumph of romantic art and of a natural society such as anarchists have preached lies hope, and that hope, Read suggests in his 1962 preface, is slight: '... to establish one's individuality is perhaps the only possible protest.' And so the pattern of Read's work is completed in romantic pessimism for the fate of man in general, and in romantic individualism, flowering in its own art under a lowering sky, as the only solace and refuge.

There is a rather sombre and Wordsworthian appeal to this volume if one follows the pattern which the author imposed in his last decade; the procession from 'the glory and the dream' of childhood to the 'clouds that gather round the setting sun' seems to fill one's vision. But that is really a distortion of what the component pieces meant when they were originally written. Thus, there are two ways to consider *The Contrary Experience*: as the collage that Read eventually produced in 1962, and as the series of individual pieces appearing at various times and viewed in biographical-chronological order and also in terms of relative formal complexity.

This means a rearrangement by which one begins with the 'War

Diary', which was written first in spite of its late publication, proceeds to *In Retreat* and 'The Raid', continues with *The Innocent Eye*
and the parts of *Annals of Innocence and Experience* other than the
war narratives, and ends, as in *The Contrary Experience*, with 'A
Dearth of Flowers', but considered as the last of a cycle of discontinuous pieces rather than as the dying fall of a life's trajectory. I suggest
that the insight it will give us into Read's practices as an artist may
justify this approach for the light it casts on the whole cycle of his
writings, which seem to surround this most central and most personal cluster of his works like shadowy megaliths circling the central
stone on which the sun shines with the most revealing intensity.

In following this discontinuous group of works which is *The
Contrary Experience*, one is aware, if not of progress in the ordinary
sense, at least of formal and technical development. The first item is
the least deliberate and polished—a series of letters, with an audience
of one, which are merely a shade less direct than a notebook written
as an author's *aide-mémoire*. *In Retreat* and 'The Raid' are episodic
pieces written for publication and for a public larger than one, but
based on actual diaries; both were composed within a few years of
the events they described. *The Innocent Eye* is a highly condensed
account of childhood written thirty years after the last of the events
described; it is inspired by the view—another version of a connection
already expressed in differing ways by two of Read's literary heroes,
Wordsworth and Proust—that 'all life' is 'an echo of our first sensations' and that 'our memories make our imaginative life'. It is one of
Read's most formally precise works, and as near as Read ever came
in prose to imagistic writing; he represents with felicity the intensely
physical world of childhood, vibrantly dominated by sensory
responses that become blunted with adolescence.

In comparison, *Annals of Innocence and Experience*, written in
1939, takes the form of reflective narrative, as it describes the formation of an artist and a thinking being; it lacks the sharp and concrete
vividness of the evocations of life in *The Innocent Eye*. Already there
has been a shift in viewpoint; the I—and the pun is inevitable and significant—is at the centre in *The Innocent Eye*, and very near the centre of 'A War Diary'. In 'A Raid' and *In Retreat*, it is moving to the
periphery, and the writer is already observing himself with the objectivity proper to a literary persona. In *Annals*, the detachment, if it is
not complete, has become as nearly so as is possible when a writer
discusses himself; the I is virtually marginal. 'A Dearth of Flowers'

achieves almost complete objectivity, for the author now talks of himself rarely. He talks rather of the history and topography of the country to which he has returned after so many years, and of what has happened to it since the days when he experienced it as the child of *The Innocent Eye*. Yet, by association, by analogy, by implication, one realizes that these oblique fragments of local history are really the history of their creator. It would be going too far to say that he had identified himself with his country, but the symbiosis between man and land has become almost total.

* * *

If one reads *The Contrary Experience* in the order Read established in 1962, there is an immediate shock as one passes from the chapters of early life to the war letters. It is the passage from the vision of the 'innocent eye' interpreted by a highly trained sensibility, to the unpolished vision of a young man of talent who had interrupted his education in mid career. Written from regimental messes in England where Read had to conceal his intellectual interests, and from the trenches, these letters reveal in many ways the insecurity of their writer and his painful emergence from a solitary dedication to literature. The presence of a being of his own age and of the opposite sex to whom he could pour out his ideas and feelings was obviously important to him, and it may well be that this means of release enabled Read to preserve the remarkable sangfroid with which he accepted the life of a serving officer in World War I. The exuberance of youth, its passing enthusiasms (for Lucien Pissaro as a painter for example), its insecure mental arrogance, are all there; there are passages of belatedly adolescent heartiness which suggest that, for all the sophistication he often shows at this early time in discussing the novels of James, the philosophy of Sorel and the criticism of Coleridge, Read was still in some ways extraordinarily juvenile for a young man of experience and in his middle twenties. For example:

> I have a jolly little cubicle which I share with one of these friends. Naturally we make it cosy (as only *men* can). Carpets, curtains, easy chairs—everything complete ...
> I also accidentally met and became very pally with Richard Aldington. He is a jolly open-faced English type—26 years old—and quite boyish. Altogether a friend to be. He showed me a lot of new poems. ...

... Osbert and Sachie turned up. They are sons of Sir George Sitwell— aristocratic, wealthy, officers in the Guards, Oxford University and what not. But *also* furious socialists, good poets (Sachie very good) and very young (about my own age). They are crammed full of enthusiasm for the future and it is with them that I can imagine myself being associated a good deal in the future. ...

No one who knew Read in later life would expect of him the bubbling enthusiasms that appear in the pages of these letters; he became with the years more circumspect in expression, and this, though it may be attributable in part to the repulses which in the end teach all of us that the sleeve is no place for a heart, was due also to the development of the kind of literary reticence that makes Read's mature writings seem to exist on the spare margins rather than in the lush central jungle of romanticism.

Yet the impulsive superficiality of many passages of the 'War Diary' should not divert one from the significance of its contents as showing Read's mental life at the most important time of his career. There is no doubt that it was in war that Read passed out of an innocence whose tatters still cling in places to his War Diary', into the experience that gave his thought an outline which persisted, no matter how its apparel of details might change over the years, with amazing consistency to the end of his life. War, in fact, was the Contrary Experience that provided the title for his complete autobiographies, and the fascination of the 'War Diary' is to be found in following the emergence, in their first unpolished appearance and under the stimulus of events, of thoughts that would be expressed with more polished style in his later writings. We see Read developing his Nietzschean beliefs, proclaiming his philosophic pessimism, declaring:

> *Man is a constituent of the divine.* The divine is not a constituent of man
> There you have my creed plain enough.

Later, thinking of death, he reacts in a way that Nietzsche, and Stirner as well, would have applauded.

> I don't want to die for my king and country. If I do die, it's for the salvation of my own soul, cleansing it of all its little egotisms by one last supreme egotistic act.

And when his correspondent tells him that she cannot understand why, with his opinions, he is taking part in war, he defends himself thus:

> I've no doubt about my position. If I were free today, I'm almost sure I should be compelled by every impulse within me to join this adventure. For I regard it as an adventure and it is as an adventure that it appeals to me. I'll fight for Socialism when the day comes, and fight all the better for being an 'old soldier'.

If Read did fight for socialism—or rather for—anarchism it was by means other than those used by soldiers. Yet even in World War II, when he had long looked on war with horror and had equally long claimed to be both an anarchist and a pacifist, he could still think that it might be necessary for young men to share in a general experience and he could write, in his poem 'To a Conscript of 1940':

> But you, my brother and my ghost, if you can go
> Knowing that there is no reward, no certain use
> In all your sacrifice, then honour is reprieved.
>
> To fight without hope is to fight with grace,
> The self reconstructed, the false heart repaired.

And this, though he could also exclaim passionately, 'I have hated the Army as such ever since the first day I knew it,' and could confess in his last book what he never revealed in his earlier writings on war— that its real horror is, as he says in *The Cult of Sincerity*, 'not death nor the fear of mutilation, discomfort or filth, but a psychotic state of hallucination in which the world becomes unreal and you no longer know whether your experience is valid—in other words, whether you are any longer sane'.

It is perhaps a measure of the shift from actuality Read has already achieved in the 'War Diary' that he should ignore such nega- tive experiences, and stress instead such positive qualities of the sol- dier's life as comradeship. He appears to have been an efficient officer, whose voice had, as he wrote in a poem long afterwards, 'the old accustom'd ring'; his friend Frank Morley once insisted to me that to understand Read one must positively remember his officer past, which gave him a sense of self-induced discipline not incompat-

ible with his anarchism. Yet he felt, as Orwell was later to feel in the
trenches of Spain, an extraordinary sense of unity with his men as
well as with his fellow officers. 'I had such friends', he said in *Annals
of Innocence and Experience*, 'as I had never had before and have
never had since—friends with whom one lived in a complete communal bond of thoughts as well as goods.' And, looking at himself
objectively more than forty years later when he wrote the introductory note to the 'War Diary', he remarked that such experiences
'might explain his instinctive beliefs in small independent units of
production, in guild socialism, in anarchism in a complete rejection
of any ideal that compromised human freedom'. It is evident that,
even though Read had first encountered anarchist writings in 1911,
and had contributed to that Guild Socialist organ, the *New Age*, as
early as 1912, his attachment to such doctrines of human brotherhood became firm in the trenches of Flanders; he then expressed his
anarchism in terms that did not alter substantially in the years ahead.

> I don't think I'm ready to discuss the change that is taking place in my
> 'political' sentiments. It is a revolt of the individual against the associa-
> tion which involves him in activities which do not interest him: a jump-
> ing to the ultimate anarchy which I have always seen as the ideal of all
> who value beauty and intensity of life. 'A beautiful anarchy'—that is my
> cry. I hate mobs—they fight and kill, build filthy cities and make horrid
> dins. And I begin to think that their salvation and re-creation is none of
> my concern, but the concern of each individual. Only so can these asso-
> ciations be broken—cell by cell, segment by segment.

And at another point he declares himself a communist in economics,
but in ethics an individualist. 'Are these two creeds incompatible?' he
asks, aware already of the underlying dialectic in his thought, as he is
on another occasion when he contrasts his views on social change
and his views of the things of the mind.

> No one is a more convinced *social* democrat than I am. But it seems to me
> Art and Thought are essentially aristocratic things.

And certainly, at this time when his original enthusiasm for Nietzsche and Blake was complicated by what he described as his 'unanticipated but complete surrender to the spiritual enchantment' of
Henry James, Read developed an élitist view of the arts. Much of his

later criticism was indeed complicated by the paradox of seeking a world in which every man would become an artist as naturally as he ate or slept, yet recognizing that in the world he inhabited art was unavoidably the province of the few. But in these early days there are few signs that such thoughts troubled him; he accepted with youthful pleasure the idea that his tastes and his talents put him above the herd, and when, in that memorable week of October 1918, he met Pound and Eliot and Lewis, he seems to have had no doubt that he had entered a kind of aristocracy. 'It has been a wonderful week,' Read noted at the end of it, and near the end of his 'War Diary': 'the most truly wonderful in my life. I have lived such a lot, learned such a lot and at last I really am on my feet and facing the world.' It was the first of a number of times in his life when events took an extraordinary compression, so that as a cumulative result of his appearance in *Art and Letters* he found himself quickly accepted into the most vital literary movement of the time, recognized as one of the imagist poets, and supported by the friendship of men like Eliot and Aldington who helped to establish his name as a professional writer while he accepted his bureaucratic drudgery as the price of the security in.which to write.

The 'War Diary' ends in appropriate anticlimax as, the following month in Canterbury, Read celebrates the Armistice, 'hopelessly sober', reading *The Sacred Fount* 'with a savage zest' while others rejoice.

* * *

In the 'War Diary' Read tells of the writings on which he was engaged while serving in the army—a novel he had begun, a short story called 'A Glimpse of the Garden'—but apart from some slight sketches based on military life, and rather symbolist in tone, none of his prose has survived, except for his fugitive political pieces in the *New Age* and *The Guildsman*, that can clearly be attributed to this time. His two war narratives, *In Retreat* and 'The Raid', appeared as we have seen, in 1925 and 1927 respectively. *In Retreat* was written in 1919, and 'The Raid' probably some time shortly afterwards, but both were examples of the 'objective' style of writing which Read claimed in the 'War Diary' he was developing, and both were based on more immediate records that have survived.

In the case of *In Retreat* the model—a mere skeleton—was the Army Book in which Read kept his officer's record of the progress of the retreat on the Somme, as he experienced it in his own very limited sector, from the early morning of the 21st March 1918 when his unit manned battle stations, following almost hour by hour the progress of the withdrawal until, on the 28th, the slight and scattered remnants of the battalion were reunited. Preserved at the Read archive in the University of Victoria, it is the merest pencilled shorthand of action, beginning on the 21st March with:

> 4.50 a.m. Man battle stations.
> 6.35 Roupy Defences. Stanley Redoubt about II a.m.—Heard that line of resistance had been penetrated ...

And so it continues, with even the most dramatic action levelled out in laconic phrases.

The adventure was (with the exception of that which inspired 'The Raid') the most dramatic in Read's experience and he wrote about it one of his best early poems, 'The Refugees', which appeared in *Naked Warriors* in 1919 and was therefore almost certainly written before *In Retreat*.

> Mute figures with bowed heads
> They travel along the road:
> Old women, incredibly old
> and a hand-cart of chattels.
>
> They do not weep:
> their eyes are too raw for tears.
>
> Past them have hastened
> processions of retreating gunteams
> baggage-wagons and swift horsemen.
> Now they struggle along
> with the rearguard of a broken army.
>
> We shall hold the enemy towards nightfall
> and they will move
> mutely into the dark behind us,
> only the creaking cart
> disturbing their sorrowful serenity.

This, of course, is the record of a movement glimpsed in the midst of action, a fragment of imagist immediacy, whose sharp concreteness is deepened by the shadow of recollected compassion.

In dealing with the wider context in which this incident was enclosed, *In Retreat*, the first work in which Read develops his chosen prose form of the brief narrative, is by contrast objective and at the same time reflective. It lacks the sensationalism that has marred so many accounts of war, yet it is not without excitement or, for that matter, without passion. Read presents mainly a record of what war so largely is, bewilderment and fatigue, interrupted by moments of searing terror and violence like this particularly perilous moment of the retreat.

I waited anxiously for B—— to take the open. I saw men crawl out of the trenches, and lie flat on the parados, still firing at the enemy. Then, after a little while, the arrow was launched. I saw a piteous band of men rise from the ground, and run rapidly towards me. A great shout went up from the Germans: a cry of mingled triumph and horror. 'Halt Eenglisch!' they cried, and for a moment were too amazed to fire; as though aghast at the folly of men who could plunge into such a storm of death. But the first silent gasp of horror expended, then broke the crackling storm. I don't remember in the whole war an intenser taste of hell. My men came along spreading rapidly to a line of some two hundred yards wide, but bunched here and there. On the left, by the main road, the enemy rushed out to cut them off. Bayonets clashed there. Along the line men were falling swiftly as the bullets hit them. Each second they fell, now one crumpling up, now two or three at once. I saw men stop to pick up their wounded mates, and as they carried them along, themselves get hit and fall with their inert burdens. Now they were near me, so I rushed out of my pit and ran with them to the line of trenches some three hundred yards behind.

It seemed to take a long time to race across those few hundred yards. My heart beat nervously and I felt infinitely weary. The bullets hissed about me, and I thought: then this is the moment of death. But I had no emotions. I remembered having read how in battle men are hit, and never feel the hurt till later, and I wondered if I had yet been hit. Then I reached the line. I stood petrified, enormously aghast. *The trench had not been dug, and no reinforcements occupied it* ...

But for the most part the experience of the retreat is lived on a curiously level plane of emotion, so that anger at the enemy is far more muted than the rage that Read finds rising within him when, cold, hungry and totally exhausted, he is refused a billet or even food by men of his own army who have stayed safe behind the lines.

Almost throughout the narrative, the style is unpretentious, spare, even somewhat *grisâtre* in tone, as befits the landscape and the prevalent mood of a subdued despair and a terror vague and ill defined, as it must often be in war, where so much is unknown. Read keeps this nebulously menacing feeling in our minds by his repeated references to the atmospheric conditions that provoke a sense of uncertainty.

> We waited for the dawn; it was weird, phantasmagorical. Again the fateful mist. As it cleared a little, the woods near us hung faintly in the whiteness.

But the visual descriptions are clear and sharp, and here and there the level is broken by some image, some vignette, that loosens the objective structure of the narrative to let in feeling. One such passage appears when Read tells of digging in with his exhausted men on a hill outside a village. They have found biscuits and wine in the houses.

> So S—— and I each took a wine glass, and starting at different points, we began to go a round of the men. Each man lay curled up in his shallow pit, resting. To each we gave a glass of wine and a few biscuits. They took it thankfully. There was a lull in the distant fighting: I don't remember any noise of fire during that hour. The sun was warm and seemed to cast a golden peace on the scene.
>
> A feeling of unity with the men about me suddenly suffused my mind.

And there is another vivid moment—a violent one this time in which sudden terror takes Read's mind back in a curious way to the peaceful world of *The Innocent Eye.* He and his men come to a canal that is narrow but deep, and they are looking for a crossing, when a machine gun suddenly opens fire on them.

> There was a good few trees about which must have obstructed the firer's view; the cut twigs, newly budded, fell into the water. We hesitated no longer: we plunged into the stream. The men had to toss their

rifles across many of which landed short and were lost. The sight of these frightened men plunging into the water affected one of those curious stirrings of the memory that call up some vivid scene of childhood: I saw distinctly the water-rats plunging at dusk into the mill-dam at Thornton-le-Dale, where I had lived as a boy of ten.

The refugees Read made the subject of his poem are not absent from the prose narrative, but they have ceased to be a centre of attention, an archetypal symbol of that ultimate horror of war—its destruction of the innocents. Instead, they provide an arresting detail embedded in the flow of the retreat and contributing to that sense of a complete disordering of the certainties of life which is at once the most exciting and the most bewildering feature of a great social disaster like war.

We assembled in the village street and marched on again. The road was busy with retreating artillery and a few infantrymen. From behind us came the sounds of firing: the enemy were attacking Ham. We trudged on, passing villages whose inhabitants were only just taking steps to flee. They piled beds, chairs, and innumerable bolsters on little carts, some hand-pulled, some yoked to bony horses. They tied cows behind. There were old men, many old women, a few young women, but no young men. They and their like proceeded with us along the western road.

The whole experience ends on a strange note of contrast, like a violent symphony quietening to a brief final adagio, when, after the enemy has been halted and Read can be sent back to rest, he reaches a corner of the land, still unspoilt by war, and takes from his pocket the book he had put into it at the beginning of the retreat and left unread for a week that seemed like a year. It is *Walden*, as good a literary antidote to the passions of war as one could imagine, and a book much in tune with the dreams of a just, peaceful and simply ordered world that filled Read's mind in those days when he was not engaged in the actual business of fighting.

* * *

'The Raid' describes an experience of doubly unique significance, for this was the only occasion on which Read felt fairly certain that he had actually killed a man, and also the only occasion when he made a really personal contact with one of the enemy. Like the retreat from the Somme, it impressed him so much that he treated it in several different ways, first as a bit of bravado in a letter dated the 1st August 1917 which he wrote immediately after the event and later included in his 'War Diary', then in the brief episodic poem 'Liedholz' which he may have written shortly after the event and which was published in *Naked Warriors*, and finally in its most elaborated form as 'The Raid'. Apart from the importance which the recurrence of the story gives it as an episode of complex significance in Read's mental life, it is interesting to observe how the way of telling was affected in each case by his purpose.

In the account that appears in the 'War Diary' he is writing for the eye of a girl who obviously cares for him and whom he wishes— however innocently—to impress. It is a tale told with a breezy jollity which minimizes the danger yet makes vivid and exciting the central incidents in which Read and his sergeant surprise two Germans, and capture one of them, an officer. Read does not say that it was he who shot at the German he thought was killed, and at the end he dwells in a rather exaggerated way on the camaraderie between him and his prisoner ('an ex-schoolmaster of some sort and a very intelligent fellow').

> We had to take him down to Brigade—an hour's walk. It was a beautiful early morning and everything was peaceful and the larks were singing. In our broken French we talked of music. He played both the violin and the piano and we found common enthusiasms in Beethoven and Chopin. He even admired Nietzsche and thenceforth we were sworn friends. He wrote his name and address in my pocket-book and I promised to visit him after the war if I ever came to Germany. By the time I handed him over to the authorities at the Brigade we were sorry to part with each other. And a few hours previously we had done our best to kill each other. *C'est la guerre*—and what a damnable irony of existence ... at any rate a curious revelation of our common humanity.
>
> I've got a beautiful automatic revolver as a souvenir.

The mood of the poem is quite different. It is laconic, reducing the capture of Liedholz to five bare brief lines of action:

> We met in the night at half-past one
> between the lines.
> Liedholz shot at me

and I at him;
in the ensuing tumult he surrendered to me.

There is no reference to human brotherhood, no touch of camaraderie; Nietzsche is a word in a list of things discussed in broken
French, and Liedholz is reduced to a dry cipher in the mind, a Span-
dau professor who is 'not too intelligible'. And all the rest is bracket-
ed between the references at the beginning and the end to the fact that
Read, when he took his prisoner, had 'black face and nigger's teeth',
and that Liedholz, who in this way becomes slightly alive at the very
end of the poem, was amused by the circumstance. The strained flip-
pancy of the whole poem suggests that it was written when Read was
in his most bitter mood and felt that war was, above all, absurd as
absurd as his own Christy Minstrel disguise.

The final prose version, 'The Raid', is much more complicated,
both formally and psychologically, which suggests that it was probably written later than *In Retreat*, giving Read more time to reflect on
his memories, with the result that the first third of the account does
not deal with the raid at all, but with the nature of cowardice, exemplified by the behaviour of one of Read's fellow officers who was
taken off the raid because of his evident fear. The point Read wishes
to make is that P. was probably a coward because 'his mind ... was
not free to lead its own existence, or to create the conditions of its
existence'. The point of introducing P. becomes evident when Read
describes the beginning of the raid and discusses his own feelings:

> I felt that I ought not to neglect a single aspect of that slow advance
> to the enemy's lines, for in those few minutes I experienced a prolonged
> state of consciousness during which I hung over a pit of fear, weighted
> down by a long and vivid anticipation of its nature, and now brought
> to the last tension by this silent agony of deliberate approach. Fear is
> more powerful in silence and loneliness, for then the mind is more open
> to the electric uprush of the animal. There is safety in action and una-
> nimity in all the noisy riot of strife—until even that safety is beaten
> down by the pitiless continuance of physical shock: then there is safety
> only in the mind again, if it rise like a holy ghost out of the raw stumps
> of the body.

He goes on to suggest that neither brute strength nor mere imagination is enough to save a man from cowardice; P., after all, had imag-

ination. One needs imagination plus faith, even if the faith be only
animal faith, even if it be merely fatalism, 'and by fatalism I mean a
resolve to live in peace of mind, in possession of mind, despite any
physical environment. ... And so in the presence of danger, and in the
immediate expectation of death, one can forget the body and its fears
and exist wholly in the mind.' This meditation on the nature and the
power of fear now becomes the centre of Read's retelling of the incident, and gives the whole narrative a quality which a few years after
its publication would have been called existentialist. Like so many of
the existentialist stories and novels, it is a study of the behaviour of
men in an extreme situation, and the central issue is the power to defy
death, and in defying death to defy the apparent meaninglessness of
existence.

The result is that Liedholz takes a secondary role. He is no longer
the centre of the narrative as he is of the poem, and the idea of brotherhood among enemies exemplified in the first 'War Diary' account
of the incident, while it is not entirely eliminated, is reduced to an
impulse of the younger Read which his elder self looks on with indul-
gence. It is interesting to compare two points in 'The Raid' with their
counterparts in the 'War Diary', written immediately after the event.
Then Read said: 'He even admired Nietzsche and thenceforth we
were sworn friends.' Now he says: 'Nietzsche was at that time still
fresh in my awakening mind, and I stammered in broken enthusiasm
about his books, but got no response.' Then he said: 'By the time I
handed him over to the authorities at the Brigade we were sorry to
part with each other.' Now he says: 'I last saw him standing at a distance from me, waiting to move. I gazed at him, eagerly, tenderly, for
I had conceived some sort of vicarious affection for this man. I had
done my best to kill him a few hours before. I waved my hand as he
left, but he only answered with a vague smile.'

These discrepancies exemplify the essential difference in tone
between the two versions. One can hardly doubt that the first of
them, which is nearer in time, is also nearer in factual truth. Yet it is
the second which, by the operation of the reflective faculty, draws a
deeper truth out of the episode, and in doing so finds an appropriate
form. The original version is an interesting document regarding the
life of the artist; the new version is a shaped work of literary art.

* * *

Read's treatment of the war incidents, each in several versions, suggests that they had acquired a special and compelling significance for him, and the only other phase of his life for which this can be said—at least on the strength of surviving literary documents—is his childhood at Muscoates. In spite of the apparent remoteness of that rustic experience from the deadly episodes of wartime, it shares with them a dramatic isolation from the rest of his life. The two war experiences were different from each other and from anything else in Read's life; their uniqueness isolated them. In the case of Read's childhood, it was isolated by his abrupt transference, at an extremely impressionable age, to an environment so profoundly different that his first ten years were encapsulated in memory, and almost sixty years afterwards, in 1962, he could say: 'The seclusion of my first ten years now seems like an age of unearthly bliss, a ring in a rock to which all the strings of my subsequent happiness are tied.' It seems likely that, if the change had been more gradual, those years would have faded into a kind of uniform past instead of shining with their special and preternatural light. Here one can only judge subjectively; I know that had I been abruptly exiled at any time up to the age of fourteen from the corner of Shropshire which enshrined almost all the happiness of my childhood, I should certainly have felt like Read a compelling desire to return and complete the divided experience; the severance did not come until I was eighteen, when outside interests were filling my mind, and then I returned after a year and found everything diminished, and wondered why I had ever thought that there was no other place in the world to live out my life.

The effect of Read's abrupt detachment from the farm in the Vale of York was to turn it eventually into a domain of the imagination. Read himself would have called it a domain of memory, for he remarks when describing it that 'our memories make our imaginative life', which is indeed true, but only if one accepts the Proustian qualification that when memory seems most vivid it is selected and suffused by the imagination. *The Innocent Eye* is the most appealing of Read's autobiographical essays, and the nearest to formal perfection, precisely because it is shaped by a passionate act of *imaginative* recollection.

Once again, when he wrote *The Innocent Eye* in his fortieth year, Read was giving final shape to a work that had already been developed on a much slighter scale in verse. The original version appears in *Eclogues*, a collection of poems published in 1919 and written between 1914 and 1918. It is called 'Childhood', and divided into two parts, the first a page of lyrical prose objectively describing the farm and its immediate setting, and the second a brief passage of verse in which the child wanders through his environment. It is a bright work, full of visual images, but it deals entirely with the surface of existence except for a single reference to the child's 'eager soul' which retreats before the passage of a fiery traction engine. It is essentially a landscape poem evoking almost nothing but the scene it represents, yet that scene, with the pond, the garden and the orchard, with green lizards under the stones by the well and red-coated huntsmen galloping over the fields, is a true sketch—as sharp as a mediaeval miniature—of the setting of *The Innocent Eye*.

The bright physical surface of things is constantly present in *The Innocent Eye* as well, for it is this aspect of the world of which the child is most conscious. Time as duration, except that it dictates the brutal ending, plays little part in the narrative, for the child grows older almost unconsciously, and what time he observes is cyclic, the swing from dawn to dusk, the repetitious weekly routines, the circling of the seasons with their clearly defined patterns of growth and farm work. It is essentially a world in space rather than in time that is presented, the farm within its surrounding landscape; the very chapters are plotted in spatial terms, and the pattern of space as of time is essentially circular, that of the mandala. The vale itself—or as much of it as the child's eye sees—is described as 'a basin, wide and shallow like the milk-pans in the dairy ...' In other words, it is a great circle, a microcosm ('my world') capable, in the child's perception, of an almost infinite shrinking as the dark falls and 'the centre of the world had become a candle shining from the kitchen window'.

Within the vale, the farm is its own realm, and within it are the various domains, each given its separate chapter. The four squares of the green, the foldgarth, the orchard and the garden, lying around the house, form the heart of the farm, a square quadruple heart like that of many mandalas; the stackyard and the cow pasture are outlying domains. Direction is important; the attention of the dwellers in the farm is drawn northward, to the green dales where their relatives own mills, and to the purple moors beyond. The other direction is less familiar.

Beyond the Ricall, which flowed rather deeply in the soft earth and was quite impassable to us, lay the mysterious land we never explored:

the south, with the hills rising in the distance, the farm with the fiery window hidden in the hills.

Within this world things and incidents are described with a
remarkable visual clarity, in a light that is perpetually summery (for
Read admits that his winter memories are few and scanty). The following passage is typical of the way in which, with an adept simplicity of language and detail, a vivid picture is built up suggesting the
strongly visual imagination that in later years would make Read so
responsive to the plastic arts.

> The farmhouse was a square stone box with a roof of vivid red tiles;
> its front was to the south, and warm enough to shelter some apricot trees
> against the wall. But there was no traffic that way: all our exits and
> entrances were made on the north side, through the kitchen; and I think
> even our grandest visitors did not disdain that approach. Why should
> they? On the left as they entered direct into the kitchen was an old oak
> dresser; on the right a large open fireplace, with a great iron kettle hang-
> ing from the reckan, and an oven to the near side of it. A long deal table,
> glistening with a honey gold sheen from much scrubbing, filled the far
> side of the room; long benches ran down each side of it. The floor was
> flagged with stone, each stone neatly outlined with a border of some soft-
> er yellow stone, rubbed on after every washing. Sides of bacon and plum-
> dusky hams hung from the beams of the wooden ceiling.

It is a very concrete world. Feelings play little part in the narrative, and Read presents the child as almost devoid of them. 'Pity and
even terror, are emotions which develop when we are no longer innocent ... The child even has a natural craving for horrors.' I cannot
decide whether Read is here imposing an adult's simplification on his
memory. Everything is recorded so sharply and clearly that one is
inclined to doubt it. But if he is not, then his childhood must have
been exceptional, for I can remember very clearly things that caused
me terror, extreme and illogical, at no greater age than three, and I do
not think I am alone.

Another aspect of *The Innocent Eye* which is related to the
absence of strong or clearly defined feelings (as distinct from 'instinctive attachments') is the fact that people are usually less clearly presented than things, and are seen at their most vivid when they come
in some dramatic way from outside, or are associated with some

novel activity. Read has only the vaguest memories of governesses
who must have been daily companions; on the other hand, figures
like Jabez, the driver of the traction engine, and the horse-breaker
Fiddler Dick are very vividly present, though their appearances were
only seasonal. Similarly the relative who emerges in the strongest
image is neither Read's father nor his mother, but his uncle who kept
the mill at Howkeld and was the master of a strange realm of antique
machinery. Read's mother—though it is evident from references in
later parts of *The Contrary Experience* that he was deeply attached
to her—hardly appears at all, and he confesses that his memories of
his father 'are too intermittent to form a coherent image'. One can
only assume an unconscious reticence at work, a censoring of memory over relationships which must have been intense and whose ending was to be so dramatically abrupt, and therefore so traumatic.

Like a map in the process of drawing, the world of Read's childhood spreads out chapter by chapter from the farm, yet memory still
keeps it within the close world of the locality. Read admits to have
forgotten completely trips to Scarborough which one would have
thought exotic to a child so rustically isolated, yet nearby Rievaulx
Abbey remains strongly in his mind; so does the church at Kirkdale,
built twelve centuries ago by the Saxon monks, and the mill where
his uncle lived in a materially self- sufficient world beside a mysterious stream that, having lost itself in the limestone caverns, came
surging up at this point to turn the mill wheel. And beyond, the exotic far point of Read's memory world, there was Bransdale, reached
only by a moorland track, and strange enough to provide the image
of a detached world that glows with strange splendour in the midst
of the narrative.

> The people who lived here were strange and dark and beautiful even to
> my childish eyes. For sometimes, when staying at Howkeld, I would go
> out for the day with the wagoners. Our load of grain and flour was
> drawn by great shaggy-footed cart-horses, their harness bright with
> brass ornaments, their manes and tails plaited with coloured ribbons—
> drawn over the wide purple Moors, where God seems to have left the
> earth clear of feature to reveal the beauty of its naked form, till we dipped
> down into the green dales and lifted our burden.

The actual bounds of the world of *The Innocent Eye* are narrow;
with modern roads one can explore it in a car between lunchtime and

tea. Yet it is astonishing how wide in Read's transfiguring memory this microcosm appears, so that when one now sees the farm at Muscoates as a stranger—when one circumambulates the small stone house, the little orchard and garden—one is disappointed at the sudden shrinking of the vision into reality. Like the world Proust describes, that of *The Innocent Eye* lives only in the transforming imagination; for even the child can never have seen it exactly as the artist does, who shapes it into an elaborately formal mosaic.

Just as striking as the physical self-containment of the vision is the sense of a world totally lost in time. I have already remarked how Read's childhood was lived in an agrarian society of a kind that was exceptional even in his day. Everything he describes—the farm and its methods, the old water-mills in their last decade of prosperity, the church with its high pews, the ruined abbey, and the hall built by Vanbrugh—combines to create an image that is pre-Victorian, the image of a world in which even the railway has no part, in which the traction engine appears as a nightmare vision, and this temporal isolation intensifies the sense of immersion in an ageless tradition, a continuity that is other than duration.

But no world is hermetically sealed from intrusion, not even the underworld of fiction from which the Green Child wanders and which Olivero finally enters. And in *The Innocent Eye* there are elements—even other than Jabez with his engine—which suggest dimensions extending beyond the purple horizons. The sense of creativity appears early, and while the cycle of natural growth on which the farm depends is accepted by the child on the thoughtless level of the instinctual life, there is an emerging consciousness of aesthetic feeling in activities like the moulding of lead bullets.

> We used the bullets in our catapults, but the joy was in the making of them, and in the sight of their shining beauty. ... fire was real, and so was the skill with which we shaped hard metals to our design and desire.

The impulses that would have led Read away from the farm, even if there had been no abrupt ending to his life there, manifested themselves, not only in his love of making solid objects, but also in a passion for music inspired by Fiddler Dick's violin, and in the enthusiasm for reading that, after his seventh year, possessed him in a household starved of books.

All the clues to Read's later development are present in *The Inno-*

cent Eye. But it would be a remarkable narrative even if there had been no career to which to relate it. Form, style and content are perfectly integrated in a work that is not only self- contained within its own circle of space and time, but also artistically self-consistent.

* * *

The tone of the remaining sections of *The Contrary Experience* is quite different from that of *The Innocent Eye* or of the war narratives, which have in common their extreme conciseness and the sense of inevitability that comes from passionate feeling subjected to a compelling discipline of form. The chapters that originally formed the latter part of *Annals of Innocence and Experience*, and carried Read's life forward from the death of his father in 1903 to the end of the 1930's, are indeed finely written and exemplary autobiography, discursive in tone and linear in form, caught in the flow of duration. They form a fascinating account of the mental development of a man who emerged from an eighteenth-century world into the lesser hell of an industrial city and the greater hell of war, who developed into the poet and critic, and who tried to live as a sensitive, creative and moral being in the chaos of a world between two wars. But there is not the same gleam and glory to this narrative as there is to *The Innocent Eye;* it is too analytical, too shadowed by experience, too passionless. Yet there are remarkable passages, and especially those in which Read discusses his development as a poet, and expounds his philosophy moulded from many influences, a philosophy not without faith, but without belief. Rejecting, as he continued to reject, the dream of personal immortality, Read substituted for it the image of the Tree of Life (though he meant by this something different from the cabbalistic symbol).

> My favourite symbol is the Tree of Life. The human race is the trunk and branches of this tree, and individual men are the leaves which appear one season, flourish for a summer, and then die. I am like a leaf of this tree, and one day I shall be torn off by a storm or simply decay and fall, and become a pinch of compost about its roots. But meanwhile I am conscious of the tree's flowing sap and steadfast strength. Deep down in my consciousness is the consciousness of a collective life, a life of which I am a part and to which I contribute a minute but unique extension. When I

die and fall, the tree remains, nourished to some small degree by my brief manifestations of life. Millions of leaves have preceded me and millions will follow me; the tree itself grows and endures.

Read was to live long enough to share the doubts of those who survive him as to whether even the Tree can endure.

These chapters of Read's middle life are most rewarding for the light they throw on the development of his poetry and politics, his philosophy of education and aesthetics, and rather than submit them now to an analysis they are too deliberately discursive to require, I prefer to use them later as evidence in the chapters on Read as poet, critic and anarchist.

* * *

There remain the chapters which form the last movement of *The Contrary Experience*, 'A Dearth of Wild Flowers'. Here the linear bond of time is again discarded. They are detached essays on the North Riding, and at first reading one is puzzled as to their real purpose, since superficially they resemble the rural essays of Georgian writers who commented in a cultured and gentlemanly way on the antiquities and the natural beauties of their chosen county. This impression is deepened by the knowledge that Read did attempt in 1949 the kind of country life which fairly prosperous writers had carried on earlier in the century, buying a large rectory, becoming a figure in the village of Stonegrave, and walking in the places he had known in childhood.

But re-reading and reflection cast a different light on these chapters. One then notices their almost complete impersonality. Read describes impressions rather than experiences, and appears in the narratives mainly to express opinions, rarely to act. He is trying, in fact, like the Second Voice in *Moon's Farm*, to recover 'the feeling of the place' and 'the sense of the past'.

Some of the essays deal with people who helped to shape the region or who expressed its spirit: Saint Ailred of Rievaulx; the Reverend Comber who ministered at Stonegrave in the seventeenth century; Laurence Sterne, with whom—poor Yorick!—Read seems to feel a special affinity as he looks at the recovered landscape of childhood's world with sadness shadowing his joy.

For much is gone 'from memory's bright inventory'. The surface
of the vale has been changed by a revolution in farming methods.
Tractor-drawn ploughs eliminate the footpaths; herbicides kill the
rich flowering of the cornfields. Even in the dales the woods have
been felled, the farms abandoned, the mills are fallen to ruin. Yet
some essential things remain: the village houses, the church, with the
Saxon stones built into its walls, above all the moors and the seclud-
ed dales. Read feels at home in this 'stone country', and, having no
love for mountains, those 'accidents of nature', he recovers himself in
the gentle wildness of the moors. For this is not the cruel Brontë
country of the West Riding. These moors 'are moulded by gentle
forces, by rain water and wind, and are human in their contours and
proportions, inducing affection rather than awe'. And here and
there, in the deserted dales, there are still paradisial corners, like the
deserted mill at Bransdale, which Read feels 'my spiritual heritage,
the "bright jewel" to which I often retire in moods of despair', and
Farndale. Long ago in ruined Flanders, Read could dream himself
back 'in Yorkshire, with the daffodils in Farndale and the brown
moor reviving with green', and now, the best part of a life later, he
still finds daffodils, growing for miles along the dale and seeming in
the sunshine 'like a golden overflow from the beck'. They are, Read
says, 'part of an Eden that should remain for ever undesecrated'.

But the very tone of his description, its nostalgic melancholy, suggests his feeling that even the daffodils of Farndale are as much
endangered as everything else of that bright world of childhood.
Continually in these chapters rings the knell-note. 'The past has vanished and we are the last outposts of a civilization in retreat.' And
while Read warns himself against succumbing sentimentally to the
feeling for the past, which 'can be destructive of a proper sense of the
present', he nevertheless sees all the elements of an undisciplined
modernity ('weed-killers, motor-cars, tractors, mechanization, tourism,
the radio, the cinema, urbanization') combining in the destruction of
a natural way of life. It is not only the child from Muscoates, but also
the disciple of Ruskin and Morris, who emerges in the lament for the
passing of the wild flowers, which is the penultimate chapter of *The
Contrary Experience* and which ends with the minatory warning
against 'the alienation of sensibility that is the inevitable consequence of mechanization'.

It is as simple as that: we have lost touch with *things*, lost the physical experience that comes from a direct contact with the organic processes of nature. The man who followed the plough felt a tremor conducted from the shining thrust of the coulter in the earth along his arms and into his heart. To dig, to harvest, to sow; to weed, to prune, to scythe; to walk, to ride, to swim; to watch the birth and death of animals; to be conscious of defecation and slow decay, bloom and rot; to participate with all one's senses in the magical rhythm of the seasons—all these are such elementally human experiences that to be deprived of them is to become something less than human. There has never been and never can be a civilization that is not rooted in such organic processes. We know it—instinctively we know it and walk like blind animals into a darker age than history has ever known.

Having said so much, Read can do no more in his last chapter, the premature testament of a man reaching seventy, than reiterate the beliefs in which he had lived: his romanticism; his sense of the need for the aesthetic view of life which sees goodness as 'living beauty', and for 'the concept of honour' as 'the personal aspect of the sense of glory'; and his conviction that his philosophy of a 'unity of the aesthetic and the moral' is 'in the proper sense of the word, existential'. It is made actual in deeds: in the deed which is the work of art; in the deed which is an inspired moral act. This leads him back to anarchism as a practical social expression of harmony with the natural law. But even in anarchism, as Read has already shown in *Education through Art*, we are dealing with the aesthetic life.

> It is the function of art to reconcile the contradictions inherent in our experience; but obviously an art that keeps to the canons of reason cannot make the necessary synthesis. Only an art that rises above conscious reality, only a transcendent or super-real art, is adequate. In this fact lies the final and inescapable justification of romantic art, and it is to the elucidation and illustration of this truth that I have devoted my intellectual energy in the years that are now spent. (*The Contrary Experience.*)

So we see a life that has come full circle and returned to the place of origin, ending in a declaration of consistency; whatever the divagations, whatever the illusions of progression, essentially it has been around the same still centre that the journey has been made.

3

The Green Child is no ordinary novel. It has been called a parable, a romance, a fairy tale, a Utopian fantasy, an allegory, and it contains elements of all these in its intricate symbolic suggestiveness. There is a bright and visionary clarity in its writing that brings it nearer to *The Innocent Eye* than to any other of Read's writings, and it also resembles that book, written only two years before, not only in its discontinuous, mosaic pattern, but also in the importance of spatial as opposed to chronological elements.

So far as the chronology is concerned it is never conventionally linear; in the first part we have time turning back on itself as Olivero returns to his native village in Yorkshire to be faced by Kneeshaw, the boy who caused his departure from the village thirty years ago, and by the Green Child, who appeared there on the day he left and who seems, as she did then, ageless. The second part of the novel inserts the intervening years, and here, though time is durational, it slows down after the exciting period of Olivero's adventures in Spain and his journey to Roncador; indeed, once he has created his almost perfect pastoral state, the sense of time passing is absorbed, as in all Utopias, in the day-to- day repetition of ordained action. This sense of stagnation is intensified in the underground world of the third part of the novel, where the Green People have almost no sense of time, and the cycle of life passes as unremarked as it is by animals.

In contrast to this muting of time, the spatial elements are of crucial importance in *The Green Child*. The action takes place in three different and clearly defined worlds: the Yorkshire moors and dales; the South American highland republic of Roncador; the immense complex of caverns where the Green People live. Each of these worlds is described in precisely concrete detail so that we visualize it in clear images. Equally important are the journeys, in which direction rather than time is the important attribute. His trip over the pampas from Buenos Aires and into the mountains is for Olivero a voyage into a new dimension of existence, and when he goes over the pass from Argentina into Roncador he translates his excitement into spatial terms:

> I was now too excited to sleep, at once eager and apprehensive, on tiptoe, as it were, at the threshold of a country which held my destiny. The grassy track at my feet, the vista of wooded hills, the vast sky above me, all invited me forward with a secret promise.

In Roncador, the calculation of spaces within the city plays an important part in plotting the downfall of the dictator, and, later when Olivero and his General Iturbide attack and destroy the bandit army of General Vargas, the whole incident is envisaged in the spatial terms of topography and the appropriate movement of forces. Most significant of all, there is Olivero's walk with the Green Child up the stream to the moors, where direction—in this case the reversed flow of the stream—becomes of crucial symbolic importance.

The dislocation of time, and the endowment of space with an enhanced and quasi-magical significance, are common attributes of romance, and romance indeed is one level on which we may read *The Green Child*, before we immerse ourselves, like Olivero, in the deeper waters of meaning. In the classic way of good romance, it opens with a matter-of-fact statement that immediately attracts our attention with the suggestion of mystery:

> The assassination of President Olivero, which took place in the autumn of 1861, was for the world at large one of those innumerable incidents of a violent nature which characterise the politics of the South American continent. For twenty-four hours it loomed large in the headlines of the newspapers; but beyond an intimation, the next day, that General Iturbide had formed a provisional government with the full approval of the military party, the event had no further reverberations in the outer world. President Olivero, who had arranged his own assassination, made his way in a leisurely fashion to Europe.

From the statement that Olivero has arranged his own assassination, we realize something out of the ordinary is about to be revealed and, as Olivero travels, we learn that he is mentally 'occupied by a landscape distant and withdrawn in the long dark tunnel of time, but bright in its crystal setting'. Born an Englishman, he is going home returning, as we are told, 'to the place where his personality had first been liberated, in circumstances extraordinary enough to make them the enduring reality of his life'. He arrives in his Yorkshire countryside. It is changed inevitably by time, but it is essentially familiar—familiar, that is, except for one circumstance, which immediately removes us into the realm of fantasy. For the water in the beck beside the village street is running in the opposite direction to that which Olivero remembered from the distant past. No law of nature can explain this phenomenon, and Olivero decides to follow the stream and satisfy his alarmed curiosity.

From this point we become irrevocably involved in the world of romance, or rather in three worlds, for *The Green Child* is a triptych of romantic genres. The first part is an example of the fairy romance, in which some being, human in appearance but not in nature, enters our life and transforms it. The stream leads Olivero to the mill, where he looks through the window and sees Kneeshaw trying to feed blood to the woman he recognizes as the Green Child. He liberates her, and, after he has extracted her history from Kneeshaw, the two men fight, the miller is drowned in his own stream, and Olivero and the Green Child follow the ascending beck until they reach the bog that is its source, and there, stepping on to a silvery quicksand, they sink below the surface of the pool.

From this ambience of elfin fantasy we move in the second part of *The Green Child* into an apparently realistic narrative of Olivero's adventuring after he leaves the village in 1830. Yet this also is romance, of another kind, the Quixotic romance of the magic journey in which the hero passes through testing perils (he is imprisoned in Spain, and captured by privateers at sea), but arrives at last in a land far distant from his own and entirely different in character. There he is mysteriously elected to power and rules over a pastoral realm like a virtuous king in an ancient story.

Finally, in the last part, we return from the apparently real to the superreal; the tone of fantasy is resumed as Olivero and Sally descend like people in a painting by Hieronymus Bosch within a bubble of air which, by another strange inversion reinforcing that of the back-ward-flowing stream, *ascends* into a pool in the realm of caverns where the Green People live. This is another kind of romance; perhaps the most potent, since we are left to speculate on the connection between the reversal of the stream and Olivero's meeting with the Green Child. Are we to assume that she herself has the power to reverse the law of nature; or that some mysterious power which controls her emanates from the world below; or perhaps that it is all Olivero's dream, in which, like the romantic artist, he deliberately transcends actuality? For the story takes on the archetypal pattern of the descent into the underworld which recurs in every mythology and almost every religion. The realm of the Green People is a kind of Hades, and if its inhabitants are not exactly 'the blurred and breathless dead' who surrounded Odysseus 'with rustling cries', they exist in a scarcely human world of uncanny order, devoid of passion. However, *The Green Child* departs from classic stories of the descent into the underworld, for, unlike Odysseus and Heracles and Orpheus, Olivero does not return to the upper earth, but lives out his life among the Green People; when he dies his body is petrified with Sally-Siloën, and he becomes

> part of the same crystal harmony. The tresses of Siloën's hair, floating in the liquid in which they are immersed, spread like a tracery of stone across Olivero's breast, twined inextricably in the coral intricacy of his heart.

They are magic sleepers who will not awake.

Yet *The Green Child* is not merely a cluster of romances, for, as I have suggested, it is related in structure to Read's autobiographies, and it represents a further phase of indirection, in which experience, having passed through the stages of immediate recording and of autobiographical artifice, is finally transformed, like the bodies of the Green People, into the crystal patterns of art. Jung was undoubtedly right when he detected that, on one level at least, *The Green Child* was about Read's inner life, and an examination of the autobiographical elements helps to elucidate its contents and liberate its allegorical significance.

The Green Child is not only rooted firmly in the world of Read's memories; more interestingly, it also charts symbolically the pattern his later life would follow, since he too, like Olivero, would return— exactly thirty years after he decided in 1919 to abandon Yorkshire and find a career elsewhere—to seek in his native county the scenes he remembered as 'withdrawn to a fantastic distance, bright and exquisite and miniature, like a landscape seen through the wrong end of a telescope'. *The Green Child*, then, not only projects the past transfigured; it also charts a future, and in doing so presents a pattern which, in its own way, life will re-enact, thus proving that Wilde (whom Read cautiously admired) may be right about life's mimicry of art, at least among those who attempt to live, as Read did, by aesthetic laws.

The links between *The Green Child* and Read's own imaginatively transfigured memories are, however, much more complex than those provided by the parallel between two men returning to their Yorkshire villages after years of wandering. One after another the resemblances build up. Read, like both Olivero and his rival Kneeshaw, came of a family of millers, and the mills of his relatives polar-

ized his childhood by presenting in opposition to the farm, which
was daily reality, the images of a life governed by a routine of primitive machinery yet miraculously self- sufficient. At the same time the
limestone landscapes of Kirkdale and Bransdale provided the natural phenomena which undoubtedly suggested the two principal top-
ographical wonders of the Yorkshire of *The Green Child*. In the real
world a stream could vanish underground and emerge to feed the
Strickland mill at Howkeld; it needed only a small stretching of probability to think of a stream that would actually change its course and
flow back to its own source. And the deep cavern near the church at
Kirkdale, with its stalactites and its dark branches stretching away
beyond candlelight and courage, became the model for the underworld of the Green People; as a child Read must often have thought
of the great cave's mysteries and of the possibility that strange beings
might survive in its depths as the extinct hyenas lived there in the
days of palaeolithic man.

The Green Child herself, of course, belongs in origin to folk literature and not to fact; in Keightley's *The Fairy Mythology*, which
Read quoted in *English Prose Style*, seven years before he wrote *The
Green Child*, she and her brother are represented as having been
found near a pit from which they have emerged into the English
countryside. Like Read's Green People, they live on beans which in
their country grow in the stalks rather than in the pods of the plants.
The boy dies and the girl survives to tell of her country where 'they
saw no sun, but enjoyed a degree of light like what is after sunset'.
Nothing more is told of the Green People in this original story, and
the Child herself does not resist efforts to feed her on ordinary
human food, as she does in Read's novel. Indeed, she changes colour
from green to sanguine, accepts baptism, and becomes 'rather loose
and wanton in her conduct'.

I suspect that this original legend was modified in part by the
influence of W. H. Hudson, whose heroine Rima in *Green Mansions*,
seen in the forest by the narrator, appears as an ethereal being of
greenish-grey colour; like the Green Child, Rima has the ability to
vanish into green bushes without a trace, and shares with her an
affinity to birds. There are other suggestive echoes of Hudson in *The
Green Child*; the description of Olivero's journey over the pampas to
Roncador recalls *The Purple Land* and *El Ombu*, while Hudson also
wrote a Utopian novel, *The Crystal Age*, whose people live an asce-
tic and passionless life not unlike that of the Green People. Even its

title has an echo in the passion of the Green People for actual crystals and for crystalline harmonies. At the end of World War I, when he was friendly with Ford Madox Ford, Read read all of Hudson's books, and he shared Ford's high opinion of *Green Mansions* and *The Purple Land*. But, if memories of Hudson's books went into the shaping of *The Green Child*, so, it seems likely, did those of Voltaire's *Candide*, another of Read's favourite books; Voltaire not only introduces, in Candide's journey to El Dorado, an inaccessible and Utopian South American realm, but also, by introducing the Jesuit communities of Paraguay, gives a hint Read may have followed when he studied the history of these communities to provide a past for his mythical Roncador.

But if the Green Child and her country, like the land of Roncador, have their origins in fiction as well as in the topography of the Yorkshire limestone country, Olivero and Kneeshaw appear both to have their origin within the writer's self, and thus to be related in more than the fact that both are the sons of millers. They are, I suggest, projections of opposing facets of Read's own personality. The resemblances between Read and Olivero are too obvious to need discussion. Both are intensely conscious of the power and quality of words. 'Words can be bright and glittering,' Olivero remarks, 'can attract men's eyes and fascinate their minds—even when they mean little or nothing.' Olivero's pilgrimage leads him to spend some years in a prison in Cadiz, a 'dark and forbidding building' which has a haunting resemblance to the orphanage school of Read's childhood. In Roncador Olivero displays military and organizational talents resembling those Read developed during his period as a soldier and a civil servant. And, denied the possibility of creating order through literature, he does so by establishing an ideal pastoral society which comes as near as politics can ever do to a work of art.

> There is no joy comparable to the joy of government, especially in circumstances of virgin chaos. Not only inanimate things—money, equipment, goods of every kind—but even human beings, are so much plastic material for creative design. A sense of order is the principle of government as well as of art.

Olivero carries out a revolution in isolation from world influences, and the isolation enables him to create the perfect political form, but he finds that this very form, elaborate it though he may,

is—like classical art—ultimately unsatisfying. He tries to introduce
the element of the unpredictable, and out of his little war with the
bandit general Vargas emerge the few romantic images of the period
in Roncador, such as Olivero's description of the night after victory.

> We then took a number of captured horses and rode away into the night.
> The funeral pyre still burned with a lurid light in the darkness behind us;
> before us the stars hung above Roncador. In spite of our victory, we were
> silent; only the creaking of our saddles, and the jingle of our equipment,
> rose above the soft thunder of hooves.

But even this experience is unsatisfying, like the experiences of
Read's life as an impresario of the arts, and Olivero deserts the world
of action to seek the shining vision of childhood which lies at the end
of memory's long tunnel.

If Olivero's nature so clearly resembles Read's own, and his career
seems like an imaginative projection of his creator's, the significance
of Kneeshaw is more oblique. He appears at first a surly, churlish
peasant. Yet on more than one occasion we become aware of elements in Kneeshaw that do not fit in with so simple a characteriza-
tion. Why, alone among the young men of the village, should he be
romantically obsessed with the Green Child? As Read describes him,
he is elementary yet complex, primitive in instincts yet not necessarily crude; he is in fact the passionate and intuitive complement to
Olivero's intellectual deliberation—a missing element of the unpredictable and spontaneous that is needed to create in *The Green Child*
the equation of reason and romance.

It should not be forgotten that Kneeshaw first appeared in Read's
writing sixteen or seventeen years before *The Green Child* was written, in an ambiguous poem entitled 'Kneeshaw Goes to War'. Kneeshaw in the poem is an introspective, withdrawn individual sucked
into the military machine, which sets his thoughts on unfamiliar
paths. Through experience and through fear he is liberated from the
prison of himself; finally, a physical cripple, he can sing his own song,
which ends:

> I stand on this hill and accept
> The flowers at my feet and the deep
> Beauty of the still tarn;
> Chance that gave me a crutch and a view

Gave me these.
The soul is not a dogmatic affair
Like manliness, colour, and light;
But these essentials there be:
To speak truth and so rule oneself
That other folks may rede.

In *The Green Child* Kneeshaw takes on more definite qualities, some of them malevolent. He has committed the act of destruction that sets Olivero on his wanderings; now he seeks to dominate the Green Child by administering the sinister eucharist of a real lamb's blood. The confrontation between him and Olivero is inevitable. They are both fascinated by the Green Child, and eventually through her each is lost in water and becomes dead to the earthly life.

At this point the deeper reason for Jung's interest in *The Green Child* becomes evident; one might very plausibly chart the novel as a parable of the Jungian process of individuation. Kneeshaw is the archetypal dark brother, the Shadow. Having confronted him, Olivero can travel on with the Green Child, who corresponds to the archetypal Anima, the soul-image, and with whom, descending into the pool, he undergoes symbolic baptism and is born again by ascending in the pool of the underworld, where he confronts the wise old men who in Jungian terms personify the spiritual principle.

It is hard to imagine that Read was unaware when he wrote *The Green Child* (published in 1935) of this resemblance between what happens in the Jungian dream world and what happens in his novel. But the resemblance is not complete, since *The Green Child* does not lead the myth of individuation to a successful end. The imperatives of the free imagination intervene, and an examination of them requires a diversion of view to the third part of the book.

Read has cautioned us against assuming that he is posing either of the quasi-Utopian visions of *The Green Child* as desirable eventualities, and the paternalistic dictatorship which Olivero establishes in Roncador is far enough from the anarchist vision for us to assume that, if there is any didactic intent here, Read is suggesting that order without 'eccentric elements', to use Olivero's phrase, leads to the frustration of spontaneity and the consequent stultification of life. But the land of the Green People seems at first a different matter, for there are attractive aspects to this underworld paradise. There are no wars, not even any quarrels; there is no possessiveness either towards

persons or towards property; literacy and timepieces are alike unknown and unneeded; the Green People proceed by a natural development from play to work, from work to philosophic dialogue, and
from philosophic dialogue to a contemplation that leads them through
deepening serenity towards death.

Their world has thus all the elements of an idyll, and yet one feels
repelled by these people whom Olivero had thought of, before he
lived among them, as 'beings half-human and half- angel, intermedi-
ate between the grossness of earth and the purity of heaven'. In fact
the Green People are neither angels nor men; they are retarded children caught in a perpetual innocence that prevents their development into men endowed with all the irrationalities of humanity; they
lack above all 'the sense of glory'.

It is to such a world that Olivero's attempt to recapture his childhood has led, and here the clues begin to weave backwards and for-
wards between the novel and *The Innocent Eye*, Read's nostalgic
vision of a childhood to which in fact one can never return. We have
already seen how Read suggests in *The Innocent Eye* that strong
emotions like terror and pity are hardly present in children.

> The child ... survives because he is without sentiment, for only in this
> way can his green heart harden sufficiently to withstand the wounds that
> wait for it.

The Green People are children *whose hearts have remained green*;
they have no attachments to individuals, the death of others raises no
feeling in them, and, because their emotions do not develop, their
intellects blossom into arid abstractions; their wisdom consists in
mechanically playing out the chimes on series of little gongs, and
contemplating crystals whose appeal lies in their subtle divagations
from the strictly natural order.

> Aesthetic pleasure was a perception of the degree of transgression
> between the artificial form and its natural prototype, and the greatest
> aesthetic emotion was aroused by those crystals which transgressed both
> within the limits of probability.

In other words, the Green People are 'classicists', and one is not surprised subsequently to learn that their only strong emotion is a dis-
gust at 'the organic and vital elements of their bodies'.

Everything soft and labile filled them with a species of horror, and above all the human breath was the symptom of an original curse which would only be eradicated after death.

Therefore they petrify the bodies of their dead, until they achieve a kind of immortality by taking on 'the mathematical precision and perfect structure of crystal'. These crystals are steadily filling up the caves; in the end the dead will crowd out the living.

Thus, under the elusive and ethereal charm of the Green People lies a negation of vital forces, an anti-organic view of existence, and it is Olivero's end to welcome death through hatred of life; most significantly, unlike the antique heroes and the gods of sacrificial religions (e.g. Osiris and Christ) he does not return from the under-world; he has been reborn into death, not into life eternal.

Once this becomes evident, Kneeshaw's role assumes its true importance, for Kneeshaw, devious, brutal and destructive, still rep-resents life and reality. Olivero's error has been to deny him. In youth he fled rather than come to terms with him; his flight led to the ster-ile achievements in Roncador. On returning he becomes the acciden-tal but inevitable cause of Kneeshaw's death and, in destroying his other self, is self-condemned to perpetual alienation from the forces of life.

Thus *The Green Child* reveals its ultimate significance as a para-ble illuminating the dialectic that runs through all of Read's works: the necessary interplay between freedom and order, between reason and instinct, on which the organic reality of life as well as of art depends. The discontinuous triptych form is appropriate to this pur-pose, as is the imagistically sharp visual quality, and the style of deceptive restraint which seems to suggest simplicity, but in fact— like the style of Stendhal whom Read so much admired—projects the sangfroid of ordered passion.

* * *

The Green Child was the only work of fiction that Read thought worth preserving. A few other fragments remain, but add little to his achievement. Most are wartime 'sketches', semi-fictionalized experi-ences or actual stories, which appeared between 1916, when Read published three of them under the title of *Fables from Flanders* in the Leeds University magazine, *The Gryphon*, and 1930, when he pub-

lished others in the Faber pamphlet *Ambush;* the latter included a
particularly lurid piece called 'Killed in Action' which had already
appeared with war poems in *Naked Warriors* (1919) and which
Read then described as a chapter from a novel. All are unsuccessful
attempts to give fictional form to immediate experience; none
approaches in effectiveness Read's two direct reportages on war, *In
Retreat* and 'The Raid'.

More interesting, and certainly more appealing, is the novella for
children, 'Penny Wise and Pound Foolish,' which exists in a handwritten notebook in the Read Archive at the University of Victoria,
and which, so far as I know, was never published, though Read made
elaborate plans for illustration. It is the story of a penny, coined at the
beginning of Queen Victoria's reign, as it passes from hand to hand
until at last, old enough to become a curiosity, it lives out its last years
among other modest family treasures. Reminiscent of the days when
Read handled the pennies of the poor as a clerk at four-and-two-
pence a week in the Leeds Savings Bank, it is filled with pleasant and
whimsical conceits, including coin's-eye views of human character,
and philosophies of monetary destiny dominated by the fear of the
great Melting Pot; it also presents a pleasantly oblique picture of the
social world of Read's youth, a half-rural world of farmers, craftsmen, little shopkeepers, taverns and leisured gentlemen who secrete
sovereigns in their waistcoat pockets. 'Penny Wise and Pound Foolish' is a pleasant entertainment that should one day be published, but
it is little more.

When one remembers Read's original ambition to become a novelist in the manner of Henry James, his surviving fiction is a scanty
harvest, and one can hardly accept his own excuse for its slightness—
that his various occupations left him little time for writing. He could
have written short stories or even chapters for a novel as easily as
essays in the time he commanded, if fiction had been the form in
which above all he felt impelled to express himself. It is clear that he
was by temperament and talent a poet and an essayist, not a novelist,
and that *The Green Child* was the kind of *jeu d'esprit* which many
poets have performed once in their lives, as a change from more
familiar genres. Walter de la Mare's *Memoirs of a Midget*, Lermon-
tov's *A Hero of Our Time*, Morris's *News From Nowhere*, and that
romance of Alain Fournier which Read admired so much, *Le grand
Meaulnes*, are all poets' holidays of this kind, and an elusive similar-
ity distinguishes them from the works of ordinary—or even extraor-

dinary—novelists. They are not involved in the ordinary fictional task of exploring a world populated by likely personalities related to the universe through varying degrees of believable perception; they do not have those worries over plausible psychology or the consistency of timetables or the authenticity of natural phenomena that pursued even such powerful and free spirits as Dostoevsky and Balzac among the novelists by profession. They can choose their own degrees of probability, their own relationships with actuality; the fact that they are poets licenses any break into fantasy or implausibility they choose to make. It is still left for the Tolstoys and Hardys and Stendhals to produce the real Niagaras of fiction. Yet the novels of poets are often fountains of rare wit and fancy which have their own very distinct places in literature. One of the features that usually distinguishes them is the way in which they use the regular methods of the poet for their own irregular purposes. *The Green* Child would not have been the small and unique classic it has now become if Read had not used in writing it his poet's complex sensitivity to words and his essayist's power to control and manipulate ideas.

The Inward Journey

Between the public view of Read in his years of celebrity, and his private view, there was a great discrepancy. To most of the people who treated his name as a classroom—if not a household—word, he was the great champion of the modern in art. The limitations he imposed on that role were hardly regarded; whatever was new, it was thought, he advocated, and his great contribution to the thought of his time seemed to lie in his enthusiasm for the revolutionary.

If Read sometimes took this estimation at face value, and saw himself as an inspired spokesman for the movement of change, he always, in the end, returned to the conviction that he was, above all, the poet. 'My criticism is, fundamentally, a defence of my poetic practice,' he once said; and all his literary achievements do in fact take on greater significance when one *sees* them clustered around that original urge which led to his use of words, the desire to be a poet. He may not appear to posterity like his friends and contemporaries, T. S. Eliot and Ezra Pound, as one of the major seminal influences on the poetry of our time. He founded no school; he had, with the doubtful exception of a few young men in the Forties, no disciples. He did not remain attached for long to the groups that temporarily attracted him, the Imagists and the Surrealists. Yet he was an originative as well as an original poet, and today his verse stands strikingly apart from the fashionable movements that flourished during the greater part of his life. It represents not only the last stage of indirection in his work, the final integration when the poem is successful—of impulse and form; it is also the central calling to which he returned constantly until the end of his life, enjoying an exceptionally long span of effective poetic creation (from World War I to the 1960's). If there was a still centre in the maelstrom of Read's life, his poetry provided it.

At first sight, there seems a contradiction between Read's deep and sustained involvement in contemporary movements in the visual arts and his progressive withdrawal from contemporary move-

ments in poetry. It was the contrast between the missionary and the
hermit, but the world has known examples enough of men who have
combined these complementary roles. If Read had been asked to
explain the difference between his attitudes towards poetry and art,
he would undoubtedly have said that the modern movement, which
in poetry was interrupted by the return to didactic motives and traditional forms in the 1930's, remained vigorous for decades afterwards in the visual arts. But I suggest that there are more profound
reasons. By the beginning of the 1920's Read had given up his early
ambition to become an artist, and if he still painted a little, it was
entirely for his private satisfaction. He could therefore stand aloof
from the actual current of creation in the visual arts, formulate his
standards and apply them with relative consistency. In poetry his
continued involvement in the process of creation established a quite
different situation, as Read confessed when in 1948 he wrote the
introduction to a new edition of *Form* in *Modern Poetry*, originally
published in 1932.

> But the critic who is also a poet is in a special difficulty. With a certain
> objectivity he has elaborated his system of scientific criticism; but at
> other moments in his life, in another mood, he has felt a creative impulse,
> and submitting to this impulse has written poetry which owes nothing to
> his critical theories.

Such a statement has to be considered in relation to Read's views
of what should happen in the creation of a poem. For him such creation is not a deliberate act, as it may be for the classical poet who
shapes a poem according to an already established pattern. He sees
as the essential feature of modern poetry its recovery of that attribute
of romantic poetry, and of all great poetry in the past, 'the form
imposed on poetry by the laws of its own origination, without consideration for the given forms of traditional poetry'. Defining more
directly the actual process, he claims, in *Poetry and Experience*, that
'the conscious poet, the poet as a personality, has to withdraw from
the scene and in a very real sense let the poem write itself'. Thus we
have the seeming paradox of a writer who believes that form and
style are quintessential attributes of any work of art, poem or painting ('form alone exists—only form preserves the works of the mind'),
and who sees art as 'discipline, definiteness, abstraction from chaos',
also contending that complete spontaneity is necessary for the act of

poetic origination. The paradox is resolved by the thought that origination alone is not enough. 'All art originates in an act of intuition,
or vision. But such *intuition* or vision must be identified with knowledge, being fully present only when consciously objectified.'

Because he found deliberate self-criticism—as distinct from the
innate sense which helped to shape his verse and to reject at the time
what was inferior—difficult to sustain, Read tended to write little
about his own poetry or even about the poetry of his contemporaries.
There is a significant example of this difficulty in *Annals of Innocence and Experience*, when he discusses the juvenilia which he published in his first book of verse, *Songs of Chaos:*

> The intensity with which I wrote some of these poems is still a vivid mem-
> ory—it was not an intensity of emotion leading to expression, but an
> emotion generated by the act of creation. The intensity was due to the
> discovery that an image could be matched with exact words. The trivial-
> ity of the image did not seem to matter. Even now, with all my literary
> and critical experience, I cannot be sure that it matters. I cannot be sure,
> for example, that a poem which now costs me a qualm to quote is not
> nevertheless a valid poem and therefore a good poem. It was called 'A lit-
> tle Girl':
>
>> I pluck a daisy here and there—
>>   O many a daisy do I take!
>> And I string them together in a ring,
>>   But it's seldom the ring doesn't break.
>>
>> O daisies rosy, daisies white!
>>   If I could string them in a ring
>> They'd make a bonny daisy chain—
>>   O why is a daisy a delicate thing?
>
> If, as a very childlike youth, I succeeded in evoking the simplicity of a
> child's outlook, even a child's insight, then the result is valid. It is only
> sentimental if as an adult I am trying to exploit childish things.

One can only comment that, as an adult critic, Read could obviously not always recognize sentimentality when he saw it. 'O daisies
rosy, daisies white' is not what a child would say or think; such apos-
trophizing belongs only to poems written for children by adults. Nor

would the sensibility of a child—particularly such a child as Read portrays in *The Innocent Eye*—lead him to ask, untutored, 'Why is a daisy a delicate thing?' One suspects the influence of those Edwardian governesses who move so shadowily through Read's childhood.

A more critical judgement led Read to reject in general terms most of the poetry others were writing in the last thirty years of his life, but it was a judgement that he rarely expressed at length or in detail, for he was temperamentally reluctant to attack the work of individuals, and without specific reference it is difficult to maintain any critical position, condemnatory or otherwise. When *Moon's Farm* was chosen by the Poetry Book Society in 1955, he was invited to write on his poetry for the Society's Bulletin; instead, he set down a series of maxims for young poets. One of them reads:

> Never write reviews of contemporary poetry—it makes you too conscious of being a poet yourself, and perhaps an inferior one.

And, indeed, though Read wrote a number of benign prefaces to books of verse, I can think of few reviews of poets anterior to Wilfred Owen. It was only in later years, in books like *The True Voice of Feeling* (1947), *The Tenth Muse* (1957) and *The Cult of Sincerity* (1968), and in *Truth is More Sacred* (1964), his volume of literary discussions with Edward Dahlberg, that he expressed at length his views even of the poets who had dominated the literary world of his youth and many of whom had been his friends—Pound and Eliot, Aldington and Lawrence and Edwin Muir; and even then he tended to be personally reminiscent rather than critical.

As we shall see in the following chapter, the vast majority of Read's critical essays on literature in fact dealt with the writing of the past, and the most important of them with the Romantics; the rest were spread over the history of English literature from Froissart to Henry James. Even the books that seem to offer guidance on his views of modern poetry and poets, and which might therefore be expected to throw some light on his own poetic development, are in fact disappointingly past-oriented.

In *Form in Modern Poetry*, for example, he tells us that 'by "modern" poetry I mean all genuine poetry from Coleridge's day to ours— and indeed all genuine poetry of all time', and he so far sidesteps the reader's anticipations that, after making a few general statements on the modern attitude to poetry, he completes his book

without having discussed the poems of any writer later than Gerard
Manley Hopkins. Only in the preface to the 1948 edition does he
even mention Pound.

In the 1948 revision of his early book, *Phases of English Poetry*
(1928), the new chapter on 'modern poetry' is again almost devoid
of references to specific contemporary poets, while saying much of
the influence of Browning, and arguing that the formal characteristics of modern poetry are the ultimate development of 'Wordsworth's theory of poetic diction, as modified and corrected by
Coleridge'.

Yet in this book Read at least discusses in general terms the
predicament of the modern poet and, by implication, his own.

> The modern poet [he says] is before all things honest. He does not write
> for fame nor for money; he would be disappointed if he did. He merely
> writes to vent his own spleen, his own bitterness, his own sense of the dis-
> parity between the ugliness of the world that is and the beauty of the
> world that might be. He is trapped in a mechanical civilization. Every-
> where about him are steel cages and the futile voices of slaves ... to be
> part of our civilization is to be part of its ugliness and haste and econom-
> ic barbarism. It is to be a butterfly on the wheel.
>
> But a poet is born. He is born in spite of the civilization. When, there-
> fore, he is born into this apathetic and hostile civilization, he will react in
> the only possible way, he will become the poet of his own spleen, the vic-
> tim of his own frustrated sense of beauty, the prophet of despair.

The stance may seem, in the 1970's, heroic, but this is perhaps a
measure of how much farther poetry has been alienated during the
past forty years from the contemporary world.

Read maintains that such poetry of spleen and frustration is 'the
only *typical* modern poetry'. He ends *Phases of English Poetry* with
the question, how the modern poet can reconcile his world and his
art and 'resume his function as the explorer and the educator of
human sensibility'. He speculates on the possibility of returning to a
communal poetry like that of the old ballad- makers which will satisfy 'the emotional needs of the populace'. But it is clear that this aim,
so frequently canvassed in the Thirties, is temperamentally repugnant to Read:

> It means a surrender of every personal standpoint, and a sacrifice of all

pride of knowledge and exclusiveness of sensibility. And at present our very conception of the poet and the poet's activity presupposes a condition of pride and isolation. Inwardly, I feel that this life of intelligence is the only reality, and that the art of poetry is the difficult art of defining the nature of mind and emotion, a veiled activity, leading the poet deep into the obscurities of the human heart.

The one essay in which Read confronts directly the predicament of modern poetry (meaning poetry after the first quarter of the twentieth century) is 'The Image in Modern English Poetry', first written in 1954 and included in *The Tenth Muse*. Here, following the doctrines of the Imagists with whom he had once identified himself, he declares that in the twentieth century 'there was one clear line of progress—the isolation and clarification of the image, and the perfecting of a diction that would leave the image unclouded by rhetoric or sentiment. To that task our greatest poets—Yeats, Pound, Eliot and Thomas—devoted their best energies.' But those poets and their successors have diverged from this creative direction, 'and once again a veil of rhetoric is drawn over the vision of the poet. Sentiment supersedes sensation, the poetic consciousness is corrupted'.

Read felt a mounting sense of isolation as a poet after the early 1930's. 'My own vision is slightly myopic,' he once remarked; 'I do not *see* very clearly beyond the poets of my own generation—Pound, Eliot, Williams, Crane, Tate and Marianne Moore.' He believed to the end of his life that the poetic principles and practices developed by Eliot, Pound and the Imagists between 1906 and 1915 represented the true movement of poetry, deriving from the romantic tradition; alone though he might be, following in his poetry a 'veiled activity' that contrasted with the actions of his public personality, he felt that it was he who sustained however humbly and intermittently the authentic modern movement in poetry, the tradition of vital and incessant experiment.

2

If Read tended to be reticent about poetic movements during the years of his maturity, and aloof in his later practice of the poetic art, he devoted some of the best pages of *Annals of Innocence and Experience* to his first introduction to poetry and his early years of verse

writing, and here he provided an invaluable background to the consideration of the war years during which he moves with amazing
rapidity from the apprentice work of *Songs of Chaos*, collected in
1915, to the clear imagistic vision that inspires *Eclogues*, published
in 1919, but probably written between 1916 and 1918.

Every poet begins to write from a unique inner impulse, but in
certain times and social ambiences the external circumstances that
help to shape the styles of poets are often similar, and the influences
that fostered Read's poetic inclinations resembled those experienced
by many lower-middle-class English poets in a period when schools
taught no modern poetry and the writing of one's first verse was likely to be a solitary activity regarded by the respectable as only slightly less deplorable than masturbation. Nothing remotely resembling a
youth culture existed, and experimental literature was carried on in
narrow metropolitan circles. Whatever natural impulse led Read to
poetry, a series of fortunate accidents produced the circumstances in
which his talents found their proper course. A teacher at the evening
school he attended while working at the Leeds Savings Bank awak-
ened a feeling for the sound of poetry which all his schooling had not
stirred. His brother's employer, the Quaker tailor William P. Read,
showed an encouraging interest in his early poems, all now lost.

> They were, I think, mostly short lyrics about flowers, birds, atmospher-
> ic moods; the more realistic of them may have attempted to catch some-
> thing of the poetry of foggy, gas-lit streets, the glow of furnaces by night,
> the clatter of clogs on the stone pavements. There were no love poems.

One finds no references to interest on the part of others than W. P.
Read at this time, and one suspects that in his first years of writing
Read drew most of his encouragement from the example of earlier
poets.

Tennyson attracted him by his meticulous rendering of intimate
landscapes; Blake provoked his fantasies and stirred him with his
splendid incantations; Ralph Hodgson misled him into whimsicality.
His *Songs of Chaos* were written under the influence of these poets,
and, as the example I have quoted suggests, there is little need to
linger over them. The first truly liberating influence—if one accepts
Read's own opinion that Donne merely provided him with 'an extension of sensibility, an education in emotional rectitude'—was Robert
Browning, whose experiments in 'the expression of intellectual concepts in the language of feeling' had a profound and largely forgotten

influence on the more important poets of the modern movement, Pound especially and even Eliot. Read retained from his early attachment to Browning a predilection for the dramatic monologue.

When he left school Read was fortunate in moving from Halifax to Leeds. The University as yet offered no guidance in modern literature, but the city had attracted men like Frank Rutter and Jacob Kramer, who were interested in all manifestations of modernism in the arts. From his meeting with these men and his initiation into the Leeds Arts Club in 1913, when he was twenty, Read dated the beginning of a 'passionate participation' in the 'immediate destiny' of poetry. He marks off 1913 to 1917 as the period during which he evolved his philosophy of composition. It is uncertain when he first became aware of Imagism. He did not meet the leaders of the movement, Pound, Aldington, Flint and Hilda Doolittle, until 1918, and he never met T. E. Hulme, though later he edited his writings. The first anthology of the group, Pound's *Des Imagistes*, appeared in 1914, but Read does not mention this in his *Annals*, and it is likely that his introduction to the movement was through the 1915 anthology, *Some Imagist Poets*, with its famous preface, calling for the use of the *exact* word, the creation of new rhythms to express new moods, the presentation of images, and the production of 'poetry that is hard and clear, never blurred or indefinite'. Read's first surviving reference to the Imagists occurs in the War Diary' on 31st July 1916, when he mentions them approvingly, with Henry James, as representatives in literature of 'the essence of the XXth century'. Later he claimed that already in 1915 he was writing in the Imagist manner, but his memory for dates was rarely exact, and the first poems he published showing an Imagist influence appeared in 1916 in the Leeds University student paper, *The Gryphon*.

If one can judge from these poems, he had as yet incompletely mastered the implications of Imagist doctrine. One alone 'Aeroplanes', is written in accordance with the canons of the movement, presenting the plane as

> A dragonfly
> in the flecked grey sky.

and the shell-bursts around it as

> smoke-lilies that float
> along the sky.

The cluster of images sustains an ironic analogy between a lily-pool in summer and a scene of war. The other *Gryphon* poems are marred by an archaic diction which Read later condemned and by the jarring introduction of abstract concepts. A good example is the opening passage of 'Ypres':

> With a chill and hazy light
>   the sun of a winter noon
>   swills
>   thy ruins.
>
> Thy ruins etched
>   with silver silhouettes
>   against a turquoise sky.
>
> Lank poles leap to the infinite
>   their broken wires
>   tossed like the rat-locks of Maenades.
>
> And Desolation broods over all
>   Gathering to her lap
>   her leprous children.
>
> The sparrows whimper
>   amid the broken arches.

The use of the first person singular, and the survival of Wildeian phrases like 'silver silhouette' and later in the poem—'vermeil flames' and 'wan harmonies', soften the clear impression of the original metaphors (the sun swilling the ruins and the poles with their wires tossing like rat-locks), while the visual unity of the poem is destroyed by the introduction of the personified abstraction, Desolation, whom we are tempted to visualize as a Hellenistic group of statuary—something like Niobe lamenting her children—in the centre of a scene of modern war.

Throughout his life Read was troubled by the difficulty of achieving a proper balance between visual and conceptual elements in poetry. He did so most successfully in his shorter poems, and some of the best of these belong to the volume of imagistic verses entitled *Eclogues* which he published in 1919. Indeed, the twenty poems published here represent such a manifest advance on *Songs of Chaos* and the *Gryphon* poems that it is difficult to accept the span of time from 1914 to 1918 which Read attributes to these poems. The well-assimilated Imagist influence suggests that the versions contained in *Eclogues* date from the latter part of the war. The first poems of the group to be published—'Curfew' and 'The Pond'—appeared in the initial number of *Art and Letters*, under the editorship of Frank Rutter and Read, in July 1917. Another, 'The Orchard', marked Read's first appearance as an acknowledged Imagist; it was accepted by Ezra Pound and published in *The Egoist* later in the same year.

Most of the *Eclogues* are poems of rural nostalgia, including 'Childhood', with its anticipations of *The Innocent Eye*, and also 'The Pond', 'The Orchard', 'Pasturelands', 'Woodlands' and 'Harvest Home'. They are most successful when they record an observation or episode sharply and clearly and hint analogically at a deeper and wider resonance. 'The Pond', justifiably one of the best-known Imagist poems, is an excellent example:

> Shrill green weeds
> float on the black pond.
>
> A rising fish
>   ripples the still water
>
> And disturbs my soul.

The image that in a sense is the poem presents a perfect example of the Imagist approach: the presentation of a vivid surface—green weeds on black water—and the fish's breaking of that surface in a way that suggests the deep correspondences between the objective world and the poet's mind.

A self-conscious poeticism still lingers in some of the *Eclogues*, as in the opening lines of 'Curfews':

> Like a faun my head uplifted
> in delicate mists ...

but there are others in which the conceptual element is entirely subsumed in the sensual, such as 'April':

> To the fresh wet fields
> and the white
> froth of flowers
>
> Came the wild errant
> swallows with a scream.

Such a poem offers a variety of legitimate responses. One can dwell merely on the visual and aural presentation; one can remember the terrible myth of Procne and Itys; one can dwell on the variety of the natural world exemplified in the contrast between the static beauty of flowers, tethered in their setting, and the free, ever-moving beauty of the animal world.

Eclogues records the transition from Read's rural childhood. Among the middle poems there are two, significantly uncertain in tone, that mark his diffident advance into another social world: 'Garden Party' (I have assumed a conscious sociability/pressed unresponding hands') and 'Concert Party'. There are also some controlled, objective Imagist war poems, the best of which is 'Movement of Troops'. Here, as Robin Skelton has suggested, the effect of the accurate portrayal of a scene is intensified by 'the shift in viewpoint from that of the speaker to that of a watcher observing what is surely a descent into the inferno'.

> We entrain in open trucks
> and soon glide away
> from the plains of Artois
>
> With a plume of white smoke
> we plunge
> down dark avenues of silent trees.
>
> A watcher sees
> our red light gleam
> occasionally.

Published in the same year as *Eclogues*, Read's other wartime volume, *Naked Warriors*, presents a mood opposed to its cool objectivity. Here Read is the anarchist, the man of his wounded time whose

cry against society and its crimes is almost a reflex action. He rebels
not only against war, not only against the social system that has led
to it, but even against the escapist attitude of pre-war writers—the
beer-drinking, Georgian cottagers, and the crepuscular bards of
Hibernia. He has pointed out that the epigraph to the volume may be
interpreted as a rejection of the early Yeats:

> War through my soul has driven
> Its jagged blades:
> The riven
> Dream fades
> So you'd better grieve, heart, in the gathering night,
> Grieve, heart, in the loud twilight

The introduction of Yeats at this point has an ironic resonance. In
later years Read admired the Yeats who remade himself as a poet,
and also, in a rather embarrassing way, he became involved in one of
Yeats's most controversial actions. When Yeats was invited to edit
The Oxford Book of Modern Verse, which appeared in 1936, he
decided—in the middle of a decade that demanded in poetry the
direct rendering of experience—to reject poetry written in the
trenches during World War I by soldier poets, including such figures
admired in the Thirties as Wilfred Owen and Siegfried Sassoon. 'He
chose', Read recollects, 'instead a poem of my own based on war
emotions "recollected in tranquillity".' As an interested party, Read
refrained from comment for thirty years. In *Annals of Innocence and
Experience*, he admitted that his war experience had modified his literary values, 'not altogether for the good', but only in 1967, in a
paragraph of *Poetry and Experience* which ostensibly concerns
Owen, did he publicly grant that Yeats was right and obliquely reject
much of the poetry he himself had written in wartime.

'All that a poet can do today is warn', wrote Owen in the preface to his
poems, and in these words he resigned the interpretative function of
poetry. When he said 'the Poetry is in the pity' he implied that it was not
where it should be, in a magical felicity expressing the physiognomy and
movement of the outward world. Owen sacrificed felicity and harmony
(the proper ingredients of poetry) for Truth, the truth about war. It may
be argued that the sacrifice was worth while, that Truth is more impor-

tant than Beauty. But Arnold's point is that Truth and Beauty must be reconciled in poetry—to give man 'a satisfying sense of reality'; to reconcile man with himself and the universe.

At this point Read clearly agrees with Arnold, and by implication with Yeats.

After the controversial epigraph, *Naked Warriors* begins with that awkward, ambiguous poem, 'Kneeshaw Goes to War'. Physically, the war has mutilated and therefore reduced Kneeshaw; mentally it has freed him from the prison of himself and has thus increased him, as, analogically, it provided for Read 'an increase of my literary experience'. But, as Read added, 'it does not need a war to effect that change in a poet: I should have been brought to it by the impact of life itself.' The real effect of war was to create a disequilibrium in experience and also in response; for thirty years the theme would assume an excessive importance in Read's poetry.

In *Naked Warriors* he was concerned with the fresh, direct experience of conflict. Apart from 'Kneeshaw ...' the book consists of 'The Scene of War', which includes some poems I have already mentioned: 'Liedholz', 'The Refugees'. Of the remainder, a few, such as 'Villages Démolis', are vivid accounts of the physical reality of war. 'Fear' is a psychological notation which anticipates the longer treatment of the same idea in 'The Raid'; a fragment of clinical introspection rather than a developed poem. 'The Happy Warrior' also is less than a poem; it is an expression of immediate anger without benefit of tranquillity.

> I saw him stab
> and stab again
> a well-killed Boche.
> This is the happy warrior,
> this is he ...

We are left with two diverse and more substantial items, 'My Company' and 'The Execution of Cornelius Vane'. In 'My Company', Read takes as his subject the sense of comradeship and of fates shared that creates the community of the trenches, and is the principal compensation for the horror and ennui of life in what is euphemistically called 'action'. The horror exists in the image of the man on the wire whose corpse his comrades cannot bring in for fear

of their own deaths; it is enclosed within the poet's monologue when
he opposes his sense of unanimity with his men to the loneliness that
leadership and responsibility impose on him. When he discusses his
own thoughts and portrays action concretely, the verse is good, but
the integrity of the poem is spoilt by outbursts of feeling which
assume a conventional, sentimental tone largely because they are so
self-consciously literary. Such shifts can be disastrous, as in the passage which begins with the description of his men carrying planks
and iron sheeting 'through the area of death', halting when flares
burst, cursing when they continue: one becomes deeply involved in
the scene, and then one's involvement is dissipated when the poet
cries out:

> My men, my modern Christs,
> Your bloody agony confronts the world.

The association provoked is literary in a ludicrous manner, for it
reminds one of the ending of Wilde's meretricious 'Sonnet for Liberty':

> These Christs that die upon the barricades,
> God knows that I am with them, in some things.

The same failure of a feeling that has not passed through the
shaping hands of imagination is evident, perhaps less crudely, in 'The
Execution of Cornelius Vane'. Here, at least, the poet is not standing
before us to express sincere thoughts with awkward directness. He
proceeds indirectly through the narrative of Cornelius Vane, a coward who shoots off his finger and avoids action until a desperate
emergency forces him into battle, and he is caught and executed. It is
an attempt to penetrate imaginatively an alternative personality, for
Read had himself overcome fear but knew the monstrous forms it
could assume in others, as 'The Raid' suggests. Human desperation
and the inhumanity of military law are opposed to each other, and
the poem stirs one's sympathy for the first. Its major flaw is the tendency to lapse into abstract Latinate language appropriate neither to
the story nor to the man Cornelius Vane.

> He was still running when he began to perceive
> The tranquillity of the fields
> And the battle distant.

Away in the north-east were men marching on a road;

Behind were the smoke-puffs of shrapnel,
And in the west the sun declining
In a sky of limpid gold.

The narrative would be more consistent with its theme if for 'perceive', 'tranquillity' and 'declining' one were to substitute words with more concrete and particular connotations like 'see', 'quiet' and 'falling'. 'The Execution of Cornelius Vane' nevertheless shows Read moving away from the original occasion into the shaping world of the imagination.

3

During World War I, Read both matured as a poet and made his first impression in the literary world. He was accepted with surprising ease by contemporary poets, most of them slightly older than himself. The friendship of Frank Rutter, and Read's own evident talent, helped to smooth his way, but there were other, personal qualities which contributed to his acceptance; he suggested them long afterwards in discussing the origins of his friendship with Eliot.

> When I first met Eliot I was, from an intellectual point of view, both ignorant and naif. I had not had the advantage of his orderly education and philosophical training. The only credit I might claim was the experience of war, and though he respected this, I was in the process of disowning it ... I do not know what he found to like or respect in someone so fundamentally different in background and temperament, but first my Englishness, I suppose. My naivety, even after the experience of war, was that of a country boy, uncorrupted by society or learned sophistication. The enthusiasm that had survived a war was but another aspect of the same naivety, and Eliot must have been aware that it embraced him with an intuitive sympathy and understanding. This poet, in spite of his reserve, was not indifferent to devotion, and he felt the need for one or two disciples. (*The Cult of Sincerity*.)

After the war Read developed as an essayist making occasional excursions into other forms of prose, but his career differed from

that of many other writers in that the prose did not kill off the poetry, doubtless because, after adolescence, Read rarely experimented
with fiction, so that his creative as distinct from his critical powers
were consistently directed into verse. After the war he published ten
volumes of poetry (including various *Collected Poems* which contained new material), and until the beginning of his eighth decade
there were few years in which he did not publish poems either in periodicals or in books.

There is a perceptible line of development in this poetry, and the
burden of it is carried in his long, rather than in his short poems.
Some of the later short poems were more complex in form and perhaps more profound in thought than the *Eclogues*, but it is hard to
show development in the 'clarity and elegance of ... sensibility'
which, as Robin Skelton has remarked, is most evidently displayed in
Read's briefer poems. It is in the longer poems that development
takes place, a development from metaphysical abstraction towards
an ever greater concreteness of vision. Read was aware of this development, for in 1932, on the eve of publishing what I believe was his
first relatively successful long poem, *The End of a War*, he wrote in
Form in Modern Poetry that:

> Poetry of any length is visual or it is tedious; it may be visual by virtue of
> its action, or by virtue of its imagery. It can never, whilst still remaining
> poetry, be merely informative or conceptual.

He was, in fact, always at his best in poems—long or short—where
action or the strong visual rendering of physical scenes was involved,
preferably brought into a detached form through an element of indirection imposed by distance in time or space.

Conflicting with this characteristic concreteness of vision was
Read's obstinate ambition to write the long contemplative work
which he regarded as the sign of a major poet. He was fascinated by
the genre of philosophic verse, and the poets he admired most, from
Donne and Traherne, through Wordsworth and Coventry Patmore,
to such innovators as Hopkins and Eliot, were all in their various
ways metaphysical. Read was ill equipped, at the beginning of his
career, to emulate them. He was innocent of religious experience,
untutored in philosophy. His mode of thought tended to be visual
rather than conceptual. He later acquired a working knowledge of
philosophy as it impinged upon his fields of aesthetic and political

interest, but he never won acceptance among professional philosophers, who regarded his thought as nebulous and inconsistent. Yet it
is often an advantage in a poet to be an imperfect logician, for this
leads him to seek the expression of philosophic truths by oblique
paths, and Read moved forward, as his Imagist origins taught him,
by a series of attempts to reconcile the visual and the conceptual, and
by the development of a style that matched his poetic personality.

He wrote, in all, twelve works that might be classed as long
poems. His poetic drama, *The Parliament of Women*, which he completed early in the 1950's, was published only in 1960 in a limited
edition. Five early philosophic monologues appeared in *Mutations
of the Phoenix* (1923). Three others were included in later collections between 1926 and 1944. *The End of a War* (1933) and *A World
Within a War* (1943) were separately published, and *Moon's Farm*,
Read's only true dialogue in verse, was produced by the BBC Third
Programme before it was published in 1955 in a collection of poems
that bore its title.

These poems fall into groups that mark fairly clearly the periods
of Read's poetic career. The first stretches from the end of World War
I to the early 1930's. It corresponds to the time when Read was finding his voice as a critic of literature and the arts; in verse as in prose
this was an interlude of philosophical searching. It reaches a partial
poetic resolution with *The End of a War*. The second period begins in
the middle Thirties and extends until after the end of World War II; it
corresponds with Read's open identification with modernist movements in the arts like surrealism and constructivism, and his political
emergence as an advocate of anarchism, and it brings his poetry into
a close relationship with the events of his time, though not into a
relationship of submission. The most successful long poem of this
time is *In the Middle of a War*. The last period is that of Read's return
to Yorkshire; it is represented by *Moon's Farm*, at once the longest of
his poems and the only one that indubitably belongs in the company
of Eliot's *Quartets* and Pound's *Cantos*.

The impression created by the long poems of *Mutations of the
Phoenix* is that Read is trying to work out a metaphysical system in
verse, rather than utilizing an existing system (as Dante did that of St.
Thomas Aquinas) as the armature on which to build a poetic vision.
In consequence one is tempted by the poet's deliberately intellectual
language and form, into seeking to disentangle the 'meaning' of the
poem. This task has actually been undertaken for all Read's longer

poems except *Moon's Farm* by two Swiss scholars, H. W. Hatiser-
mann (in an essay on 'Herbert Read's Poetry' which formed part of
Herbert Read, edited by Henry Treece, 1944), and his disciple Ray-
mond Tschumi (in *Thought in Twentieth-Century English Poetry*,
1951). As these assiduous interpreters, who worked with Read's
approval, have provided as accurate explications as are likely to be
given, there is clearly no object in repeating their task, particularly as
telling us what the poems are about does not eliminate one's sense of
an essential disunity, between the intellectual and the visionary, in
these works where the concentrated impact of the image, as it
appears in Read's shorter poems, is perilously dispersed.

The title poem, 'Mutations of the Phoenix', is a series of meditations on the temporal guises of the spirit. It begins diffusely by evoking the common fire that burns within us and 'has burnt the world ...'
and proceeds through varying images of flame and spirit, to the question 'Why should I dwell in individual ecstasy?' and thence to a series
of abstract considerations on the nature of consciousness:

> Mind wins deciduously,
> hibernating through many years.
> Impulse alone is immutable sap
> and flowing continuance
> extending life to leafy men.
> Effort of consciousness
>   carries from origin
>   the metaphoric clue.
> The cap is here
> in conscience human unique;
> and conscience is control, ordaining the strain
> to some perfection
>   not briefly known.

This is neither thought eminently well expressed, nor feeling poeti-
cally conceived, and only towards the end of the poem, when 'the
metaphoric clue' is taken up in the vision of the place where the meditation on the phoenix has unfolded, does the pattern of images take
on a final visionary quality:

> This is holy phoenix time.
> The sun has sunken in a deep abyss

her dying life transpires.

Each bar and boss
of rallied cloud the fire receives.

Till the ashen sky dissolves.

The mind seeks ease
   now that the moon has risen
      and the world itself is full of ease.

The embers of the world
   rustle, fall: a bird's wing, a dry leaf.
There is a faint glow of embers
   in the ashen sky.

These stars
   are your final ecstasy,
and the moon now risen
   golden, easeful ...

But here one misses the immediacy that appears in Read's earlier
shorter poems, 'the structure of events' which, in another of his
longer poems, 'Beata l'Aima', he declares 'alone is comprehensible'.
Whether that is the case with other poets, it is certainly so with Read.
A poem contained in an event, even if the event is merely seeing a fish
rising, is in his hand more telling than many pages of philosophic
variations worked out in a macaronic language of concept and
image.

Compare, for example, the lines from 'Mutations of the Phoenix'
last quoted, with a short poem written not long afterwards, 'The
White Isle of Leuce'.

Leave Helen to her lover. Draw away
before the sea is dark. Frighten with your oars
the white sea-birds till they rise
on wings that veer
against the black sentinels
   of the silent wood.

> The oars beat off; Achilles cannot see
> the prows that dip against the dim shore's line.
> But the rowers as they rest on the lifting waves
> hear the revelry of Helen and a voice singing
> of battle and love. The rowers hear and rest
> and tremble for the limbs of Helen and the secrets of
>   the sacred isle.

Here is no attempt to distill an intellectual formula. The poet presents an event caught at a moment of dramatic suspense. One visualizes the scene made sharp and definite by white birds against the black and silent wood. One catches the resonances of the singing and Helen's laughter, and there, framed in the tightness of the poem's form, the vision stands with need of no more explanation than the feelings aroused by the sound of words and the associations set ringing in the mind by names and images. There is not a syllable out of place or unnecessary or incomprehensible; all is in balance and in tension, and it is hard to think of poetry that uses more subtly the classical virtues of spareness and economy to record the echoing distances of romantic feeling.

For the solution Read eventually found for the long contemplative poem he was indebted to Browning; it lay in the substitution of a personal for an impersonal voice, which immediately set the poem within 'the structure of an event'. For this reason, the most successful of the early long poems are 'John Donne Declines a Benefice', which appeared in *Mutations of the Phoenix*, and 'The Lament of Saint Denis', first published in *The Criterion* in 1926 and included in the same year in *Collected Poems 1913–25*. In both of them the language is idiosyncratic, considerably less abstract than in poems like 'Mutations of the Phoenix', 'The Analysis of Love' and 'The Retreat', and in both the speaker assumes the density of a visual as well as a vocal presence.

'John Donne Declines a Benefice' is the less convincing of these two poems, for Read has neglected Browning's caution in taking as the speaker of a dramatic monologue a figure whose literary voice we do not know. We know how Donne wrote (even if we do not know exactly how he spoke), and this knowledge undermines the credibility of the poem. Its harshnesses of diction, abruptnesses of rhythm, and startling concatenations of images create a superficial resemblance to Donne's *manner*, yet the way Read uses these devices is different from Donne's way.

> So shall the soul invade
> The world of the imaginary divine
> In which the fanatic can abandon selfhood.
> But a sick pride calls the act profane—
> To rid this soul of its compact kingdom
> And give it a crystal nothingness,
> The boy left, a wickless mass
> Of inchoation. There's some divine amalgam
> Of flesh and spirit, an alloy
> Which I must find—must make my God
> Invisibly from spit and clay.

That does not suggest even an imaginary Donne seeking (as Read imagined him doing in *Annals*) 'to bridge the separate worlds of intellect and feeling ...' It is too obviously none other than Read, struggling with his main poetic problem how to write contemplative verse without introducing the destructive element of abstraction. Even the jerky, awkward speech and tortuous vision, so different from the limpid diction and the visual clarity of his shorter poems (but present in all the longer poems of this early period), are symptomatic of the same unresolved problem.

'The Lament of Saint Denis' is distinctive because, through the Saint's eyes, Read presents the truth in visually exciting hallucinatory visions. The Saint never appears, but in his mind we see phantasmagoric processions of mankind seeking salvation and peace, finding only terror, and meeting on their way an ominous being with severed head. The head speaks; he is not a storm-quelling spirit, for he contains the storm, as he contains the essential contradictions of light and dark, order and chaos. Read's speech flows out in a tone of authority that might be compared for its clarity and assurance with that of Eliot. The tortuosity and obscurity have vanished; a poem that to its climax is visually conceived, reaches through its own intrinsic inevitability a clear point of intellectual statement, but a statement implying that such moments of penetrating rationality can be attained only by visionary paths.

I am chaos and dark nothingness;
The storm you met on the way
Is now held in me.
In this lightless body,
Uncrowned, ungrac'd, devoid,
The tumult reigns. In a moment,
In any other moment,

The storm will issue,
The chaos will be without
In the past and in the future,
Yesterday and tomorrow.

And in that moment I shall stand
In ordain'd radiance.
A visible exaltation shall possess my limbs,
My lips shall be rosy and the porch of life,
And my eyes the light of reason.

Tschumi, Read's Swiss exegete, remarks with evident regret: 'The full meaning of the poem cannot be extracted in the form of philosophical statements: it is a poetical meaning, which prose is unable to express.' That, I suggest, is its virtue. The fault of the earlier long poems was precisely that Read was trying to express in verse thoughts better said in prose.

Read's first successful long poem, even according to his own criteria, was *The End of a War*, which first appeared in *The Criterion* at the end of 1932, and was published separately in the following year. The date is significant, for since 1926, when 'The Lament of Saint Denis' was published, Read had proclaimed his literary affinities with the Romantics, and had established in works like *Wordsworth* and *The Meaning of Art* his position as a critic of literature and the visual arts; by leaving the civil service, he had also liberated himself from political inhibitions. This meant that he had acquired both the freedom and the ability to develop his philosophy through the form of the essay. In addition to his release from an uncongenial employment, there had been another change in his life whose implications in terms of guilt and liberation must be worked out eventually by his biographer. His first marriage had failed, and by the time he wrote *The End of a War* the relationship was coming to an end. Thus *The End of a War* is a poem that closes an era; as its title suggests, it is the summing-up of the period in Read's life dominated by the memories of the war that matured and haunted him. By the time it appeared, a new series of public events had begun to change his private vision.

The End of a War is in form a discontinuous dramatic dialogue. It is based, as Read's prose 'Argument' tells us, on an actual incident on the eve of Armistice, when the British were advancing in pursuit of the retreating Germans. A battalion comes to a village, outside which a severely wounded German officer lies propped against a tree. He tells the scouting party that the village has been evacuated. The officer in charge signals back to the battalion, who march into the village square; massed there, they are fired upon by machine guns stationed in various houses and in the church. A hundred die; the rest slaughter the ambushers and then kill the German officer. Later they find in one of the cottages the naked body of a young girl, her legs and one arm severed. The British officer who had first come to the village investigates the crime, but cannot solve it. He goes to sleep exhausted; in the morning he awakens to the sound of the bells celebrating the Armistice.

There is no possibility of this being a disguised account of an episode in which Read took part, since on Armistice Day he was in England. The episode came to his notice indirectly, but it formed an appropriate framework in which to make a final statement on events that had changed his own life.

Read arranges the poem in three parts: the German officer, the French girl and the British officer all speak, but not to each other; the two officers speak in separate but parallel 'meditations', and the French girl in a dialogue between her body and her soul. The intent is philosophic; the poem is a triptych (a form shortly to be repeated in *The Green Child*) in which each episode is related to a personality and a predicament, and in which the poem loops in a circle from light to light, though the German officer's light at the beginning is a fading one and the British officer's at the end is a grace that

> ... descends and wakes the mind
> in light above the light of human kind
> in light celestial
> infinite and still

eternal
bright

The German officer has fought with gladness, unable to believe in
a personal god, but dedicated to 'the Father and the Flag, and the
wide Empire' which call the world 'to one Life, one order and one living'. He is one of those for whom battle has been an ecstasy :

> The throbbing of guns, growing yearly,
> has been drum music to my ears
> the crash of shells, the thrill of cymbals
> bayonets fiddlers' bows and the crack of rifles
> plucked harp strings. Now the silence
> is unholy. Death has no deeper horror
> than diminishing sound—ears that strain
> for the melody of action, hear
> only the empty silence of retreating life.
> Darkness would be kinder.

He considers his friend Heinrich, whose religious renunciation he
cannot understand. To place God first is outside his nature. One
begins with faith in the self, and goes on to faith in the State. Only in
service to the State could he imagine God,

> in the end of action, not in dreams.

Since he has thus made God, God dies as his own light dies. He triumphs over death only by dreaming to the end of 'an Empire in the
West'. But that dream fades with life and the darkness that embraces
him is the 'void of Nothing' in which this world is

> so infinite
> so small
> Nichts

If the 'Meditation of the Dying German Officer' is also the poet's
meditation on the relationship between the worship of human collec-
tivities and nihilistic despair, the 'Dialogue between the Body and the
Soul of the Murdered Girl' touches in a particularly moving way the
subject of innocence, at this time much in Read's mind, for *The Inno-*

cent Eye was written shortly after *The End of a War*. The French girl, as Read had been, is a child torn suddenly by events from the rural innocence of her origins; loathing of the enemy and the love of God grow up together in a mind that is a soil

> tilled
> for visionary hate.

It is the hatred that through some awkward attempt at spying brings her to death. The dialogue ends in a disturbing ambiguity of feeling. Soul insists that the men who have died unblessed by faith in a cause are no less martyrs than the rest. Body replies:

> Such men give themselves not to their God but to their fate
> die thinking the face of God not love but hate.

And Soul answers:

> Those who die for a cause die comforted and coy;
> believing their cause God's cause they die with joy.

But we remember that the German officer died for a cause, and died without joy. And there is a double connotation to the word 'coy' which leads one to suspect a deeply ironic intent.

The German officer dies; the French girl is already dead. The English officer awakes to find himself alive, with the bells that celebrate Armistice breaking in on his dreams, and the voices of the old peasants singing in thanks for peace. He feels reborn out of an existence in which he had felt his individuality destroyed

> and I myself a twig
> torn from its mother soil
> and to the chaos rendered.

He considers what life holds for him now that he has come through, and remembers the German officer:

> Your gentian eyes stared from the cold
> impassive alp of death. You betrayed us
> at the last hour of the last day

> a smile your only comment
> on the well-done deed ...
> But you are defeated: once again
> the meek inherit the kingdom of God.
> No might can win against this wandering
> wavering grace of humble men.
> You die, in all your power and pride;
> I live, in my meekness justified.

It is unfortunate that Read did not end the poem here, for the tone is true and the argument complete. He continues to an ending spoilt by awkward conceptualizing, as the officer realizes that his early longing to fight on for justice has vanished, and now sees the alternatives as surrender to a malign and mechanical force or acceptance of the obscure purposes of God; it is the worship of God that he chooses. The choice would have been a false one in terms of Read's own life, for this was not the conclusion he himself reached, and it is untrue in terms of the poem because it seems accidental and unnecessary. Yet, flawed though it is, *The End of a War* was the best long poem Read had yet written.

4

Read rejected the characteristic attitudes of the dominant trend in English poetry during the 1930's. Though he took an active part in the Surrealist movement, with its insistence on a revolutionary art, and made public before the middle of the decade his hitherto private adherence to anarchism, he did not accept the idea of art as propaganda, and consistently rejected the doctrines of social realism fashionable at the time.

In age and experience, Read really belonged to a half generation between the classic 'modern' writers—Eliot, Pound, Lewis, Joyce— and the younger poets first introduced as a group through the publication of *New Signatures* in 1932. Despite the aristocratic element that often tinged his thinking, he retreated into none of the varieties of conservatism that Eliot, Pound and Lewis each in his own way adopted, nor was he tempted to follow Joyce into an aesthetic *cul-de-sac.* He retained his pacifism, he broadened his anarchism. And the poems he wrote between 1933 and 1945 reflected as deep an awareness of the social problems of the time as anything Day Lewis or Auden wrote. As late as the 1950's when both these poets had long abandoned social revolution in any form as a theme, Read was still, in such a poem as " The Death of Kropotkin," asserting his anarchist faith.

The circumstances of the time in fact fostered a poetic activity in Read which resulted in the production, in the twenty years between 1935 and 1955, of a series of poems superior to any but a handful of very short pieces from the preceding decades. His vision deepened in intensity and clarity; his expression sharpened in intelligibility, and in the best works of these two decades it fused feeling and form into constructions so harmonious and economical, and yet so emotionally active, that one is unsure whether to regard them as perfect examples of classicist form or perfect expressions of romantic feeling. In these poems, more than in any of his other writings, Read in fact achieves that synthesis of the abstract and the organic which had always been his goal.

The best—with one or two exceptions—are works that in some way reflect the collective perturbations of the age. Among the shorter pieces they include that ominous unrhymed sonnet, 'A Northern Legion', written in the early Thirties and ostensibly describing a Roman war party marching over the scorched earth of Northumbria, their bugles calling in the desolate eagle- haunted valleys:

> Endless their anxiety
> Marching into a northern darkness: approaching
> a narrow defile, the waters falling fearfully
> the clotting menace of shadows and all the multiple
> instruments of death in ambush against them.
>
> The last of the vanguard sounds his doleful note.
> The legion now is lost. None will follow.

'A Northern Legion' appeared in *Poems 1914–34;* there are other poems in the volume which indicate Read's political apprehensions at this time of Fascist ascendancy; while his realistic pessimism is reflected in the refrain to 'A Short Poem for Armistice Day'—'I have no power therefore have patience.' A cynical gloss on that patience appears the intent of 'The Brown Book of the Hitler Terror', one of a small group of satirical poems he wrote at this time.

In Bednib's shop I picked up a book
An actor came in in a floating gown
He gave me an objective look
I put the book down.
And went into the sunlit streets
Where cars like shuttles passed my eyes
Discreet, I cried, discreet, discreet
And only Socrates was wise.

By 1940 when Read published his next volume, *Thirty-five Poems*, the Spanish Civil War had run its tragic course, and World War II had begun. The best poems of the volume are again related to the political events of the time. There are two short pieces on the Civil War which, a generation afterwards, shine out among the few good poems that event inspired: 'Bombing Casualties in Spain' and 'Song for the Spanish Anarchists'. Equally enduring in their appeal are 'To a Conscript of 1940' and 'Herschel Grynszpan', the latter addressed to a now forgotten assassin, a Jewish boy of seventeen who in 1938 killed a German diplomat in Paris. These four pieces are among those rare occasional poems that survive to become monuments to their occasions. They do so because in them—as in the two longer poems of this period, *A World Within a War* and *Ode Written during the Battle of Dunkirk*—Read persuades us by projecting events and images rather than by enunciating arguments. The 'Song for the Spanish Anarchists' does not express directly a single anarchist doctrine, but in that moving picture of bucolic liberty all we need to know about the anarchist communes in Spain and the faith by which they lived is in fact implied.

The golden lemon is not made
  but grows on a green tree:
A strong man and his crystal eyes
  is a man born free.
The oxen pass under the yoke
  and the blind are led at will:
But a man born free has a path of his own
  and a house on the hill.

And men are men who till the land

and women are women who weave:
Fifty men own the lemon grove
    and no man is a slave.

The effectiveness of this poem, and of 'Bombing Casualties in
Spain' and 'Herschel Grynszpan', is enhanced by the quality of
invention that irradiates them. Read never saw a commune of Spanish anarchist peasants; he saw the bodies of the children who are
mourned in 'Bombing Casualties in Spain' only in a smudged news-
paper photograph; but he created in the mind images that are more
telling than any precise description of an event seen. It is because of
the surrealist incongruity of the metaphors in 'Bombing Casualties in
Spain' that the poem lives on in harrowing reality.

These are dead faces.
Wasps' nests are not so wanly waxen
wood embers not so greyly ashen.

They are laid out in ranks
like paper lanterns that have fallen
after a night of riot
extinct in the dry morning air.

Such images do the work of which conceptual statements are inca-
pable. They make a moving poem into vivid historical statement.

In the Spanish poems Read stands outside, letting the event create
its own image; in 'Herschel Grynszpan', he projects himself as an
intermediary between the assassin and the world. Grynszpan's act,
he recognizes, has unleashed a situation in which 'violence is
answered by violence', but, in Sorelian mood, he regards this as the
breaking of the unwholesome mock-calm with which the rest of the
world has accepted the crimes of the Nazis. And so:

This beautiful assassin is your friend
walking and whispering in the night beside you.
His voice is the voice that made you
listen to secrets in the night around you.

In the other poems I have mentioned from this period Read
appears as the old soldier observing a conflict to which he is no

longer actively committed, but in which he is involved by the sense of
shared perils and shared complicity. In the fifteen years from 1918 to
the writing of *The End of a War* he had absorbed the experience of
World War I, and had made what inner reckoning he could. *The End
of a War* was the one poem he wrote of that event which, to quote
Wordsworth with the exactness on which Read insisted, took 'its origin from emotion recollected in tranquillity'. The act of composing it
was a kind of emotional immunization, and in World War II he was
able, despite his genuine concern over the horrors that were being re-
enacted, to regard events with that combination of feeling and
detachment which is conducive to good poetry. The *Ode Written
during the Battle of Dunkirk* adopts the recollective tone, creating
the scene and atmosphere of a sunny May at Broom House, letting
war's fury emerge in an image of distant sound, and then allowing
the reminiscent—not the arguing—mind to play over the past of old
guns remembered and the present of new guns heard and to find
eventually the unassailable nucleus of hope.

> The self perfected
> tranquil as a dove
> the heart elected
> to mutual aid.
>
> Reason and love
> incurv'd like a prow
> a blade dividing
> time's contrary flow.
>
> Poetry a pennon
> rippling above
> in the fabulous wind.

   A World Within a War is the better of the two longer poems, with
its strongly personal and strongly visual recreation of the poet's ideal
life in Broom House as an island of peace in a world at war. I stress
the ideal quality of the vision, for the existence shown in the poem,
with its active consciousness of the ambient natural world, and its
picture of the poet inditing his book of hours concerning freedom-
exalted mystics, and walking in free times 'through the woods with
God', is hardly a literal representation of the life Read was leading at

this time, hurrying between Beaconsfield and London to attend to his publishing and taking on constantly heavier public duties. (That is merely hinted in two inconspicuous lines:

> The busy routine kills the flowers
> That blossom only on the casual path.)

Yet it has its imaginative reality, as the picture of a mental hermitage with outside it a world

> Of alarm and horror and extreme distress
> Where pity is a bond of fear.

But through the dark and terrifying wood, which is an imaginary extension of Read's own acre of beech copse, goes the 'ancient road' followed by the martyr and the man who makes him one. It is the path of a quest that leads to the seizure of the grail and, in Shelleyan vision, to the building of

> A crystal city in the age of peace
> Setting out from an island of calm
> A limpid source of love.

It was passages like the last that led Robin Skelton (whom I mention again as one of the few writers who have actually criticized Read as a poet rather than merely trying to explain him) to dismiss *A World Within a War* as 'marred by sententiousness'. I agree that the poem contains passages which considered individually might be dismissed as sententious, but there is a unity of voice and an interplay of evocative imagery which make such passages seem natural, indeed inevitable, in their place within the poem read as a whole. Had *A World Within a War* ended in the lines I have quoted, it might have seemed merely shallowly optimistic. But it carries on by admitting the reality of what we fear, and finding the antidote to anger and destruction as in the last part of *The End of a War* in the power of the meek, which triumphs even when the meek are destroyed.

> Should the ravening death descend
> We will be calm: die like the mouse
> Terrified but tender. The claw

Will meet no satisfaction in our sweet flesh
And we shall have known peace
In a house beneath a beechwood
In an acre of wild land.

As a footnote to that vision, consider another poem, '1945', written when the explosion at Hiroshima had shaken Read's hopes of a crystal city beyond the war. His children come running over the sands, delighted they have found samphire.

But I saw only the waves behind them
  Cold, salt and disastrous
Lift their black banners and break
  Endlessly, without resurrection.

5

It may well have been the event at Hiroshima that turned Read's poetic view decisively away from the evil present and the shattered golden future of collective humanity towards a personal and a historic past. Though for a brief time at the end of his seventh decade he was more politically active in a direct way than he had ever been before, his very actions during his association with the Committee of 100 had an air of desperation enhanced by the fact that they were accompanied by no parallel urge to express his social idealism in either poetry or prose. *Moon's Farm*, with its theme of finding oneself through returning on oneself, is intensely personal, a poetic counterpart to *The Green Child*. The 'Poems mostly Elegiac' which were published with it in 1955 hover over the semi-legendary past, Bethlehem, ancient Greece and China, with even Kropotkin crystallized into a myth rather than an activist symbol. They are grave, melancholy poems, some of them among the best Read ever wrote, visions shining clearly at the end of long caves of remoteness like Olivero's memory of home, and attracting us because the caves reach back into a past that unites us with the archetypal figures of mythology.

I saw you then
Iphigenia or some legendary girl
Crouched over a fire of withered thyme

In Agamemnon's tomb. The flames
Were brief: and left a darkness
Deeper than the night: into which we walked
Strangers to our separate dooms.

His return to Yorkshire in 1949 was the consummation of Read's separate doom. Like Olivero, he had been into the world, he had done his Utopian tasks, finding the results meagre, and as a poet in his prime years he had avoided the frustration of retreat which he detected as one of the causes of Wordsworth's decline; he had lived according to his own dictum that 'poetry is a mode of communication between one man and his fellows … a state of mind buttressed by social contacts—a point of intersection of individual and group: in some sense a concentration in the individual of social or universal consciousness'.

But by the end of the war the hope he had always nurtured to return to the countryside where he was born had strengthened into a resolve. He began to write poems about the North Riding: one on Orm, the Saxon who rebuilt the first monk's church at Kirkdale and whose carved stone is still part of the present fabric, and another, 'The Ivy and the Ash', recording in clear pictorial images an exile's memory of the land's nature.

Descend into the valley
explore the plain
even the salt sea
but keep the heart
cool in the memory
of ivy, ash
and the glistening beck
running swiftly through the black rocks.

An 'Exile's Lament', written probably in 1945, was even more explicit in its expression of nostalgia:

Here where I labour hour by hour
The folk are mean and land is sour.

God grant I may return to die
Between the Ricall and the Rye.

Read got his wish, and *Moon's Farm* was the nearest he came, in poetry at least, to the reckoning with existence that prepares one to accept death. It is more than a philosophic poem, though in the strictest terms less than a religious poem, since it confesses its author's lack of conventional faith; perhaps it can best be defined as the devotional testament of an unbeliever.

It is a dramatic dialogue set on the site of a vanished farm in one of the dales behind Muscoates. In fact Moon's Farm still exists—or did when I went there a year or so after Read's death: a solid stone building standing forlorn and broken-windowed with the brambles clambering to the door. Read took the licence of exaggerating the desolation of the setting, for in his poem there is no stone on another where Moon's Farm stood: only bare, ragged ground and memories. Three voices speak. The First Voice, attached to a being who looks like a female tramp, is given as 'Place' in a note on the proofs of the poem at the University of Victoria; the Second Voice, that of the returning native, is 'Self'; the Third Voice, attached to a male tramp, is 'Time', and 'Place' refers to him as 'Father'.

There is one interesting minor way in which, quite apart from the general theme of return, *Moon's Farm* resembles *The Green Child*; here again there is an apparent confusion of direction, when 'Self' meets 'Time' who has come to meet him but also to catch him up, and 'Time' near the end of the poem remarks:

And the way up and the way down are the same.

Such lines in *Moon's Farm* remind one of the tone of Eliot's philosophic poems; given the personal closeness between the two poets, this is not entirely surprising. But the echo is only occasional, and *Moon's Farm* stands in its own right as the best of Read's long poems, working out with moving honesty the progress of thought through which experience had led him to the realization that the aesthetic philosophy, which he had come to regard as a way of living, is also a way of dying. He might die in pain, weariness or despair:

But if at the last moment
I could see some perfect form
  it might be this fern at my feet
or a sparrow flickering past my window
or a painting on the wall

or some poet's vision of eternity
  like a great ring of pure and endless light
  all calm, as it was bright ...
Granted that I could at the last moment
see some bright image
  I should die without fear or trembling.
It is when we look into the abyss of nothingness
  infinite nothingness
that we lose courage
  and die swearing
    or die praying.

'Place' answers him, 'Yes: men should hold on to tangible things.'
'Time' says: 'Live in the moment of attention.' 'Place' adds: 'Live in
the presence of things.' And the poem ends with 'Self' recollecting in
clear and imagist detail what Moon's Farm looked like when he went
there to gather daffodils as a boy.

This is a resolution far more true to Read's way of existence than
the conclusions of any of his previous long poems, truer because it is
the most personal of all—and when we approach matters of life and
death we come alone. And it resolves the dilemma posed by *The
Innocent Eye* and *The Green Child;* for what a return to the place of
the past can give us is not a continuation of a life we left decades
before, but a landscape that has special emotional resonances in the
present, and an acceptance, as Read puts it at the end of *The Contrary Experience*, of 'the laws implicit in the visible and material universe', made manifest for the poet in the image which is also a symbol
linking us to the collective consciousness of mankind and to that
unknowable All which we call God.

6

There remain two sharply contrasting works which Read wrote during the 1950's, neither of which fits into the customary patterns of his
writing. The first is the only play he ever completed and published,
The Parliament of Women. From his student days in Leeds, Read had
intermittently attempted playwriting, but apart from *The Parliament
of Women* the only surviving example I have discovered, and that a

fragment, is the beginning of a play about extra-sensory perception called 'old Lover's Ghosts' (it exists in a notebook in Victoria); references to the bombing of Hiroshima place it in the later 1940's, round about the time Read was beginning to work on *The Parliament of Women*. He mentioned the latter work to me in 1950, when I had told him I was experimenting with a poetic play.

> I too [he wrote] have been writing a verse (free verse) drama, historical in subject-matter, but I regard it as a trial piece and I am not sure that I shall ever publish it. There seems to be a generally diffused impulse to write drama now and I think it is more than a fashion.

He kept the play for almost a decade before he allowed it to be published by a private press; then the edition was so small and so discreetly distributed that it aroused little attention, though some of his friends—Stravinsky, Wilson Knight, Muriel Spark—expressed their enthusiasm, and Robert Speaight gave it a public reading. Eliot, to whom he diffidently submitted it in 1955 (urging him to 'treat it as a Ms from an unknown provincial author, and let it take its normal course at the office'), did not think it good enough to accept for publication by Faber & Faber.

I have found it a poem rather than a play, at once attractive and disconcerting. It is uncompromisingly literary; Read even denies in his preface the intent of stage-craft, and implies that he is seeking the kind of dramatic quality that survives off the stage, the quality of *The Cenci* and of *The Borderers* which are still read for their poetic moments, rather than for the quality of theatrical immediacy which characterizes most plays that succeed on the stage.

The setting and the theme are surprising in their archaism, until one remembers the remoteness from ordinary contemporary life that characterizes all Read's major imaginative works. For it is no farther to the mediaeval Morea in which *The Parliament of Women is* enacted than it is to the republic of Roncador or the land of the Green People.

The Parliament of Women, then, is a play about lords and monarchs, not about anarchists; it is essentially a knightly play, and it reminds one that when he started to write criticism Read found the sense of glory projected with a purer intensity in the chivalrous chronicles and fantasies of Froissart and Malory than in any later work. It is coincidence, of course, that he should have written the play three years before he himself became a knight, but when one reads it, and realizes how much virtue he sees in a chivalrous conception of life, the coincidence seems singularly appropriate. If the anarchists who condemned him for accepting a knighthood had read this play, they might still have condemned him, but they would at least have understood him.

The major plot of *The Parliament of Women* is entwined with the theme of political morality. William Villehardouin, crusader Prince of Achaia (and thus a remote and devious successor to Agamemnon), sets out from his capital of Mistra to take part in the internecine quarrels of the Byzantine dynasty of the Palaeologi. He leaves his Greek wife, Anna, to rule his realm in consort with the wives of the twelve French barons of Achaia. Betrayed and deserted by his allies, he and his barons are captured and held for three years by the Emperor Michael Palaeologus. They are only released when Anna and her ladies, who rule absolutely in their lords' absence, agree to ransom them by giving up the strategic castles of Morea to the emperor's men. They act from the desire for a life of peace, only to discover that Prince William and his barons regard peace as a mere strategy and contrive to twist honour in such a way as to regain their power. The interaction of feminine instinctualism and masculine rationality, the ambiguities of honour and glory, create the real dramatic structure of the main theme, into which is intertwined a subsidiary amorous theme in the troubadour tradition: the love of Geoffrey de Bruyère, one of William's barons, and Helena, the Greek wife of one of his knights. This lesser plot never really rises above the conventionally romantic, and it is in the main theme of William and Anna, of honour and power, that the play seems to fulfil Read's own definition of the characteristic that distinguishes drama from fiction 'that it abstracts the universal elements from life and constructs from these a rarefied and artificial life of the intellect, which is also in some undetermined way the life of the instincts'.

Apart from its general effect, which at least proves Read's competence as a man of letters to handle any literary form with skill, there are fine individual passages of verse in *The Parliament of Women*, such as the speech of the old knight, Sir Pierre, as he gives the fugitive lovers his blessing:

Sorrow I no longer feel, nor joy
As I stand here where the stairs divide

Waiting to go down for the last time.
Your passions, children, are green leaves
That dance in a sudden breath of wind.
The same wind once drove my ship
Over the restless waves, then died.
It is difficult to remember its drift
And I have made no charts—would not,
For a rigid course breaks the baulks
To let salt waters in. Stillness will return.
I too had a wife, a fair wife,
Sons and daughters that I loved;
But all have passed me on these stairs,
Left me gaunt and cold … Pray for the sun
To warm your young limbs; pray for privacy.
Be mutual in your fantasies; other men
Let pass unheeded, unless they are poor
Or old, or broken by the wars.

Eliot, who despite their differences of viewpoint accepted the validity of most of Read's writing, was equally unresponsive to his other experiment of the 1950's, the group of poems known as 'Vocal Avowals'; it was eventually included in Read's *Collected Poems* of 1966, but only with great misgivings on Eliot's part. The misgivings were not without cause, for Read, long fascinated with the idea of pure poetry (whose possibility he had discounted in his younger ideas), had at last embarked on the extreme experiment of—as he called it in a phrase borrowed from Paul Valéry—'absolute poetry'.

When Read sent Eliot the 'Vocal Avowals', he explained 'they are like abstract painting in that one either sees the point of them or they are altogether meaningless'. Only Stephen Spender, apparently, did see the point of them at the time of writing, and published a group in *Encounter* in 1959. They are poems that certainly defy the exegete and challenge the critic. Here is a typical example.

cradle song
shell leaf lifania
leaf kiss condone
trident syllabic
system restrain

marlowe meridian
lissom lodore
buddha barbaria
now alone

   The point of such poetry is of course that it has no logical point;
it has slipped out of the continuities of thought that are necessary in
prose; in doing so it has abandoned grammar and syntax, though it
has not abandoned formal elements proper to poetry, such as
rhythm, alliteration, a measure of syllabic regularity, and, above all,
the image. At last the words and the images stand out, detached from
all the accretions of rationality. We can savour the words for their
sound and form, we can arrange them as they could never be arranged in a clause or a sentence, and by juxtaposing words that nor-
mally never consort together, we can produce new resonances. The
need for abstract words, for colourless conjunctions and preposi-
tions vanishes; every word is also an image heavy with connotations,
and when the connotations chime together they produce a strange
music in the mind.
   Such work, of course, represents the withdrawal of poetry into its
ultimate privacy, the absolute opposite of the communal verse of ballad makers and oral epic bards in which poetry began. It meant for
Read the last act in that revolution which the 'modern' movement in
poetry represented for him; he went alone on this final stage of the
Imagist journey, but he reached his destination. However disconcerting they may be to those who seek rational meanings in poetry,
'Vocal Avowals' have their beauty of sound and suggestion and, on
each re-reading, strike wider resonances in the mind. Spender suggested they represented a fusion of Read's preoccupation with art
and his poetry; 'your critical awareness of something very pure and
beautiful in abstraction suddenly flowering in your poetry'. Except
that this final departure in poetic form was in actuality the result of
long preoccupation rather than of sudden flowering, Spender's insight may well be correct; in these small, intense and vivid poems we
may find the microcosms of Read's imaginary life, the grains of sand
in which worlds are contained.

4

The Sense of Glory

If to the end of his life Read considered himself primarily a poet the description applied only to a minor proportion of his work. Most of his writing, in volume as in numbers of titles, he did as—in his own description—'a critic and philosopher of art and literature'. Professional philosophers have often been disinclined to grant him the second part of the title, but, though Read followed the example of other libertarian thinkers, in avoiding the creation of a metaphysical system, he established effectively his claims to being regarded as more than a critic. He went beyond the contemplation of actual works of art and literature to seek the sources of artistic creativity and to establish the relationship between the work of art and the percipient mind. And these very studies led him to the point where his aesthetic philosophy took on an ethical character, and became synthesized with the political philosophy of anarchism which he had already evolved in his youth.

Yet it is no rigid structure of metaphysical architecture that faces us when we seek Read's philosophy. It is rather a kind of coral growth, a symbiosis of attitudes related by a common urge that can perhaps most accurately be described as the dynamic equilibration of freedom and order. It was not in the nature of Read's mind to marshal his thoughts into a single summational work, even of so undisciplined a structure as Coleridge's *Biographia Literaria* which was for long his critical bible. It was his method to work out the facets of a subject in separate essays and afterwards to bring them together; a collection established in this way he regarded as a more organic entity than a book constructed on a mechanically logical plan. He did not reject the systematizers; indeed, he borrowed their ideas without concealment, but he found that in the fields of thought where he was working, so near to the spontaneous urges of creation, his own approach was the more fruitful. And in the end, if there is no system,

there is certainly a recognizable pattern, a philosophy of the relationships between the arts and human society, which spans the whole
horizon of human creativity from poetry where Read's criticism
begins in the judgement of his own art, to the politics of the unpolitical where it emerges as a criticism of all civilization.

In the chapters that follow I shall trace the pattern in a sequence
which I think follows the directions of Read's thought without
imposing an uncharacteristic rigidity or an unintended consistency.
His criticism of literature and the visual arts leads naturally to his
insights into the relationship between art and society, hence to the
aesthetic basis of a libertarian ethic, and finally, by way of education
considered as a function of art, to the society that right education
might produce—the free society of ordered anarchy.

Read the critic, the aesthetic philosopher, the anarchist and edu-
cationist, is essentially Read the essayist, for it is in these fields that
he principally uses the form which, apart from the poem, he found
most congenial. His essays fall roughly into two classes, differing in
volume, tone, even in pattern.

In the introduction to his *Collected Essays in Literary Criticism*,
in which he gathered most of the longer critical pieces he had published up to 1936, Read made some illuminating comments on the
nature and future of the 'polite' essay, the category in which he then
considered his own prose writings had their proper place. The quotation is long, but it throws light on his own practice, and for this reason I reproduce it unabridged.

> During the last quarter of a century we have witnessed the death of
> the 'polite' essay. A hundred years ago, in the hands of Macaulay, it was
> the very voice of authority, solemn and orotund. A generation later
> Arnold and Bagehot gave the form its last refinement; with Pater it was
> already in decline, expressive and subtle, but overwrought and literary.
> Since Pater's time there have been good essayists, but gradually the
> form has been sacrificed to the increasing tempo of the press. The quar-
> terly and monthly magazines, the only effective patrons of this kind of
> journalism, have given way to the weekly reviews and daily newspapers;
> and though two or three of the old magazines still survive, they are mori-
> bund in the sense that they no longer appeal to a vital public. The excep-
> tions, in my own time, have been the *Times Literary Supplement*, which
> until recently published every week a leading article of essay length, and

the *Criterion*. It was in these two journals that most of the essays now reprinted first appeared.

The essay length is from 3,500 to 5,000 words. Less than 3,500 become an article or sketch—and to meet the exigencies of the daily or weekly it is generally much less,—1,000 to 1,500 words only. The upper limit of the essay is no doubt also determined by journalistic considerations: anything more than 5,000 words is disproportionate to the fixed dimensions and miscellaneous character of a periodical, and is probably as much as the ordinary reader is prepared to absorb in a provisional format. Speaking from the writer's point of view, I would say that this upper limit also represents as much as any one with a sense of form would want to write on a given subject—as much, that is to say, unless considerably more. Five thousand words give one room to turn around, to examine the various aspects of the subject, to summon the relevant evidence and to draw the necessary conclusions. It is a general view that the essay gives—not a biography nor a critical analysis, not a history nor a treatise. It is personal in its approach, but not intimate; objective rather than discursive. On any subject of permanent interest it should give the point of view of an age or generation; it should revise accepted opinions in the light of new knowledge.

Its function cannot be taken over by the 'feature' article or sketch. If the essay is to disappear from our literary practice, a very definite instrument of culture will disappear with it. The scholar will remain, for he has leisure or opportunity to study a subject at the sources; and there will be crowds round the literary snack-bars. But the figure in between, the amateur of letters, the man of cultured tastes, whose predominance gives a nation its degree of civilization—this type will lose its sustenance and disappear.

This was a reasonable assessment of the situation towards the end of the Thirties, when Read assembled the *Collected Essays*. It was the depression decade; publishers were cautious; literary journals were dying or amalgamating; even *The Criterion* had only one more year to limp when Read wrote these words. Yet in one way he was to prove himself wrong, and, in another, events were to perform the same task.

In spite of the deprecatory view he expresses of the 'article or sketch', Read had already, by the mid Thirties, made himself a master of this useful vehicle of criticism. His weekly art chronicles in

The Listener, his reviews of books and exhibitions, the brief pieces
which—after his flight from academic life—he learnt to write on
occasion and on demand, were literary journalism of the highest
order, and in this genre he developed into a public critic in the same
class as V. S. Pritchett, Cyril Connolly and Edmund Wilson. Such
short pieces showed the breadth of his knowledge and his resource-
fulness in utilizing it; they caught and kept the reader's interest by
rhetorical virtuosity without debasing the theme Read had accepted; and the most familiar subject would be renewed by a mind as
unpredictable as it was accurate in its insights. The most readable—if not the most memorable—of Read's books of criticism are
indeed those miscellaneous volumes, like *A Coat of Many Colours*
and *The Tenth Muse*, in which he gathers the best short occasional pieces of a decade, and pieces them together into a random
mosaic whose surprising juxtapositions of painters and poets create a mental continuum of changing, shimmering brilliance like a
well-assorted kaleidoscope. Reading such volumes, and similar collections embracing merely the visual arts, such as *The Meaning of
Art* and *The Philosophy of Modern Art*, one realizes how much Read
contributed to the popularization of art during the past generation,
in a manner that in no way compromised the dignity of the works
he discussed or his own critical integrity. It was serious, arresting
literary journalism, whose very brevity developed a concise and
vivid eloquence, a highly personal tone, that characterized Read's
short occasional writings.

At the same time, Read was unduly pessimistic in prophesying
either the death of the long essay or the decline of the amateur of letters. During the 1940's there was an unanticipated resurgence of
quarterly journals, particularly in North America. Many of them
were devoted to narrowly scholarly interests, but others encouraged
the essay that was not bounded by academic specialism, and in these
particularly in the *Sewanee Review* Read was able to continue publishing his longer critical pieces to the end of his life.

Yet, though the form continues, there is a striking difference of
tone between the essays which Read wrote in his early years for *The
Criterion* and *The Times Literary Supplement*, and published in such
volumes as *Reason and Romanticism* and *The Sense of Glory*, and
those which formed the critical volumes he published after World
War II. The earlier essays have something of the genial and relaxed
manner that survived from the days of Hazlitt into the Georgian era;

they are quiet in pace, and deliberately graceful in phrase and metaphor; it is hard to imagine such essays as those on Froissart or Malory being written by Read after Hiroshima or, for that matter, after the outbreak of the Spanish Civil War.

The later essays are more solemn in tone and dense in texture, in spite of the fact that most of them were delivered first as lectures. After 1945 Read's engagements abroad required a constant supply of new themes, which in turn provided material for the many and varied works of criticism and aesthetics he published during the 1950's and 1960's. Most of the audiences were academic, either at American universities or in the erudite gatherings of Jungian scholars at the annual Eranos Tagung at Ascona.

There are, I suggest, several reasons for the opacity one sometimes senses in these papers. Read was inclined to think in visual and tactile terms, a tendency related to his adherence to Imagism, his passionate interest in painting and sculpture, and the particular vividness with which, in his poems, his autobiographical essays and *The Green Child*, he evokes the visible world. He was the opposite of his contemporary, Aldous Huxley, whose almost completely non-visual mind thought naturally in concepts and who was able to express them convincingly and eloquently. Read, who declared himself for the 'organic' as opposed to 'abstract', who leaned towards the romantic rather than the classical view, seemed often at the edge of his depth when he was writing conceptually, and at such times (in discussing theories of aesthetics for example) his writing tends to lose its luminescent quality. Quite apart from this lack of ease with abstract concepts, Read's form of essay, which was a kind of serious literary causerie, did not have the structure needed to develop the form of argument it was sometimes used to sustain. There would be an arresting start, but the essay would then level out in tone; engrossed in unravelling his arguments, the writer would forget the need to elevate the reader's interest, and the ending, instead of rising on a crescendo of revelation achieved, would come indecisively and even anticlimatically. And though, as we shall see, Read's interest in psychology and in some of the other para-sciences widened his scope of understanding as a critic, it often in the practice of writing hindered his ability to transmit that understanding. He was inclined to interpolate long quotations in the opaque, Germanic style, favoured by psychologists and their translators, and, by contagion, his own writing would sometimes in these circumstances take on an uncharacteristic density. Yet, even in such circumstances, insights would often emerge with a sudden and blinding clarity, which is why one continues to read even the most opaque of Read's essays, much as one continues to read Coleridge, because they proceed from one of the great generalizing intelligences of our age.

2

'I myself am sometimes accused of eclecticism,' said Read in *The Tenth Muse*. 'I do not object to the charge. The essayists I most admire—Bacon, Hazlitt, Bagehot—they too were eclectic. If one has a beam of intelligence, let it play where it lists, so long as it has power and penetration and a fixed centre.'

Often despised in an age which worshipped the expert and deified specialization, the eclectic critic has won a renewed respect in recent years; we have begun to realize the need for synthesis in a world where the progressive division of functions has resulted in the frustration of intelligence and the fission of culture. It is true that our condition is different from that of the Renaissance when the sum of knowledge was still small enough to be embraced by a single mind as broad and deep as Leonardo's. Today, such comprehensive awareness is no longer possible, but it is still possible to create meaningful relationships between the various spheres of knowledge, and in such a task the courage and even the foolhardiness of the eclectic become essential.

Read rejected, for his own purposes, all the academic orthodoxies of criticism. 'Sympathy and empathy feeling—*with* and feeling *into*', were for him the primary processes of criticism, and this meant that 'there can be no immutable canons of criticism, no perfect critics. Criticism is good and sane when there is a meeting of intention and appreciation. There is then an act of *recognition* and any worthwhile criticism begins with that reaction.'

If Read objected to the kind of critical categories that seek to delimit the individual character of the work of art (and even at times rejected such broad classificatory terms as 'romantic' and 'classical'), he was equally opposed to the imposition on criticism of the scientific method (as distinct from the insights of scientists, e.g. psychologists, considered on their own merits).

The critic with a head but without a heart, armed with instruments of precision but without love, is the monster who killed Keats [he said] . He has had a numerous progeny, and I fancy that the species has found a particularly congenial habitat in American universities (but we have enough to spare for export in England) . In so far as he confines himself to textual criticism, he can perform a very useful service. Analysis of Hopkins's metre, exegesis of Eliot's mythology—these are types of necessary activities that one must not for a moment despise. But they should not be confused with criticism proper, which is a philosophical activity, concerned, in Acton's words, with the 'latent background of conviction, discerning theory and habit, influences of thought and knowledge, of life and descent'.

Similarly the critic will avoid a sociologically dominated criticism, and a criticism that aims at moral judgement.

But this does not mean that he will lack moral perception, and, while he will not allow a scientific or sociological approach to dominate his criticism, he will not deny that science or sociology can contribute in a secondary way to the task of the critic. Thus the psychologist helps to explain what a work of art does, but only the critic can explain what it is; the psychoanalyst can tell us about the work of art in becoming, but only the critic can interpret it in being.

It is Read's willingness to embrace the insights of psychoanalysis that academic scholars have been inclined to accept as his characteristic contribution to modern criticism, in so far as they have been willing to recognize him at all, which is more rarely than one might expect. Before I began to write this passage, I took down from my shelves eleven surveys of modern criticism to test my impression of the extent of this academic neglect. Six of them, including David Daiches's *Critical Approaches to Literature* (described as a 'comprehensive study'), do not even mention him. Kenneth Burke, in *The Philosophy of Literary Form*, briefly attacks *Poetry and Anarchism* but does not notice any of Read's more directly critical work. René Wellek and Austin Warren, in *Theory of Literature*, and George Watson in *The Literary Critics*, merely mention him in footnotes. In a single sentence in *Five Approaches to Literary Criticism*, Wilbur Scott credits Read with having been a pioneer in the 'use of psychology in literary criticism', but ranks him even in this respect after Conrad Aiken, Max Eastman and Robert Graves. And in that monstrous compendium of half-digested ideas on critical method, *The Armed Vision*, Stanley Edward Hyman combines two quite inaccurate references to Read (one of which classes that most earnest *book Wordsworth as* 'ironic') with a superficial and misleading comment in which he accuses Read of rarely utilizing the psychological insights he so enthusiastically hails.

It is clear that, in spite of Read's seasonal appearances at American universities, his distrust of the academic critics was reciprocated. But the scanty references show at least that his use of psychoanalysis as a means to critical insight had aroused too much attention to be easily ignored, and since this is indeed an important aspect of his criticism I will discuss it briefly before considering his essays in themselves.

Read's interest in psychology is almost contemporaneous with his interest in literary criticism, for he dates it to the reading of Bertrand Russell's *The Analysis of Mind* in 1921; this led him, he says, 'straight to Freud and Jung'. In *Annals of Innocence and Experience* he suggests that he was already predisposed towards psychoanalysis by the critical approach he had begun to evolve on his own initiative.

> Even before I read Freud, I tended to probe beneath the surface of the work of art, my conviction being that the work of art is either an objective phenomenon which we accept integrally and sensuously and therefore without intellectual understanding; or that alternatively it demands for its understanding, not merely a measured view of its external aspects, but also a complete analysis of the circumstances in which it came into existence. This latter type of criticism I have called genetic, and it may, if so desired, be separated from aesthetic criticism. But an adequate criticism must include both methods, for we must understand, not only form, rhythm, harmony, composition, texture, handling, etc., but also imagery, allegory, analogy, motivation, social significance and many other aspects of the work of art to which psychology alone can offer the right approach.

Read was so impressed—'alarmed' is the word he actually uses—by his first encounter with the psychoanalysts that in 1924, 'with more discretion than enthusiasm' as he later remarked, he wrote for *The Criterion* an essay entitled 'Psychoanalysis and the Critic'.

Despite his later reservations, he continued to regard this as one of the crucial essays of his career, publishing it in *Reason and Romanticism* in 1926, again in 1938 under a new title ('The Nature of Criticism') in *Collected Essays in Literary Criticism*, and finally in the *Selected Writings* (1963) under yet another title 'Psychoanalysis and Literary Criticism'.

Throughout the essay Read emphasizes that while psychology is interested in mental processes, criticism is interested in their products, and that for this reason the critic merely 'raids' psychology in the interests of his own science, if indeed criticism can be described as a science. As the discussion continues, with its speculations on the nature of inspiration, and on the creative conjunction that takes place when images emerge spontaneously from the unconscious and are subjected to an ordering process by the conscious mind, we realize how closely related to Read's romantic tendencies is his view of psychoanalysis, which, he argues, enables one to restate the concept of inspiration in rational or nonreligious form; he welcomes psychoanalysis, in fact, because it appears to give the insights of romanticism a scientific basis.

It is significant that while, in the 1930's, in books like *Art and Society* and *Annals of Innocence and Experience*, Read talks almost entirely in Freudian terms in so far as he uses psychoanalytical concepts, in this early essay written in 1924 he already shows a wide knowledge of the theories of Adler and Jung as well. While he credits Freud with having satisfactorily explained the functioning of inspiration through the actions of the id, the ego and the super-ego, he argues that Adler, in his theory of the inferiority and superiority complexes, has given the better explanation of the specific abnormality of the artist. Jung's particular function he *sees* in the resolution through his theory of psychological types of the 'blind difference' between romanticism and classicism. ('The critic, like the psychologist, should take up a position above the conflict,' Read remarks—a resolution he rarely succeeded in sustaining.) Jung's approach is also valuable in suggesting 'the further possibility of relating the types actualized by the poetic imagination to their origin in the root-images of the community'. Finally—and here Read credits its practitioners in general—'psychoanalysis finds in art a system of symbols, representing a hidden reality, and by analysis it can testify to the faithfulness, the richness, and the range of the mind behind the symbol'.

In the end it was towards Jung that Read felt most strongly drawn, as he moved deeper into the symbolic interpretation of the visual arts, and found in the writings of the Swiss psychologist not merely the ideas that assisted him, such as the seminal theory of the collective unconscious, but also a knowledge of the varieties of symbolism, in art, in religion, in primitive magic, of a richness unparalleled in any of his rivals. 'Jung' is the best guide ... because his knowledge is the most eclectic and his exposition the most detailed.' His links with Jung became close and personal when in 1953, as a publisher, he began to supervise the publication of Jung's *Collected Works* in English, and through this later association he came to regard Jung as not merely a psychologist, but also a great philosopher, a kind of modern seer. It is doubtful if any other individual influenced Read's mental development in his mature years so strongly as Jung.

Read's preoccupation with psychoanalysis has often been criticized as a manifestation of literary fashion; indeed, in an essay on Hawthorne whose first version appears to have been written in 1928, he issues his own ironic warning. 'The frequent introduction of mesmerism and spiritualism as factors in the plot', he remarks in discussing Hawthorne's novels and short stories, 'merely shows the contagion of contemporary enthusiasms, and is a warning of how psychoanalysis in modern fiction may strike a reader fifty years hence.' Applied to his own non-fictional works the warning was accurate, for the passages in his critical and political essays that now seem most dated are those in which he relies most heavily on psychoanalysis, like the rather grotesque 'Defence of Shelley' in which he seeks to represent the poet's preoccupation with incest as the result of repressed homosexuality. His best psychological interpretations are those in later works of aesthetic philosophy like *Icon and Idea* and *The Forms of Things Unknown*, in which he remains open to the discoveries of the professional analysts, but uses them only obliquely, remembering that in literature there is a long tradition of amateur psychology whose insights, in writers like James and Proust, not only anticipate those of the professionals, but are also far more subtle and revealing. Indeed, it is precisely because of their failure to give due importance to the aesthetic element in human life that he eventually finds even the most congenial of psychoanalysts wanting. 'But what I find lacking in Jung's psychology, and indeed in any of the psycho-

logical systems of today,' he remarks, 'is any suggestion that the integrated personality must be an active, creative personality, giving substance to its thoughts, making out of the plastic materials of the
external world symbols to communicate its state of consciousness.'

One result of the mosaic construction by which Read built up his
books has been an exaggerated impression of the amount of criticism
he actually wrote. For a mosaic, unlike a book written in sequential
chapters, can be taken apart and its components rearranged, and this
in fact became Read's practice.

Thus, his first book of literary criticism, *Reason and Romanticism*, was not reprinted in its original form. Instead, the essays that
comprised it were divided up, and, while some were included in *Collected Essays in Literary Criticism* of 1938, the remainder were not
reprinted until 1967, when three essays from the early book
appeared in *Poetry and Experience*. *Collected Essays* was basically a
union of *Form in Modern Poetry* (1932) and *The Sense of Glory*
(1929), which formed respectively the first and second parts of the
collection. But individual essays from *Reason and Romanticism* and
In Defence of Shelley (1936) were used to reinforce both sections,
though the title essay of the last volume was itself excluded and did
not appear again until 1953, when it was included in *The True Voice
of Feeling*. The first part of *The True Voice of Feeling* consisted of
recently written material—a series of lectures on romanticism in
poetry delivered at Princeton in 1951; the second part included, as
well as 'In Defence of Shelley', two works which had already
appeared as separate small volumes—Coleridge *as Critic* (1949) and
Byron (1951), together with a lecture on 'Wordsworth's Philosophical Faith' which had been delivered at Leeds in 1950. Outside this
pattern of reconstructions and rearrangements stands a group of
works which were not cannibalized to produce books with new
titles. These are *English Prose Style* and *Phases of English Poetry*,
both originally published in 1928, and *Wordsworth*.

The essential core of Read's literary criticism is in fact contained
in three volumes—*Collected Essays in Literary Criticism*, *Wordsworth* and *The True Voice of Feeling*. *English Prose Style* is an
excellent handbook on rhetoric whose sensible admonitions Read
himself did not always follow. *Phases of English Poetry* is a slight
study in the changes in English poetic style since the days of the
ballad-poets; it is marred by the very tendency towards categoriza-

tion which Read deplored among academic critics, e.g. one period is shown as producing a poetry of Love, another a poetry of Sentiment, yet another a poetry of Nature. Both these books are peripheral to Read's preoccupations, and are useful mainly for the glancing lights they cast on them.

The three central volumes project two main themes. One is the study through its literary productions of the civilization of Western Europe; the other is the examination of what Read variously called 'the modern movement' and 'romanticism', by which he meant the liberation of poetry which he saw beginning with Wordsworth and culminating in the evolution of a viable free verse by the Imagists and their successors. Of the civilization he was a committed member; of the movement a dedicated supporter. Detachment, in the sense of standing aside and analyzing with a cool and ironic eye, was no part of Read's critical theory or method; whether in terms of sympathy or empathy, he saw criticism as a form of commitment, and if he appeared at times as the advocate of what he criticized, this was largely because he could never interest himself deeply in anything that did not positively move his feelings. He was fascinated by Swift's *saeva indignatio*, but he could not imitate it, and he excused Swift by dwelling upon his angry idealism, by adopting the approach of sympathy rather than analysis.

3

The essays that deal with western civilization comprise the second part of the *Collected Essays*. From *The Sense of Glory* came the essays on Froissart, Malory, Descartes, Swift, Vauvenargues, Sterne, Hawthorne, Bagehot and Henry James. *Reason and Romanticism* contributed pieces on the Brontës and Smollett; essays on Coventry Patmore, Gerard Manley Hopkins and Swift were added from *In Defence of Shelley*. None of these studies had appeared in any form before 1925, when 'Charlotte and Emily Brontë' was published in the *Yale Review*. They represent Read's first decade as a mature critic, for the last of them appeared in 1936. Even so, the later pieces, taken from *In Defence of Shelley*, seem out of place among the earlier studies. They are concerned with poetry, whereas the others are concerned with prose, and while in a religious sense the essays on

Patmore and Hopkins deal with the idea of glory, it is not the same glory as that which Read envisages when he is writing on Froissart or Henry James. There is, however, among the essays on prose writers a unity of tone and assurance, identified by Kathleen Raine, when she said that they 'seem nearer to his natural vein than what came later'.

These are certainly the essays one can relate most closely in style and mood to Read's best works of imaginative prose, *The Innocent Eye*, *The Green Child* and *In Retreat*. They have the same preternatural clarity of description, the same vision unclouded by theory, the same reliance on unsupported natural sensibility. They represent the authors who in prose have spoken most directly to Read, and as we read them we recognize complex affinities. Some of the subjects, like the Brontës and Sterne, shared his experience of the Yorkshire dales. In Sterne, he found a precursor of his interest in the psychological elements in literature, and in the Brontës an example of the 'amazing quality of *innocence*' which he was shortly to explore in terms of his own life. Bagehot combined with a rare literary sensibility the Toryism of Bolingbroke and Burke, to which Read himself had once adhered, and when he quotes Bagehot declaring that 'the essence of Toryism is enjoyment', and praising the Cavalier mind as 'brave without discipline, noble without principle, prizing luxury, despising danger', one feels that he is not only looking back to the positive aspects of his war experience but also forward to that anarchism of which, still a civil servant, he could not write openly. Vauvenargues, enduring the worst of war and emerging without despair, is perhaps even nearer, at least in personal experience, to Read.

But the sympathies these essays chart are not entirely those of shared experience, or even shared attitudes, for Read can write with understanding of Descartes, whom he blames for the anti-poeticism, the denial of aesthetic values, implicit both in the scientific attitude and in the ethics of Puritanism. But, once understood, a writer can be all the more easily rejected, and the rejection of Descartes, whose theory led to a concept of beauty as 'only ... mechanical harmony, devoid of spiritual animation, deficient in the sense of glory', is essential to Read's strategy for *The Sense of Glory* which, as its title suggests, is devoted more than anything else to exemplifying in its varying forms the splendour of our civilization from its beginnings in the age of chivalry to its last declining blaze which Read, like many who have succeeded him, believed he was witnessing.

Such a 'sense of glory' is a secular phenomenon, a glory of man quite unlike the glory of God that Patmore and Hopkins seek to celebrate, even though they may do so, as Read shows in the case of Hopkins, by the 'tributes of the senses'. It is a glory that emerges from courage, not from meditation, and that arises when we say: 'Let us put the matter to the test of our own valour, and whom God is with, will prevail.' It is a conception analogous to the wisdom enunciated by Krishna in the Bhagavad Gita, and proclaimed by Read long afterwards during World War II, in his poem, 'The Contrary Experience':

> But even as you wait
> like Arjuna in his chariot
> the ancient wisdom whispers:
> Live in action ... .
>
> No resolve can defeat suffering
> no desire establish joy:
> Beyond joy and suffering
> is the equable heart
>
> not indifferent to glory
> if it lead to death
> seeking death
> if it lead to the only life.

Relating form to feeling, Read could not doubt the reality of the spirit that made Froissart's pages 'vivid with the personal radiance of men who achieve glory'. That glory he saw, whether described in action by Froissart or recorded as part of the mythology of a departed order by Malory, as a 'disinterested and individual passion' which could not—as Sorel tried to do—be converted into 'the animating force of a faction'. It was in the end, exemplified by Cervantes in that quintessential errant Don Quixote, a matter of vision, of being able to 'see beyond the futility of what is to the glory of what might be'.

There is an inconsistency in Read's treatment of the theme of glory. At the end of his essay on Froissart he declares that for us the idea of glory, which for Froissart was 'the measure of all things', has become 'remote and elusive'.

We have lost the sense of glory because we have lost the habit of faith. We neither love deeply enough, nor feel deeply enough, nor think deeply enough, to enjoy life's most impressive sanction.

Yet though Read admits that over the centuries the sense of glory becomes less 'settled' than it was in the age of chivalry, it lingers in these essays—revealed or implied—to the end. Vauvenargues passionately clings to it; Descartes betrays it; Hawthorne makes it a quality of the literary imagination; and in the end there is Henry James with his magnificent sense of civilization.

When we reach James it is possible to look back over *The Sense of Glory* and to consider the boundaries of that civilization and the manifestations it has assumed in literature. Read takes only English and French writers as his subjects (James he regarded as English, since he disputed to the end the argument that there could be such a thing as a separate American literature) and, since France and England were the countries in which the rules and myths of chivalry were developed, the choice is appropriate. Nevertheless it is significant that Read wrote this most limpid of his criticism before he had come under the deep influence of German psychologists and aestheticians; French moralists have always had a better sense of the relationship between style and thought than scholars from beyond the Rhine, and it becomes evident, when we compare *Reason and Romanticism* and *The Sense of Glory* with a book written even so shortly afterwards as *Wordsworth*, that what is best in Read's prose style was developed while he was most under the influence of the English prose writers he admired—the men like Swift and Smollett of the 'clean impersonal mode'—and of the French writers of that transitional period which embraced Descartes and Diderot and ended in the splendid isolation of Stendhal. Implicit in Read's treatment of the period that western civilization embraces—from Froissart hailing the dawn in the fourteenth century to James celebrating nightfall in the early twentieth century—is the sense of a culture that not only encouraged the emergence of men who, as Smollett said of himself, 'stand upon their own foundation, without patronage, and above dependence', but also expressed its best values through their individual sensibilities.

The variety of sensibilities which Read exhibits exemplifies the richness of that civilization. There is Smollett, whose 'mind is innocent of ideas, and indeed of abstractions of any sort, and he is at the best but an arranger of the objective facts of existence' (and not necessarily inferior, Read hastens to add, to 'minds of a more intuitive or speculative order'). There is Swift, to look into whose 'dark pain and bitterness' is 'to resign the cloak of innocence and the mask of ignorance'. There is Sterne, that classicist precursor of romanticism who makes spontaneity a literary virtue in 'a prose that is vivid, nervous and swift', and who creates characters, Uncle Toby and Corporal Trim and Mr. Shandy, who 'are, like Odysseus, at once mythical and human, and therefore held by us in a peculiar relation of both grandeur and intimacy'.

And, among these essays so full of bright glancing insights, there is that curious study of the Brontës, a study of the triumph of art over neurosis; it is curious because, though it pretends to treat of both the great sisters, it is in fact concerned almost entirely with Charlotte and devotes two perfunctory and platitudinous paragraphs to Emily in what is otherwise a most perceptive and original essay, even down to a remarkable comparison between Charlotte and Jane Austen. Yet we know that Emily fascinated Read; long afterwards he confessed to Edward Dahlberg that *Wuthering Heights* was the one novel he could read often, 'and the reason why I can always re-read this book has nothing to do with its literary qualities to explain the reason would be to explain myself'. He never did explain the reason, but it is obvious that the strong personal emotions which this Yorkshire novel stirred explain why Emily Brontë was the one prose writer he discussed inadequately in what otherwise is a series of essays at once perceptive and graceful, dominated by no literary ideology and uninterrupted by the divagations into psychological theory that sometimes obscured his later essays. Those essays developed their own virtues of depth and complexity, but rarely again did Read achieve the limpid insight or the crystal utterance that distinguished almost every page of *The Sense of Glory*, nowhere more irradiated by sympathy than in the brief study of Henry James in which Read ends the book and acknowledges his debt to the great expatriate.

James he regards as beyond rival the exemplar of 'the art of fiction at its intensest creative point', the complete literary craftsman, the Master in a literal sense, for in him 'the style and method are perfect, but also perfectly adapted to the subject-matter'. James is the great creator as well as the great teacher of fiction, for beyond this matter of craft there is the world James creates, that splendid world of the imagination whose 'burning heart' is the sense of moral dignity, and whose special achievement is perhaps its evocation of the 'general glory', the spiritual reality of the civilization James entered when he chose to abandon America for the 'continuous tradition of culture which Western Europe inherited from the ancient world'.

The essay—and the book—ends with a long paragraph in which Read not only completed his circle by implicitly joining Froissart's vision of glory to that of James, but also rose to *a* historical insight which, when one remembers that he was writing almost half a century ago, can only be regarded as prophetic. I quote the paragraph in full, since it shows how a good literary critic, without stepping out of his subject, can cast a searching light upon the darkness of his world.

Civilization was in his view a phenomenon of ever-increasing complexity, and to refuse the effort required to comprehend and develop this complexity was to deny the life of intelligence itself. Of two such denials he was conscious in a sure but intuitive manner. One is represented by the America he deserted, and the other, as well as by anything, by the Russia that confronted him in Tolstoi and Dostoievski. His attitude towards America was, as we have already seen, the animation and activation of his whole life and work; his attitude towards Russia was no less real, though it never occupied his attention to the same degree. It was a blind reaction which showed itself in an almost violent scorn of the two writers just mentioned—'fluid puddings, though not tasteless, because the amount of their own minds and souls in solution in the broth gives it savour and flavour, thanks to the strong, rank quality of their genius and experience'. And in another place he says: 'I think it is extremely provincial for a Russian to be very Russian ... for the simple reason that certain national types are essentially and intrinsically provincial.' Perhaps he would have made that overworked label suffice as a connecting-link between his antipathies. Perhaps nowadays we can see stronger and more essential links: such links are being forged by events, and the process of 'americanization', which carries with it all the determinate forces of materialism and mechanism, nowhere seems so irresistible as among the comparatively traditionless peoples of Russia. The deepest significance of the Russian revolution is surely to be found in its renunciation of Europe. The force and effectiveness of that revolution can be explained only by a recognition of the historical fact that there has been no merging of the national ethos in any wider concept of humanism, but rather a renewal of it in all its integrity. Russia has retreated into her own fastnesses. The political doctrine with which the new regime is identified,

although of European origin, is one which even its European adherents
would admit to be totally disruptive of the cultural traditions of the
West. To one who had solemnly declared his adherence to this tradition
there could be no further vacillation: that declaration had been too
deeply confirmed by anguish of mind and force of emotion. If today we
wished to take from the world of literature two antithetical types representing the dominant but opposed forces of the modern world, we could
not find two so completely significant as Dostoievski and Henry James.
In the one is all energy, all nihilism, obscurity and confusion, the dreadful apocalypse of a conscience that has lost all civilized sanctions and has
no foundations to its world; and in the other, calm, dominant, reticent
and fastidious intellect, ordering the gathered forces of time to a
manifestation of their most enduring glory.

4

'The best poetry is objective,—it is aloof,' Read once remarked. The
same might be said of criticism, and in Read's essays on English and
French prose writers sympathy and objectivity are in fact perfectly
balanced, so that each illuminates the other. But when he writes on
poetry he is not objective; he is, more even than towards anarchism,
deeply engaged. It is not merely that—as he said in 1928—'English
poetry, as a living and developing organism, is my greatest interest'.
It is even more that he was himself a poet, 'and as a poet I am aware
that my criticism suffers from the suspicion of being written in self-
defence'.

Suspicion stated in such narrow terms would in fact be unjust,
but, if Read may not actually defend his own work in books like
Form in Modern Poetry, The True Voice of Feeling and Wordsworth,
he does advocate a type of poetry which he himself practises and he
defends one of the two great poetic traditions, though with misgivings which are the inevitable consequence of practising at the same
time two vocations so close, yet so unlike in their processes, as criticism and poetry.

The incompatibility between the critic's detachment and the
poet's engagement haunted Read. In both Phases of English Poetry in
1928 and Form in Modern Poetry in 1932 he showed a reluctance to
accept openly the romanticist label. 'My experience cuts across the
classical-romantic division,' he said, and in Form in Modern Poetry

he began by arguing that the terms *classical* and *romantic* should be
used only historically, and that in describing contemporary poetry or
poetry in general one should adopt the terms 'Organic form' and
'Abstract form'. This argument also seems unconvincing, particularly when one remembers that Read had recently edited the posthumously collected works of the Imagist pioneer, T. E. Hulme, and that
Hulme had defined romanticism and classicism in such a way that
Read's entire philosophy, of life and politics as well as of art, was
neatly encapsulated in the first:

> Here is the root of all romanticism [said Hulme]: that man, the individ-
> ual, is an infinite reservoir of possibilities, and if you can so rearrange
> society by the destruction of oppressive order then these possibilities will
> have a chance and you will get Progress. One can define the classical
> quite clearly as the exact opposite of this. Man is an extraordinarily fixed
> and limited animal whose nature is absolutely constant. It is only by tra-
> dition and organization that anything decent can be got out of him.

In fact, by the time he had argued his way through Form in *Modern
Poetry*, Read had moved to a defensive and defiant acceptance of his
romanticist inclinations in so far as poetry was concerned:

> I am aware that I shall be accused of merely dressing up the old romanti-
> cism in new phrases; but forced into this academic discussion I might
> then accept 'the rehabilitation of romanticism' as an adequate descrip-
> tion of my aims.

Here Read sets up an imaginary opponent who makes grossly
over-simplified accusations. What one can reasonably claim on the
basis of his writings on poetry, is that in the contemporary world he
sees two basically irreconcilable directions of expression, not merely
in poetry, but in the other arts as well, and that in defining these two
directions in *The True Voice of Feeling* (1953) he left no doubt which
he followed.

> Throughout the history of human culture we are continuously made
> aware of two possibilities of aesthetic expression or communication, one
> being what Keats called 'the false beauty proceeding from art' which is
> expression conceived as an elaboration of selected elements of percep-
> tion and feeling; the other being what Keats called 'the true voice of feel-

ing', which is expression conceived as the direct communication by precise symbolic means of the configuration of perception and feeling, 'the
pattern of sentience'. There can be no compromise between these two
conceptions of art, one being the classical conception of art as artifice or
play, the other being the romantic conception of art as the communication of an increasingly acute awareness of the nature of experience, or art
as the cult of sincerity.

I do not personally agree that the history of poetry, or any of the
other arts, in fact demonstrates that there can be no compromise
between what we call the romantic and the classical; writers who represent both attitudes can work at the same time (Auden and Dylan
Thomas might be taken as an exemplary pair) and the two attitudes can
mingle in the same writer (as Byron, Sterne and Eliot all demonstrate
and as Read himself was to show in the case of painters like Picasso).
Nevertheless, it is evident that Read himself sees the division between
true and false as clearly drawn in terms of poetry, and that he regards
the truth as lying with the romantics. By the middle of the 1930's when
he pledged support to Surrealism and hailed it as an expression of 'the
romantic principle in art', he had clearly taken his side.

Insecurely camouflaged in his earlier writings on poetry, osten-
tatiously displayed in the later essays, the partisanship is never absent, as it so often is when he discusses the visual arts which did not
involve him as a practitioner. But this does not mean that Read's discussions of poetry lack depth or erudition; they merely lack balance.
Read displays a panoramic familiarity with poetry in several living
and dead languages, and he has obviously read all the texts since the
Renaissance that give support to his theories; he deploys them well,
but he engages in manoeuvres rather than battles, for he gives little
attention to the advocates of opposing views, and one might assume,
from reading the books I am discussing, that the advocates of classicism are far more timid and far less resourceful than is indeed the
case. Too often we seem to be reading the polemics of poetry rather
than its criticism, and the impression is intensified by the fact that,
except for biographical purposes, comparatively little attention is
paid to actual poems, and a disproportionate amount, especially in
The True Voice of Feeling, to expounding the philosophies on which
the defence of romanticism has been based.

Three major themes are worked out in Read's writings on poetry.

The first is historical, based on the thesis that in 1798 Wordsworth performed a revolutionary act by breaking with the artificial poetry—or wit-writing—that had been dominant since the Restoration, and that by this act (which was also a re-establishment of contact with the lost tradition of Chaucer, Shakespeare and Milton) he started the 'modern movement' in poetry, sustained by the later Romantics, continued by Browning and Hopkins, and brought to fruition by the Imagists. The second theme is a formal one, based on the thesis that the shape of poetry must emerge from the creative process and not be imposed by tradition; this means that free verse, developed from Coleridge's experiments in irregularity, is the only organic form in which poetry that faithfully expresses feeling can be written and is 'the specific form of modern poetry'. The third theme is a psychological one, based on the thesis that fluctuations in the vitality of a poet's writings can be traced to concealed dislocations of his mental life.

Wordsworth's revolutionary act has to be seen in the context of romanticism, and romanticism for Read was far more than a movement in poetry or even in the arts in general. It was a lifestyle, a veritable philosophy of life, for which in later years he would make sweeping claims. Speaking at Yale University in 1954, he asserted that romanticism was 'the only attempt since the end of the Middle Ages to construct a universal philosophy ... essentially a philosophy of immanence, as Catholicism had been a philosophy of transcendence'. The same year, speaking over the Columbia Broadcasting System to celebrate the second centenary of Columbia University, he told American listeners that 'the Romantic Revolution is more than a change of fashion or of style; it is the discovery of a New World, and as a consequence the Old World can never be the same, can never return to its former limits'. Romanticism, he added in the kind of apocalyptic words that in recent years have been exhausted by cultural prophets, 'was a sudden expansion of consciousness—an expansion into realms of sensibility not previously accessible to the human imagination'. Poetry was its instrument, and in poetry, as in everything else connected with romanticism, the form, not the content, was essential. 'To identify form with substance—that is precisely the romantic revolution.' Such fervours were not typical of Read, and in his longer essays on romanticism and modernism the tone is more often that of quiet conviction, and the arguments tend to be specific, relating to individual poets or particular aspects of the poetic process.

The two individual poets with whom Read deals most closely are
Wordsworth and Coleridge. Shelley, Byron and Keats are each discussed at length in specific essays of *The True Voice of Feeling*, but it
is obvious that in Read's mind they are lesser figures in what—with
an inevitable mixing of epithets—one has to describe as classic
romanticism, to distinguish it from the grander movement of which
Read sees it forming the vanguard. After the Romantics, Read sees
the nineteenth-century literary landscape dotted with a curious collection of half poets—Arnold and Patmore, Clough and Browning.
Whitman and Lawrence make barbarically yawping appearances as
writers of rhapsodic prose who have mistaken themselves for verse-
writers. Real poets appear again with Hopkins, Yeats and the Imagists, and the record ends with Pound and Eliot. The Thirties, and
even the Forties when Read thought he saw signs of a reviving
romanticism among the younger poets, are as ignored as the dead
decades of the eighteenth century when poetry languished under the
tyranny of the Great Cham, Samuel Johnson.

The agent of Read's enlightenment regarding romanticism was
Coleridge, who first made him aware of the significance of Wordsworth's poetry. Unlike most mental events in Read's life, this enlightenment is clearly recorded. It took place in 1918, and is described in
one of the letters of the 'War Diary', dated June 2nd. I quote the passage at length, since it shows clearly the reservations that from the
beginning tempered Read's admiration for Wordsworth. It begins
with a criticism of the metaphysical chapters of the *Biographia Literaria*, and continues:

> You will find, as I did, that the most interesting part of the book is
> concerned with Wordsworth. It is a magnificent criticism, so exhaustive
> and final that one wonders how a contemporary could have done it. ...
> One criticism of Wordsworth he makes is exactly my feeling (predomi-
> nant in my case more than in Coleridge's—who only thought it a minor
> fault) and that is the 'matter-of-factness' of Wordsworth's poetry. I quite
> realize the immense task Wordsworth set himself in ridding poetry of its
> flamboyancy and bombast. He did incalculable good there. But he went
> to the other extreme his simplicity *did* become simpleness.
>
> My other feeling about Wordsworth is one that Coleridge couldn't
> very well detect as he himself is tarred with the same brush: that is the
> *unreality* of his moral sentiments. They are magnificent, noble, sublime.
> I can see how beautiful and ideal was the philosophy of Wordsworth—

he thought in terms of immaculate virtue. But he would not have recognized it when he met it in the street, if ever he frequented such a low place. His whole life was so sheltered from reality that the only way he had of creating a philosophy and a world-view was by looking into the imaginative purity of his own mind. ...

But Coleridge has shown me the beauties of Wordsworth's poetry and I am ready to admit my past blindness ...

The influence of both Coleridge and Wordsworth worked slowly but continuously in Read's mind, and we know that, in his early years as a critic, he read and reread the *Biographia* as a kind of literary bible. Yet for a decade there was little evidence in his writing of the depth of his interest in Wordsworth. As a poet Read was already formed by the conjunction of natural inclinations and early influences. One can tell from his poems that he had once been enthusiastic about Blake and Donne, that he had—as he confessed—fallen under the fragile spell of Ralph Hodgson, that he had passed through the revelatory fire of Imagism. But the only remote trace of an influence of the original Romantic poets can perhaps be found and here so diluted as to be almost unrecognizable in the attempt in his longer poems to discover a poetic equivalent for conceptual thinking. As a critic he wrote his earliest apprentice work on the Imagists, and between 1920 and 1929 he wrote short journalistic pieces on a variety of poets including Whitman, Blake, Swinburne and W. H. Davies, but nothing on the Romantics, nor does *Reason and Romanticism*, despite its title, contain any specific article on them, though there are tangential references in some of the more general articles on poetry and criticism.

The first substantial indication of Read's commitment to Wordsworth as the precursor of the modern movement in fact appears as late as 1929, the same year as he started his Wordsworth lectures at Cambridge, in *Phases of English Poetry*. Still uncomfortable about the epithet *romantic*, he attempts a 'more positive' classification by discussing the Romantic poets in a chapter entitled 'Poetry and Nature', to distinguish them from their predecessors, who are herded under 'Poetry and Sentiment'. But it is in the final chapter of *Phases of English Poetry* that he states explicitly the role Wordsworth will henceforward take in his historical view of English poetry.

In formal characteristics, modern poetry is a further development of

Wordsworth's theory of poetic diction, as modified and corrected by
Coleridge. Wordsworth's drift was all in the direction of sincerity of
expression, and if his passion for sincerity drove him to such an exagger-
ation as that 'there neither is nor can be any essential difference between
the language of prose and metrical composition', it really only remained
for Coleridge to point out that there were two kinds of sincerity, the one
proceeding from impassioned meditation and possessing the rhythm and
originality of creative expression, the other proceeding from rational
observation, and possessing the evenness and clarity of logical and in-
formative expression. Wordsworth was right in spirit, and his influence
was fundamental and revolutionary; it is impossible to conceive the
development of English poetry during the last century without Wordsworth. The implications of his theory are only now in the process of
being worked out; Browning was a progress in one direction—the direction of flexibility, of making diction follow the subtleties of an unusual
imaginative vision. But only within the last years has the doctrine of sincerity in poetic diction been resumed with all Wordsworth's insistence.

Read rejects two of Wordsworth's leading arguments. Wordsworth went too far, he suggests, in attempting to equate poetic diction with the natural diction of everyday speech; he argues that 'the
language of poetry differs legitimately from the language of everyday
speech, because it is the language of a heightened state of sensibility,
and above all, because it is the language of a creative adherence to
metrical conventions', pointing out that in practice particularly—in
The Prelude—Wordsworth departed from his own precepts.

> It is perhaps no more than the old question of the scansion of blank verse,
> but my contention is that blank verse always tends to scan irregularly,
> and, generally speaking, that the more impassioned and poetic the verse
> becomes, the more irregular or 'free' becomes the metre.

All that Read has later to say about Wordsworth as a pioneer of
modernism is no more than an amplification of these paragraphs
from *Phases of English Poetry*, but he does, particularly in *Wordsworth* and *The True Voice of Feeling*, make a more direct critical
examination of the great Romantics, using a multiple view of the
work of art which is most concisely defined, not in any of his essays
in literary criticism, but in *The Meaning of Art*.

> We may conclude [he says there], that besides purely formal values such
> as we find in a pot, there may be psychological values the values arising
> out of our subconscious life; and beyond these, philosophical values
> which arise out of the range and depth of the artist's genius.

As I have already suggested, Read has comparatively little to say,
in the sense of technical examination and exposition, on the formal
qualities of the work of any of these poets, partly because the academic critics had already explored this terrain intensively. What formal
analysis he does make is aimed principally at demonstrating how
irregular blank verse developed stage by stage, from Wordsworth and
Coleridge, through Browning and Patmore and Hopkins, into free
verse. Read's underlying traditionalism emerges in this process; like
most of the anarchists, and like the Surrealists whom he later supported, he paid enduring service at the altar of intellectual ancestor worship. In the particular genealogy he charted for the modern movement
in poetry, Read differed from at least some of those very modern poets
whom, in *The True Voice of Feeling*, he tried to establish as spiritual
descendants of the Romantics. He then placed Eliot in the direct line
from Wordsworth, and thus implied his concealed romantic affilia-
tions, but twenty years later, in *The Cult of Sincerity*, he had to admit
Eliot's own claim to being a classicist in literature with distinct affinities to that archetypical anti- romantic, Dr. Johnson.

In the case of Hulme he used positively Procrustean methods to
ram that long and angular frame into an ill-fitting bed. He attempted
to equate Hulme's view with Coleridge's, and when Michael Roberts
claimed that Hulme's method was the reverse of romantic, accused
him of a 'confusing use of the word romanticism'. But it was Read
who caused the confusion by neglecting entirely, in his chapter on
Hulme in *The True Voice of Feeling*, the latter's lecture on 'Romanticism and Classicism' which he himself had edited early in the 1920's.
Hulme's argument in this lecture is based on the conviction that
'after a hundred years of romanticism, we are in for a classical
revival', and by the 'classical revival' he means precisely that Imagist
movement which Read marshals into the romantic succession. 'I
prophesy [Hulme says] that a period of dry, hard, classical verse is
coming.' He sees romanticism as an exhausted movement, a 'split
religion', and declares categorically, 'I dislike the romantics'.

Hulme in fact, like Eliot, and like Sorel whom he admired so greatly, was a neo-classicist of a peculiar post-Nietzschean type. And one could, if one wished to raise a controversy, put a case—at least as convincing as Read's—for tracing the true succession from Wordsworth and Keats not through Eliot, Pound and the Imagists in general, but through the better Georgian nature poets, such as Hardy, Robert Frost and Edward Thomas (that excellent poet whom Read inexplicably neglected), and hence through the later Yeats and Edwin Muir, to Dylan Thomas, Vernon Watkins, Norman Nicholson and Kathleen Raine.

This raises the validity of Read's other thesis—that the progression towards free verse is in fact the only way towards the liberation of poetic inspiration and the enrichment of the poem itself. It is important to emphasize that Read's view of free verse was a rigorous one. It meant liberation, but not licence; it meant the recognition that the abandonment of metre did not result in the interchangeability of poetry and prose. Far from this, Read held a high Shelleyan view of the role of the poet and of the distinctive nature of poetic language, which he once defined as a kind of *ursprach* (ancient speech), relating it to the metaphorical speech of early man.

> Poetry [he said in *Wordsworth*] is a divine ichor, a distinct essence, and it differs from prose, not in mechanical structure, but in a quality derived from the presence, within the poet, of a different state of mind, determining a different approach to life, to the universe, to language, to every aspect of existence.

And he claimed further that 'Poetry *is* the culture of the feelings … their education, their growth to fullness and perfection, to harmonious life and rhythm. This is, under the aspect of poetry, merely the process of all art.'

Such of course is the romantic viewpoint, as originally stated by Schelling. Even if one is not a classicist, it may be difficult to accept the belief in all its extremity, but it is possible, without granting such an exalted role to the poet, to accept Read's point that poetry is a special mode of communication between man and man, and that it places the poet in a special relation with the social and universal consciousness. That relation has obviously much to do with the manner of the generation of poetry, which is not an act of wit but an act of intuition or vision. As every poet knows from experience, the primary material of a true poem is not devised consciously; it emerges

from what we conveniently call the unconscious, and it shapes itself
in symbolic forms which have a meaning in the collective as well as
in the individual imagination. But, as Read acknowledges, 'such
intuition or vision must be identified with *knowledge*, being fully
present only when consciously objectified'. In other words, the final
shaping of the poem is the work of the conscious mind, and in that
shaping not only words, the basic element, have their place, but also
'structure and conception—structure which is the embodiment of
words in a pattern or form; and conception, which is the projection
of the poet's thought into a process from which, or during the course
of which, words are generated'. Here we reach the heart of Read's
argument. Order and restraint are necessary in poetry, but they must
emerge from the poem's own necessity. This is what is meant by
organic poetry. 'It is the form imposed on poetry by the laws of its
own origination, without consideration for the given forms of traditional poetry. It is the most original and most vital principle of poetic creation; and the distinction of modern poetry is to have recovered
that principle.' This means that freedom and spontaneity are the very
life of poetry:

> Poetry ... can die into the symmetrical forms of regular metre and
> verse; or it can live and give significant form to an evolving human con-
> sciousness, by creating symbols that represent a state of mental aware-
> ness or an act of perception. Such symbols in poetry—as distinct from
> the signs used in discursive language (prose)—are determined by feeling
> (or intuition), and are not logically analysable. They 'read' only as com-
> plete expressive units (the poem-as-a-whole, for example).
>
> The creation of such verbal 'gestalts' is the function of the poet, and
> it is a like function that creates a unity of melody and harmony in music,
> or a compositional unity in painting or sculpture, each act of creation
> being unique, and not typical. Poetry is the representation, in verbal sym-
> bols, of a unique mental situation.

Out of such arguments Read draws the conclusion that free verse,
which means life, is essential if poetry is to continue its task of
expanding human awareness beyond the boundaries of the conscious mind. Ideal 'instantaneous' poetry, the product of total freedom and spontaneity, 'must necessarily be written in free verse'.

But this, it seems to me, is not the only possible conclusion of
Read's theory of the creation of poetry. The mind—even the uncon-

scious mind—can and does think naturally in regular patterns; consider the mandala, which Read himself showed to be a persistent
form in the arts of children and primitive peoples alike. The practice
of writing verse in metrical or syllabic pattern is too widespread not
to have some similar basis, and the same applies to certain poetic
devices like alliteration and rhyme, which satisfy one aspect of the
human passion for analogies. I am not reversing Read's position and
claiming that all poetry should be written in regular forms; clearly
that would lose us as much good verse as his procedure. What I contend is that certain poets can and do give exactly the same kind of
spontaneous expression to their feelings, and do create exactly the
same kind of original symbols as he demands, by means of personal
adaptations of traditional shapes. As Kathleen Raine points out, in
discussing Read's poetic theories, Edwin Muir, Dylan Thomas and
Vernon Watkins, 'precisely the most imaginative poets' of the generation following Yeats, chose to use traditional forms; one might include Miss Raine herself in the same company.

I suspect—and another comment by Kathleen Raine gives support to the suspicion—that Read's obstinate and almost exclusivist
advocacy of free verse was due to a deficiency in his own experience
as a poet. He appears to have been unaware that with many poets
whole verses in regular form often appear fully made in their minds.
This apparently did not happen to Read, and Kathleen Raine's comment may suggest the reason. 'Herbert once confessed to me the difficulty he had in memorizing verse, even his own; a defectiveness of
the inward ear which may in part have accounted for his bias.'

In the long run the attempt to prove a historical continuity
between the Romantic movement and twentieth-century poetry, and
the search for a canon of form appropriate to modern verse, may be
less important in Read's discussions of poetry than his venture into
an original form of psychological criticism that verges very closely on
the biographical. 'In Defence of Shelley' contains an excellent description of this type of criticism as Read envisaged it. He is discussing Eliot's argument that 'literary criticism should be completed
by criticism from a definite ethical and theological standpoint'.

> I do not deny [he says] that such criticism may have its interest; but the
> only kind of criticism which is basic, and therefore complementary not
> only to technical exegesis but also to ethical, theological, philosophical
> and every other kind of ideological criticism, is ontogenetic criticism, by

which I mean criticism which traces the origins of the work of art in the psychology of the individual and in the economic structure of society.

While Read deploys his investigations into the effects of the economic structure of society, and of the collective psychology, mainly in his writings on the visual arts and on the arts in general, it is in these essays on poetry that he investigates most deeply the origins of art in the personal psychology of the artist. *Wordsworth* is his most significant exercise in this vein; it is a rewriting of Wordsworth's career according to the assumption that the failing of his poetic powers was the result of a mental conflict which he assiduously concealed from the rest of the world.

At first it seems curious that Read, a writer given to conciseness and clarity, devoted to the sharp clear image and dedicated to anarchism from youth to old age, should have been so attracted to Wordsworth, who as a poet was rarely less than verbose, and whose political apostasy had appalled men like Hazlitt toward whom one might have thought Read more likely to be drawn, in sympathy.

Yet there was much in Wordsworth's background that helped to create a sense of affinity in Read's mind. Wordsworth was a northerner, he had been brought up in a rural setting surprisingly like that which Read inhabited a century later, and his mother's death—like that of Read's father—had made a sharp break in his life early in childhood. Though born in Cumberland, he was even, like Sterne and the Brontës and Read himself, of Yorkshire stock, and had the racial disposition of the Yorkshireman, which Read described in such a way that, seeking to present Wordsworth, he paints what to anyone who knew him will seem uncannily like a portrait of the artist.

> Yorkshiremen are imaginative, like all northmen, but a matter-of-factness, a strong sense of objectivity, a faculty for vivid visualization, keep them from being profoundly mystical. The same qualities make them wary in their actions and canny in their reckonings. But their most extraordinary characteristic—a characteristic with which in the process of time they have leavened almost the entire English race—is their capacity for masking their emotions. It is not a question of suppression, nor of atrophy; the normal feelings of the human being are present in more than their normal force, but banked up against this impenetrable reserve. No doubt, as a protective device, this iron mask has had historical advantages. And in the domestic sphere it ensures a business-like despatch of

those affairs, such as birth, death and marriages, which tend to choke up the existence of a more expansive people.

In all this, Wordsworth was a true northerner. Indeed, it is almost impossible to understand his life and character unless we remember his racial capacity for masking the strength of his feelings. Wordsworth, as his sister Dorothy once said, was a man violent in affection. But it was necessary to affirm that fact. Outwardly he was cold, even hard. Inwardly he was all fire. But true to his type, he was not going to give himself away—not even in his poetry, not even in the most inspired moments of his creative activity. Passion, of course, does blaze from many a poem of Wordsworth's; but not the direct passion of profane love, not even the direct passion of sacred love, but passion transmuted into impersonal things—rocks, and stones, and trees.

That is Read almost to the life—even down to the scantiness of his true love poems ! The resemblance was increased in situational terms by the fact that Wordsworth's youth, like Read's, was spent in a time of extreme crisis; that if Read went to war Wordsworth went to revolution; that if Read became a follower of the anarchist Kropotkin, Wordsworth became a follower of the anarchist Godwin; that both went from their native fastnesses into the world with no thought but that of in the end returning to the soil they loved, symbolized for both of them in the golden beauty of wild daffodils.

But there is a point where the resemblance ends. Wordsworth changes his political views, he ceases to write inspired poetry, and he develops into an arrogant and graceless man with whom Read no longer feels any sympathy. Why has the change taken place? Read was interested in those curious intermittences of genius by which a poet can cease to write for a lifetime, or can cease for twenty years like Milton and then return as a different kind of poet, or can even, like Yeats, change from one kind of a poet to another without any interruption in the poetic process. Wordsworth's seemed one of the most extraordinary of these cases, and a mass of clues lay to hand in a book which a few years before had added sensational new facts to Wordsworth's biographical record—*Wordsworth and Annette Vallon* by Emile Legouis (1922).

To put the matter briefly, Professor Legouis had found evidence which proved that in 1791, in Orleans, Wordsworth fell in love with a girl of a respectable royalist family, Annette Vallon, and that in 1792 she bore him, out of wedlock, a daughter Caroline. Wordsworth returned to England at the beginning of 1793, evidently intending to rejoin Annette, but war intervened in February. Later in the year, in October, it appears that Wordsworth found his way as far as Paris, in spite of the war, but was unable to travel on to Orleans because of the Terror, during which he witnessed the execution of the first of the Girondin deputies to be killed by the Jacobin oligarchs. He returned in despair to England, and during the nine years of war that followed the years when he wrote his best poetry—his affection for Annette declined, and at last, in 1802, after having visited France in the company of his sister Dorothy and having met Annette and Caroline, he came home to marry Mary Hutchinson.

Read's thesis is that Wordsworth suffered intense remorse which he concealed from those around him and eventually from himself, that the remorse bred resentment of its object, which was transferred so that Wordsworth came to hate revolutionary France instead of Annette, and that finally, by destroying his power of feeling and making him a kind of hollow man, it robbed him of his poetic powers.

By re-examining the evidence, and by supporting the facts with well-chosen extracts from Wordsworth's poems which show his obsession with remorse, Read makes a persuasive case. Short of the discovery of some explicit statement from Wordsworth on his relationship with Annette (and it is unlikely that the poet ever committed himself so far even in secrecy) the case can never be proved. But remorse can work terribly in the human heart, as Shakespeare knew when he wrote *Macbeth*, and Read's hypothesis does more than any other that has so far been advanced to explain the desiccation of Wordsworth's poetic talent. True or not, it is an excellent demonstration of the use of psychology by the literary detective.

But *Wordsworth* is also a work that might one day help the biographical detective reverse the situation and make Read the subject of similar investigation. For in his studies of the psychological aspects of writers' lives, Read shows a peculiar interest in precarious marital situations. Not only does he discuss the breakup of Wordsworth's relationship with Annette and his cool but reasonably happy marriage to Mary Hutchinson. 'In Defence of Shelley' later culminates in an examination of Shelley's desertion of Harriet Westbrook for Mary Shelley. Another essay of the same period, 'Diderot's Love Letters', dwells on the way in which the French encyclopaedist found solace for a dreadful marriage in his passionately platonic relationship with Sophie Vallon. And the first essay of *The True Voice of Feeling*, which

concerns Coleridge and is entitled 'The Notion of Organic Form',
culminates in a study of Coleridge's 'Dejection', which reflects the
predicament of the poet who 'had married in haste and repented at
leisure' and who now, in love with Sara Hutchinson and loved by
Dorothy Wordsworth, was so deeply religious that 'his convictions
forbade him any thought of divorce'.

It is impossible not to associate these essays, and their preoccupations with broken or intolerable marital or quasi-marital relationships, with those details of Read's own life that have escaped
through his barriers of reticence. Read may not have made his first
marriage in such haste as Coleridge, but he certainly repented it at
leisure. In his writings he makes only one reference to it, when he is
discussing Eliot's equally unfortunate first marriage and the unhap-
piness it aroused when his wife Vivien 'developed the hysterical psy-
chosis to which she finally succumbed'.

> My own first marriage [Read adds] was to break up under very similar
> circumstances and that too, as time passed, increased our mutual sympa-
> thy. Eliot, however, could not accept my drastic solution, which was the
> dissolution of the marriage. Though eventually legally separated, he
> remained single so long as his first wife was alive.

Read's first marriage came to an end in 1933. He wrote *Wordsworth* in 1929, published 'In Defence of Shelley' and 'Diderot's Love
Letters' in 1936, and gave his lecture on Coleridge in 1947. The scenario I would present is that when he wrote *Wordsworth* he was
already unhappy with his marriage, yet dreaded the remorse that
might afflict him if he ended it; he proceeded to exorcize the remorse
by externalizing it in his study of Wordsworth. By 1933 other circumstances had arisen which precipitated the final break-up of the
marriage and led Read immediately into a happier second marriage
and a more productive life in which, away from academic frustrations, he lived in the close and fruitful association of Parkhill Road
with artists he admired. This, I think, is what Read is trying to
express in the ending of 'In Defence of Shelley', and I believe that he
projects himself and challenges those who criticized him when he
writes of Shelley after his elopement with Mary Godwin:

> Out of the fullness of his heart and the strength of his philosophy he
> chose to assert his individual liberty. He earned immediate opprobrium

and more than a century of calumny; but he lifted himself out of a premature old age of exhaustion, into a bright element of intellectual vitality, and into a new lease of poetic inspiration.

I believe also that out of the same surge of feeling came Read's poem 'Night Ride' (first published in 1935), with its description of two lovers travelling by bus at night, and at the end awakening to dawn.

> Slowly the bus
> slides into light.
> Here are hills
> detach'd from dark
>
> the road uncoils
> a white ribbon
> the lovers with
> the hills unfold
>
> wake cold
> to face the fate
> of those who love
> despite the world.

If this interpretation is correct, then 'Diderot's Love Letters' and the discussion of Coleridge's 'Dejection' might be taken as evidence of a continuing preoccupation with the situation, as Read speculates on alternatives to the action he took—on the possibilities that might have existed of finding at least a measure of fulfilment if not of happiness within an apparently impossible marriage. But those questionings are surely answered with finality in *The Parliament of Women* in which, however the Prince may warn them, Geoffrey and Helena desert their stale allegiances and ride off into a calm and moonlit night of exile.

5

Art and the Critic

If Herbert Read was not the *poète manqué*, he was certainly the *peintre manqué*, yet it would be hard to think of a frustration in the end more fruitful. Not only are Read's books on the visual arts more numerous and more voluminous than the whole of his other forms of writing combined. They also lead to some of his most vital insights not only in aesthetic but also in ethical and social terms. As a critic of literature Read was intensely personal; he wrote almost entirely of the kind of writing which he himself admired and sought to practise. But despite his 'Futurist' experiments in the teens of the century, the realization that he was no born painter liberated his vision when he discussed the arts he loved but could not successfully practise. (On music he remained curiously silent, though his poems and autobiographical writings suggest that he was deeply moved by it, and his second wife was an accomplished musician.) Thus he was able to observe painting and sculpture with a degree of detachment he found impossible when he approached poetry or even prose fiction.

At the same time he had strong preferences which he did not conceal. He confessed on occasion that he found himself personally so much out of sympathy with mannerist painting and baroque sculpture that he felt an almost physical repulsion on entering St. Peter's. The artists he names as those who most stirred his personal feelings—Seurat, Juan Gris, Léger, Picasso in some of his moods, Henry Moore, Gabo—are, as he said, 'conscious and intellectual', rather than 'magical or sentimental'. 'Rhetoric', he says elsewhere, 'intimidates me, and what is intimidating cannot be lived with.' He states his preference for an 'intimate' art, an art that 'belongs to a private world'. 'The greatest truth was ever spoken in a still, small voice,' he says elsewhere. 'The great mystics are not long-winded. Great poetry is never sustained beyond a page or two of print.'

All this leads one—as his own sparsely worked poetry does—to see Read as a classicist of a singularly pure kind, devoted to the quiet precision of the form as he is to the laconic simplicity of the word. Yet he is a classicist who recognizes that, once the formal disciplines he prefers become a matter of rule rather than of choice, the life of art dies. Just as in poetry he defends the romantic attitude because it keeps clear the channels that lead upward from the Castalian well of the unconscious so in painting he explains 'to the best of my ability' those expressionist modes that do not mirror his own personality or his own practice as a poet. He takes here in literal seriousness the injunction he formulated, but failed to observe with regard to poetry, in *The True Voice of Feeling:*

> In the presence of any work of art, whether it be a statue, a painting, a drama, or a poem, the recipient must abdicate for the moment—must surrender his independent and outstanding personality, to identify himself with the form or action presented by the artist. Only in that way do we penetrate to the heart of the mystery that is a work of art.

We cannot be sure that Read always made this abdication in the full sense, the sense of feeling, but it is hard to think of a critic who more thoroughly weighed the intellectual justifications of the works of art he considered. He was often a good critic; he was always a fair and painstaking apologist, and he resisted very conscientiously the temptation to evaluate painters comparatively, since he believed that each had a unique potentiality and failed or succeeded in relation to that personal touchstone. The breadth and suppleness of his understanding made him a critic peculiarly fitted for an age when the visual arts developed in so many differing directions. He justified the tolerance of his approach by means of his own peculiar dialectic:

> The greatest art includes both realism and romanticism, both the senses and the imagination. The greatest art is precisely this: a dialectic process which reconciles the contradictions derived from our senses on the one hand and our imagination on the other.

Elsewhere, discussing the apparent conflict between the classical and the superreal (a term he used often to describe in painting what he would have called 'romantic' in poetry), he declared:

I do not see why both types should not be practised by one and the same artist, though I believe that in general the plastic arts will tend towards rationality and the poetic art towards superreality.

Read recognizes the persistent duality of abstract and organic approaches throughout the modern period in painting which he takes as his special province. In part he bases his attitude on the theories of the German aesthetician Wilhelm Worringer, who claimed that the people of the harsh northern lands tend to prefer abstract form because it represents a symbolic taming of a hostile natural environment, whereas southern peoples tend towards a more serene and organic art. In part he is also guided by Jung's theories of psychological types.

But Read eventually moved away from strict Jungian typology as one can observe by comparing two essays in *The Philosophy of Modern Art*, written within a very short time of each other. In 'Human Art and Inhuman Nature', towards the end of the 1940's, Read is talking in orthodox Jungian terms of 'various types of artist, more or less constant in their appearance throughout history' and suggests that 'psychological characteristics are stronger than period characteristics'. But in 'Realism and Abstraction in Modern Art', written about 1950, he admits that he no longer accepts 'the simplest explanation ... that the two modes of expression correspond to opposite dispositions in the human personality'. While a correspondence may exist between temperament and expression, it does not exist along the axis of realism and abstraction, nor does it require 'any deep psychological revolution' for an artist to move from one to the other.

> It is merely a change of direction, of destination. What is constant is the desire to create a reality, the will to form. ... It is merely the difference of the particular resonance expressed in that moment when, naked and comfortless on the abyss of nothingness, we question the meaning and the nature of existence. We answer as answer we can—that is to say, according to our particular psycho-physical constitution. We answer with wonder or we answer with dread; and for each answer there is a separate language. But the poetry is in the freedom with which we answer; the art is the affirmation, the acceptance and the intensification of the life.

If this passage has a special resonance, it is surely that of the existentialist philosophy which Read in a rather individual way shared with many of the aestheticians of his time, and notably with André Malraux, with whom he agreed on the conception of art constituting man's only true answer to the absurdity of death. Read, indeed, went somewhat beyond Malraux in defining the special meaning that art gives to human existence when, in his later and more philosophic works, like *Icon and Idea* and *The Forms of Things Unknown*, he elaborated Conrad Fiedler's fragmentary suggestion that 'art has been, and still is, the essential instrument in the development of human consciousness'. Yet art, for all its freedom, is bounded by the limitations of the very consciousness which it has so notably helped to create.

> The truth is that art has no limits. Art is anything that can be imagined, and expressed. But living as we do in particular circumstances and with particular desires and experiences, the art of our time is not so indeterminate. It is something determined by our social and economic conditions, and by the ideas and habits we inherit from the past.

Read's looser allegiances in the visual arts were only one reason for the breadth of his sympathies. He was moved also by the very variety and vigour of European art during the period between the great wars. Language creates barriers that do not exist in painting and sculpture, and in any case the great age of modern poetry had passed with the 1920's; by 1932, Read could say with justice that 'There is ... no adequate literary equivalent in England for the impressive organization and intellectual content of the modern movement in painting.' Picasso with all his versatility seemed the very type of the era. What is perhaps amazing is not that Read should have been so fascinated with the art whose varieties he sought to bring together in a great structure of synthetic criticism, but that he should have been so comparatively unchallenged as its prime interpreter, at least in the English language.

But his scope excelled the desire to interrelate all the innovative trends and artists of his period, for his interest in the visual arts led him into fields far beyond the merely aesthetic. Not only did he discuss the role of art in the general cultural history of the race; he dwelt on the relationship of the artist to the community, and, by extension, on how the community must be changed if it is to allow the insights of the poet, the painter or the architect to enrich the lives of its members. Aesthetics thus led to ethics and ethics to politics, and out of this process emerged Read's interest in education as a transforming process, and in the social forms that would allow each man to develop the harmonious virtues that make of life itself an art.

Indeed, with the notable exception of *Poetry and Anarchism*, it was mainly through his thoughts on the visual rather than the verbal arts that Read became so powerful and versatile a social critic. And though at times he might complain of the diversion of time and interest from his real vocation of poetry that this involved ('All this art criticism has been for me ... a substitute activity forced on me by economic necessity,' he once told Kathleen Raine), there seems no doubt his discursive writing on the arts came from inner impulses as insistent as and more abundant than the spring that fed his poetry. It was not that he wrote less poetry because he spent too much time writing on art; it was rather that poetry took comparatively little of his time, and his urge to write found more expansive expression in a field related to and yet separate from his poetic vocation. Such a division of time and effort was not entirely without its benefits, for it provided a constantly interesting occupation and maintained those ties with the world that Read always regarded as necessary for the writer, so that he never suffered the temptations which he observed at disastrous work in Wordsworth's career to become a recluse concerned only with writing poetry, and to produce bad verse when the inspiration failed rather than produce nothing. Read was not a fluent poet, as the spare style of his verse suggests; it is unlikely that even in the best of circumstances he would have written abundantly in this genre, and his occupation as the interpreter and philosopher of arts other than his own gave him, one could not help feeling, a 'sense of glory' he would not otherwise have won, for in the artist he came to see the 'Silver Knight' of his boyhood fantasies, in whom alone lay hope for humanity threatened by physical destructiveness and alienation.

2

Read called himself a critic and philosopher of art, but, broad as these categories may be, they do not embrace all his achievements in this field. He was also a capable historian, as his first work in the field, *English Stained Glass* (1926), demonstrated, while his last, *Arp* (1968), was a biography of that congenial adept in many arts, Hans

Arp. During the four decades between those two books he wrote or
edited almost forty publications relating to the visual arts, some mere
pamphlets, others collections of reproductions with introductory
monographs, but at least half of them substantial volumes, dealing
with many visual arts, and tracing the reverberation of those arts in
men's secret and public lives. To discuss all these works in any detail
is impossible; to discuss even the most important in a single chapter
is difficult. I shall therefore leave for later consideration those which
deal with art in its social context and as a means of education. In this
chapter I confine myself to the books in which Read deals specifically with artists and their artifacts.

Read's interest in the theory of art became manifest early in his
career, for already in 1918 he was discussing in rather simple terms
with Jacob Kramer the validity of the 'spiritual propensities' which
Kramer sought to project in his own works. Comments on painting
distinguished more by enthusiasm than by discrimination are scattered through his 'War Diary'; he was so impressed by a visit to the
studio of Lucien Pissaro that he prophesied: 'In another ten years
people will talk of a Pissaro landscape as they now talk of a "Turner
Sunset" or a Whistler nocturne.' Yet, although he was one of the
founding editors of *Art and Letters*, and corresponded on modern
painting with fellow writers like Wyndham Lewis and Sacheverell
Sitwell, it is doubtful if he thought seriously of art criticism as an
occupation until he joined the staff of the Victoria and Albert Museum in 1922.

He was posted to the Department of Ceramics, 'a subject of
which I then knew nothing', and having no training in either aesthetics or in museum work he had to rely on his innate sensibility and his
native intelligence to carry him through. He discovered in pottery
and glass, those 'humblest and least conscious' of the arts, a wholly
unexpected interest.

> I found the close and systematic study of one branch of art an ideal
> approach to an understanding of art in general; and ceramics has this
> unrivalled advantage—its material has rarely suffered by the passage of
> time: it does not decay or fade, and one has the knowledge that the object
> presents to its present-day beholder exactly the same basis of sensation
> that it had for the artist who made it.

Read quickly accumulated a fund of knowledge, and achieved an
accuracy of perception, that enabled him to write articles as work-

manlike and unassuming as the pots he cared for. They first appeared in 1923, in the *Burlington Magazine;* he published short notes on 'The Labours of the Months: A Series of Stained Glass Roundels' and on 'The Blés Collection of English and Irish Glass'. For several years he was content to work as a specialist in the field where chance had planted him. In 1924 he collaborated with a colleague, Bernard Rackham, in an elaborately illustrated history of English pottery, still a standard work; the exact division of labour is now hard to determine, but it is likely that Rackham provided more of the knowledge and Read more of the style. Five years later, in 1929, he produced his own work in the field of ceramics, *Staffordshire Pottery Figures,* a folio of illustrations accompanied by a monograph mainly concerned with tracing the various workmen and their styles, but illuminated with some interesting comments on the genuine beauty sometimes achieved by peasant craftsmen working without any consciousness of producing what will later be accepted as art.

Between the two books on ceramics appeared the work that first drew attention to Read's quality as an art critic: his *English Stained Glass.* Not only did it display a comprehensive knowledge of the extant examples of stained glass in England and of the existing literature on the subject; it also revealed in Read a historical sense that enabled him to identify and separate convincingly the various phases of the art, and also to relate its products formally to changes in architectural style and iconographically to the philosophic developments of a period that embraced the theology of Saint Thomas, the poetic revivalism of St. Francis, the humanism of the Reformation, and, in its decline, the self-conscious aestheticism of William Morris. It is more than a monograph on stained glass; it is a historical study of the relations between the characteristic art of a period and the general cultural setting. It does not neglect the primary fact that art works through the senses of individual men, but it shows how in the period when stained glass was developed art became impersonal through 'a surrender of personality and the suppression of all those desires which, especially in an artist, seek the aggrandisement of the self'.

Art, like philosophy, was the servant of religion; and just as philosophy, through the instrumentality of reason, attempted to construct a system of knowledge, consistent with the revealed doctrines of Christian

faith, so art, through the instrumentality of the senses, attempted to give
to that system and that revelation the appeal of beauty. But in each case
the mould was rigid, and was universal and thus it came about that activities which are by nature wayward, individual, and discordant, submitted to a discipline serenely international in form.

Read discovered that his employment at the Victoria and Albert,
far from diminishing his literary activity, in fact increased its scope,
since he found endless affinities between the criticism of literature
and the criticism of art.

> It was because I could not make any distinction between these two activ-
> ities [he says in *Annals of Innocence and Experience*] that I inevitably
> became a critic of art; and since the criticism of art has been relatively
> neglected in this country since the time of Ruskin, I found plenty to occu-
> py my attention.

Art criticism became an alternative form of expression, a literary
form which inevitably had its effect on the rest of his writing, since he
had both 'to abjure the impressionistic graces of a Ruskin or a Pater'
and 'to incorporate the revolutionary discoveries of anthropology
and psychology', whose intractability in the writer's terms Read recognized.

> Precision and efficiency necessarily take the place, in a modern prose
> style, of euphony and symphonic rhythm. These new qualities are aes-
> thetic too; but as in modern architecture, the public is slow to recognize
> them.

3

Recognition as a public interpreter of the visual arts came quickly
and easily to Herbert Read, but before reaching that point of success
I would like to return to *English Stained Glass* for its evidence on the
influences which helped to determine his development as a philosopher of art, for the two writers from whom he derived most inspiration—with the sole later exception of Jung—are already abundantly
present in this early work.

One is Ruskin. Read was conscious, particularly in his later years, of carrying on Ruskin's task as a philosopher who combined with the study of art a radical criticism of society as it existed, and who extended his aesthetic view of life so as to embrace the ethical and the political. Apart from Baudelaire, Read tells us, Ruskin was the only critic of art whose work, in the days before he understood German, he 'could at once read and respect'. He acknowledges that Ruskin created no great system of aesthetics, but he credits him with a masterly power of generalizing from a broad and exact knowledge of particulars. Read admired Ruskin's power of historical interpretation, and he also found endlessly suggestive his theory of art as language. He recognized in Ruskin the rare ability to look at a picture and to transmute a perception of its visual form into writing, and he tried to emulate this achievement, but his characteristic distrust of extravagance in expression inhibited him, and nowhere in Read's work are there descriptions of paintings or sculptures so richly and exactly evocative as Ruskin's presentations of Turner's masterpieces.

There were other critics besides Ruskin for whom Read had found an admiration by the time he joined the staff of the Victoria and Albert. In Baudelaire it was less a power of description or even a theorizing ability that he found attractive than a sensibility aroused to the level of enthusiasm; he found Baudelaire's romanticism sympathetic and especially his appreciation of the naif as opposed to the sophisticated in art. While he had reservations about Pater's florid style he appreciated him as a pioneer—working without the tools presented by the psychoanalysts—in the interpretation in depth, as distinct from Ruskin's surface description, of works of art. He even recognized the profundity that underlay Wilde's wayward manner; and especially appreciated Wilde's point that nature imitates art, in the sense that we perceive in nature what art has taught us to seek. To William Morris, as well as to Ruskin, he was indebted for his first introduction to the difficult relationship between art and industry, a relationship that must be brought into equilibrium before a balanced and organic way of existence became possible for the majority of men.

But apart from Ruskin and Morris the critics I have mentioned played little part in *English Stained Glass*, where the most important influence of all is that of the German art historian, Wilhelm Worringer. When he started to work at the Victoria and Albert, Read recognized immediately the wealth of writing in the field of aesthetics that was locked away from him in untranslated German, and between 1922 and 1925 he patiently taught himself that language. The result was a vast enrichment of his fund of information and ideas not only in aesthetics but also in psychology and anthropology.

Of all the writers to whom his knowledge of German introduced him, Worringer was the most important in shaping his development as a philosopher of the arts.

Worringer wrote three important books: *Form in Gothic*, *Egyptian Art* and *Abstraction and Empathy*. *Abstraction and Empathy* in particular was a significant and even prophetic work in the interpretation of modern art. First written and circulated as a thesis in 1906, it was published in Munich in 1908, two years before Wassily Kandinsky began painting in that city the works which initiated the modern abstractionist movement in the visual arts. At this very dawn of the modern movement in painting, Worringer recognized and described the presence of two complementary trends in the arts— towards abstraction and towards naturalism. He taught in *Form in Gothic*, as well as in *Abstraction and Empathy*, that at periods and in places where man finds his world congenial, he will tend to reproduce the images it presents to him; when he finds it hostile or threatening he will retreat into a geometric or non-figurative art which represents a symbolic re-ordering of the universe. Worringer recognized that both trends could exist together, and that rarely did either exist in its pure form, but he suggested that in general northern and desert cultures, where life is rigorous, are inclined towards abstraction, whereas southern cultures, where climatic conditions are genial, tend towards a condition of empathy with the natural world.

The theory has obvious limitations. It does not cover the prehistoric case of the palaeolithic hunter who projects in his painting a clear eidetic image, or the contemporary case of the Eskimo hunter who creates in the world's most adverse physical conditions a sculpture that renders in both visual and tactile form the image of the animal on which he depends for his existence. Later, in *Icon and Idea*, Read was to provide an answer to this point in his suggestion that the primitive eidetic image is in fact pre-formal, a first response to existence by a being who has not yet drawn a distinction between himself and the phenomenal world, and that the dialectic interaction of abstraction and realism really begins at the point where man as cultivator and craftsman first sees himself in an ambivalent relationship with the world where he is condemned to find a reason for existing.

Read appears to have become aware of Worringer's theories through T. E. Hulme's introductory lecture on the German aesthetician, delivered in 1914 and edited by Read at some time prior to 1924, since it appeared in *Speculations*, the collection of Hulme's papers he published that year. His knowledge of Worringer's theory in general outline therefore existed before he understood German. By 1925 he was in correspondence with Worringer, who wrote in March of that year regarding *Speculations*. It seems likely that they also discussed matters of wider interest, for in the introduction to *English Stained Glass* Read makes a special acknowledgement of his debt to Worringer; moreover, when the latter's *Form in Gothic* appeared in 1927 in its English translation, it was edited by Read and accompanied by his introduction. In 1928 Read stayed with Worringer in Bonn; afterwards they kept up a fairly regular correspondence, though they met only once again, at the Henry Moore exhibition at Munich in 1960.

Read always regarded himself as Worringer's disciple, and was frank—as he always was regarding writers whose ideas had influenced him—in admitting his debt. As late as 1951 he dedicated *The Philosophy of Modern Art* to Worringer as 'my esteemed master', and in 1963, replying to a letter from Worringer congratulating him on his seventieth birthday, he remarked: 'Your work remains with me and I scarcely write a book in which I do not draw upon it for support and inspiration.' This admission was no mere phrase of politeness; Read had an almost Godwinian conception of sincerity and did not indulge in empty courtesies. He was acknowledging, warmly and humbly, the fact that Worringer's speculations on the nature and role of abstraction in the visual arts became the keystone to his own aesthetic philosophy.

There were other scholars whose work Read studied with profit, and just as scrupulously acknowledged. Apart from the psychoanalysts whose presence is frequently visible—Freud and Jung but also less-known figures like Trigant Burrow and Ernest Jones—he accepted the insights of Burckhardt and Berenson, of Suzanne Langer and Ernst Cassirer and—as we have seen—of Conrad Fiedler. Above all, he bowed, as an ultimate pioneer, to the eighteenth-century antiquarian Giambattista Vico, whom he regarded as the creator of 'the genetic method—a method that studies art in relation to its origins, its history and distribution—in brief, the empirical method itself. The whole of the modern tradition in art is a direct result of such an

approach.' Here we have the clue that draws together all the influences. For Read, like Vico, became a genetic aesthetician, and therefore necessarily an eclectic, so that he always stood apart from those
of his contemporaries, like Clive Bell, who sought a pure aesthetic of
significant form. He was even ready, while rejecting the idea of art as
propaganda, to admit that 'I regard the ideological content (granted
that this may be very abstract and intellectual, as well as religious
and sentimental) as a normal ingredient in works of art.'

If Read stood apart from Clive Bell—whom he rarely mentions—
he was closer to Roger Fry, whose place as a mediator between contemporary artists and the fragmentary public that showed an interest
in them he was to assume in the early 1930's; it was even something
of a formal succession, for in 1933 Read took over the editorship of
the *Burlington Magazine*, which Fry had founded, and when Fry
died in 1934 he wrote important obituary articles in *The Spectator*
and *The Listener.*

There were obvious differences between the two men, most
important perhaps the fact that Fry belonged by many personal ties
to the Bloomsbury mandarins, while Read had entered the world of
literature and the arts from the outside. Yet they were alike as *pein-
tres manqués,* and both recognized that the scientific method had
much to offer the study of the arts. 'Doubtless because he had been
trained as a scientist,' Read said of Fry, 'there was a novel scientific
approach in his art criticism something drastically different from the
vague emotional appreciation which had served the purpose for a
century or more. Fry was the first critic in this country to use the
method of formal analysis at least, the first to make it a popular
method of exposition.'

By availing himself of the insights of psychoanalysis, Read broadened the scientific approach Fry had introduced; where Fry applied it
to the work of art, Read applied it also to the process of creation. At
the same time, he was aware of the weaknesses of his predecessor's
approach, of the lack of a consistent philosophy which resulted in
Fry's criticism rarely being much more than impressionistic. He realized too that Fry had limitations in perception which belonged partly
to his generation and partly to his practices as a painter. Fry understood Cézanne and the other Post-Impressionists; he was also the
first English critic to draw attention to the virtues of African and pre-
Columbian sculpture. Yet, though an ardent formalist, he was never
able to accept the experiments of Kandinsky and the Constructivists;

while the symbolic undercurrents of the visual arts, which to Read were so important, had little meaning for him. Welcoming the revolutionary artists of his youth, and courageously advocating them when they were first introduced to an uncomprehending English public, he stayed on to defend a Post-Impressionist citadel already won, and in the end, as Read suggested, he became almost a reactionary in artistic terms:

> ... faced with the machine, mass-production and universal education, he could only retreat into the private world of his own sensibility. He did, more and more as time went on, attempt to find a universal philosophical justification for this private world, and he had at his command an ingenious mind and a patient experience of his subject. But all this effort did not bring him into any very vital or sympathetic relationship to his own age.

When Read wrote these lines at the time of Fry's death he was himself entering a period of involvement in political movements and in other public endeavours to sustain and develop the social relevance of the arts. He could hardly be expected to sympathize deeply with Fry's point of view, but a time would come, in his own later years, when he would understand it more deeply.

It is hard to say how much actual influence Fry may have had on Read. Immediately after World War I, when Fry was involved in disputes with Wyndham Lewis and his followers over that ill-starred adventure in the applied arts, the Omega Workshops, Read's sympathies were more with the Vorticists than with Fry, and perhaps the most one can say is that, like many English artists and connoisseurs, he was influenced in a very general way by the change in the climate of opinion brought about by Fry's advocacy of the Post-Impressionists, and that Fry's formalism and his willingness to consider a painting in quasi-scientific terms affected his approach. But even in a scientific sense he owed far more to Jung than to Fry, and throughout his career Worringer remained his real master in aesthetics and Read the faithful and honest disciple. Yet Worringer really gave him, at best, the sketch of a system. It was Read who developed out of it his own more complex method, and his own highly flexible approach to the work of art, which made possible a catholicity of appreciation he never attained or perhaps wished to attain towards his own art of poetry.

4

The publication of *English Stained Glass* effectively established Read as an authority in the particular branch of aesthetics he had followed since he joined the Victoria and Albert Museum, and it was only after he had consolidated this position that he began to emerge as a critic of the arts in general. In 1927 he published his first comment on the art of painting, outside the little magazines of his youth, as a review in *The Observer* of *Old Masters and Modern Art* by Sir Charles Holmes; he entitled the review 'Two Schools of Painting'. It quickly became clear that, while he was far from rejecting the Old Masters and all they represented, his closest interest lay with the Moderns. He wrote a few small pieces on aesthetics, on the meaning of beauty, on the letters of van Gogh, and then, in September 1929, published as a special supplement to the BBC's new periodical, *The Listener*, a lengthy essay on 'The Meaning of Art'. This was the real beginning of his career as an interpreter of the visual arts in general. Early in 1930 he started his regular commentaries in *The Listener*, a series of reviews of books and exhibitions, and occasional essays on general aesthetic problems, which lasted into the 1940's and on which he drew copiously for his first general work on the visual arts, which was also called *The Meaning of Art*.

The Meaning of Art is not a collection of essays so much as a mosaic of extracts from Read's published reviews and articles, arranged to present in clear and readable form an introduction to the aesthetic background of modern painting and an informal history of the arts from primitive man to Henry Moore and Barbara Hepworth. *The Meaning of Art* was three times revised and expanded up to the edition in the year of Read's death, and even today that final version remains one of the best descriptions of the nature of art available to the layman seeking instruction. It states in sharp and often aphoristic form the theoretical bases of modern aesthetics, and never strays so far into theoretical abstraction as to take us away from the thought of the work of art as a concrete object or the artist as a creating and living being. Much of its vividness and utility springs from the fact that Read has not entirely streamlined the mosaic into a continuous narrative. Each section on an idea or an artist or a movement stands apart, linked with the rest by affinity rather than linear connection, so that, though a time sequence exists, one does not have the sense of an inexorable chronological progress; the vividness of a patchwork, in which each individual piece can if necessary be considered separately, still remains. This feeling of each work and each artist being considered anew is perhaps the outstanding quality of Read's presentation in this first work, and in so many books that follow it. Equally striking is his willingness to open his mind to any work that has the one quality of vitality, so that there are unexpectedly sympathetic assessments of such movements as Rococo. He admits the difficulty of classifying and categorizing artists who are in proportion to their creativity individual and original human beings. Thus, in writing of Delacroix, after stressing the romantic elements in his painting, he goes on:

> But in the philosophy and criticism expressed in his journal he reveals the baffling duality of his genius, for here all his praise is for order, reason and clarity, in one word, classicism. ... All this merely shows how difficult in the case of a talent like Delacroix's, it is to use party labels like 'romantic' and 'classic'. For inasmuch as a genius depends on the physical and emotional features of the one type, he will seek to create the intellectual features of the other type.

The Meaning of Art is full of vivid and clear definitions, e.g.:

> I would say that the function of art is not to transmit *feeling* so that others may experience the same *feeling*. ... The real function of art is to express feeling and transmit *understanding*.

It contains a series of brilliant clarifications on points that still puzzle those who first face the verbal as well as the visual language of contemporary art.

> We must not be afraid of this word 'abstract'. All art is primarily abstract. For what is aesthetic experience, deprived of its incidental trappings and associations, but a response of the body and mind of man to invented or isolated harmonies? Art is an escape from chaos. It is movement ordained in numbers; it is mass confined in measure; it is the indetermination of matter seeking the rhythm of life.

It is full of sharp revelatory insights into individual artists. On Matisse for example:

Matisse is not interested in the model as a living being; nor in the scene for the sake of its architectural properties; but these things have suggested a pattern, and the pattern achieved is not only a legitimate work of art, but also an intuitive apprehension of the subject far more vivid than any imitative representation could make it.

Such a passage may not convert one to a passionate commitment to the painter in question (though Read himself was committed to Matisse) but it does help to resolve difficulties which are likely to come to the mind of the person who first views the work of such a painter.

This, as Read admitted freely and frequently, is peripheral to the direct and instantaneous experience through which the feeling in a work of art is transmitted to the viewer. All that the critic can do beforehand is to prepare the mind of the viewer by removing intellectual prejudices; all he can do afterwards is to help clarify the experience by his genetic explanations. And if there appears a rather simplistic tone in certain passages of *The Meaning of Art*, it is partly because Read feels that his duty is not to reveal so much as to elucidate, but partly also because the book was originally compiled at a time when popular ignorance of modern works of art was so dense and universal that the clearest and purest of lights was needed to dispel it.

The Meaning of Art was the first of a group of guides to the uninitiated that Read would periodically revise to fit the changes in the world of art and also in the climate of popular appreciation. *Art Now*, *in* which he traced the theoretical basis of contemporary art and mapped out the maze of movements into which it had divided since Cézanne, first appeared in 1933; it was revised in 193 6, 1948 and 1960, and was steadily expanded to include later movements like Abstract Expressionism and Action Painting. Where *The Meaning of Art* is descriptive, *Art Now* tends to be apologetic, a work of justification as well as explanation. *Contemporary British Art*, first published in 1951, appeared again in 1964 in an edition which not only brought Read to the movements such as Pop Art and Op Art which were flourishing in the early 1960's, but also led him to sound the first of the warnings he felt constrained to pronounce, with increasing force as the decade continued, on the disintegration which he saw overtaking the modern movement. Observing how the methods

of Dada were being revived without Dada's justification or its concealed longing for meaningful form, he concluded:

> Lacking any formal or even ideological basis, such a pictorial activity
> tends to become amateurish, flippant, vulgar. It is no doubt an expres-
> sion of a longing to return to figurative imagery, but in the 'icons' it
> selects, from science fiction, card games, advertisements, horror films,
> press photographs, etc., it is not 'popular' in the sense of having a direct
> appeal to the masses, but is a highly sophisticated disorganization of
> commonplace imagery. As such, it may have an appeal to the unhappy
> few.
>   The critic may protest, as I do, that art is always a question of form,
> and not of content. But he does not thereby identify himself with those
> foolish people who would pour new wine into old bottles. The artist does
> not work in that way, and never has worked in that way except in deca-
> dent periods. Original experience provokes unique modes of expression.

Having seen the Thirties as a time of decay for the contemporary
spirit in poetry, Read watched that process overtaking the visual arts
by the Sixties. And it is difficult, when one observes the accelerating
progress into futility since 1964, to disagree with his view that (quite
apart from moralistic judgements) we live in a decadent age, even
bearing in mind that in the arts decadence is a matter of form more
than of content.

All the books I have mentioned differ from the works of earlier
interpreters of the visual arts in their sobriety and conciseness, qualities determined largely by the different circumstances in which Read
was writing. Because techniques of reproduction were rudimentary,
writers like Ruskin and Pater had to write elaborate descriptive and
interpretative comments on individual works of art; Read could fill
his books with reproductions to support a text devoted largely to
questions of historical and psychological background and the nature
of the creative process, and concerned less with the actual form of a
work in descriptive terms than with its symbolic implications. This
approach made Read an effective aesthetic historian. His final works
in this genre, both published in the last decade, were *A Concise History of Modern Painting* (1959) and *A Concise History of Modern
Sculpture* (1964), abundantly illustrated volumes in which Read
used the simple insights he acquired from Worringer to bring an
impressive order out of the apparent chaos of contemporary artistic

trends, and to demonstrate how far modern painters and sculptors, dedicated to formal values and hence to clarity of perception, have, without moralistic intentions, carried out a task whose moral implications are in fact incalculable. He ends *A Concise History of Modern Painting* in a peroration which in this way links the actual work of painters with the wider relevance of art as a regimen of social health:

> The modern movement in art has so often been presented as in itself corrupt that it may seem paradoxical to represent it as a purifying influence. But such it is and has been from the moment that Cézanne resolved to 'realize his sensations in the presence of nature'. In retrospect the whole of this movement, in spite of its deviations and irregularities, must be conceived as an immense effort to rid the mind of that corruption which, whether it has taken the form of fantasy-building or repression, sentimentality or dogmatism, constitutes a false witness to sensation or experience. Our artists have often been violent or destructive, inconsiderate and impatient, but in general they have been aware of a moral issue, which is the moral issue facing our whole civilization. Philosophy and politics, science and government, all rest finally on the clarity with which we perceive and conceive the fact of experience, and art has always been, directly through its artists and poets and indirectly through the use which other people make of the signs and images invented by these poets and artists, the primary means of forming clear ideas of feelings and sensations. Individual artists may have introduced confusion into the general aim, but in the minds of the great leaders of the modern movement in painting—Cézanne, Matisse, Picasso, Kandinsky, Klee, Mondrian, and Pollock—there was always a constant awareness of the problem of courage, always a constant alertness to false solutions. To present a clear and distinct visual image of sensuous experience—that has always been the undeviating aim of these artists, and the rich treasury of icons they have created is the basis upon which any possible civilization of the future will be built.

The implications of such a view are expanded in the books, such as *Art and Industry*, *Art and Society*, *The Grass Roots of Art*, *Icon and Idea* and *The Forms of Things Unknown*, in which Read explored the various dimensions of the artist's relationship with the society that conspires with his personality to shape his style, and on which he in turn operates as a shaping force. But this aspect of Read's aesthetic philosophy will, as I have said, be discussed later; at present we are concerned with the way in which Read's views are expressed in his judgement of individual artists.

5

As a writer, Read divided his activities between the spontaneous, lyrical approach of the poet and the logical, discursive approach of the essayist. His views on poetry tended to the romantic; his practice in prose was inclined to the classical. Poetry was a private activity; prose led him into the public world, the world of lecture rooms and conferences against which his poetic self put up a ritual fight which was doomed from the beginning to defeat.

One can trace an analogous division within his attitude towards painting and sculpture. There was in Read the academic philosopher of the arts who lectured at universities and addressed the Eranos Tagung, who wrote such profound works of aesthetic theory in his last decade as *Icon and Idea* and *The Forms of Things Unknown*. But there was also the *aficionado* who responded lyrically to the concrete object, the actual work of art, and who mingled with this appreciation an intuitive sense of the relationship between the artist and the artifact.

One can observe this interplay throughout Read's career. It begins with the period of direct youthful involvement in the arts, from 1913 to 1922, when Read first became acquainted with practising artists in Leeds, when he himself aspired to be a painter and actually exhibited some of his work, when he helped to found *Art and Letters* and eventually claimed his place in the modern movement as an artist who found that his most congenial medium was words. Until 1922 he was as much a 'Sunday artist' as his friend T. S. Eliot, working like him in an office by day and writing during evenings and weekends. At the Victoria and Albert, his vocation and his employment came closer together, for he was working by day with artifacts whose appeal was visual and tactile, and creating verbal artifacts in his spare time. He accepted the discipline of study which his work involved until he became as expert in ceramics as any academically trained museum director, while his winter of lectures on Wordsworth at Trinity College from 1929 to 1930 proved so well his ability to

function academically that by the end of the year Richard Aldington
was writing to congratulate him on the publication of the lectures (in
Wordsworth) but also to issue a warning that is appropriate in the
light of Read's career:

> I thought the book extremely well done of its kind, but I hated you being
> seduced into doing that kind! My feeling is that when the *bourgeoisie*
> (particularly Cambridge) get hold of an artist they try to make a profes-
> sor out of him. It seems to me they've buggered poor old Tom Eliot up,
> and turned him from the poète des professeurs, into the professeur des
> poètes. It's a damn shame, because he has genius. For Christ's sake don't
> let them do that to you, Herbert. A poet is a man who produces poems ...

Barely six months later Aldington was writing lukewarmly to
congratulate Read on his appointment as Watson Gordon Professor
of Fine Arts at Edinburgh University ('You'll not have to feel the
damaging atmosphere of Ox. or Cam ...'). Eliot, who had been
instrumental in getting Read invited to give the Clark Lectures at
Cambridge, was also deeply involved in this appointment, for it was
he who acted as intermediary in 1929 when Herbert Grierson suggested proposing Read for the Professorship. Had Aldington known
this he would doubtless have argued that Eliot was passing on to
Read his own infection with academicism; certainly, when Read did
resign from the Edinburgh post, Aldington was far more enthusiastic than he had been at the time of appointment.

> This is great news [he wrote] and I send my warmest congratulations and
> hopes for the future. I haven't any doubt about you, with your talents,
> your courage, your energy and your self-control.

In all this, one can see Eliot as the representative of the scholarly side
of Read's literary persona, and Aldington as representative of its
poetic side.

By 1933, Read had certainly found the academic life ('the cruel
rack of the curriculum' as he once called it) too heavy in its demands
and too constraining in its disciplines: the most that he appears to
have gained from the Edinburgh interlude was practice in lecturing
and an insight into the problems of education which he would put to
use a decade later in developing the revolutionary proposals embod-

ied in *Education Through Art*. His ability to write on a scholarly level
had already been exhibited in *English Stained Glass* long before his
brief career as a practising academic.

When Read left Edinburgh it was to enter directly into the world
of contemporary British art. He not only became editor of the
Burlington Magazine, but also took up residence in Parkhill Road in
Hampstead, which was then an important physical centre of the
'modern movement' in the visual arts in London. There, as we have
seen, his neighbours were Ben Nicholson and Barbara Hepworth,
Henry Moore and Paul Nash, artists who were to give British painting and sculpture an originality and a power it had not known since
the days of Constable and Turner, and who were to regain for these
arts an international reputation.

Read's immersion in antique pottery and glassware at the Victoria and Albert Museum had not meant a loss of contact with the contemporary arts. He remained in touch with painters and sculptors,
but he had comparatively little sympathy for the Bloomsbury
painters—such as Duncan Grant and Vanessa Bell—who at this time
most prominently represented the contemporary movement in
Britain. It was rather to painters like Paul Nash, whose images of war
projected into visual form what he himself tried to express in words,
that he was attracted. But his first published article on a living British
artist was not on Nash; it was on Henry Moore—a short piece published in *The Listener* in 1931—and it foreshadowed an involvement
that in the end was to outweigh Read's interest in any other single
artist.

During his two years at Edinburgh, Read had little time for writing of any kind, and less opportunity than he would have wished to
keep in contact with English painting and sculpture at a period of
considerable and original productivity; his only writings in that field
while at Edinburgh were an article on Roger Fry and a brief introduction to an exhibition of sculpture by Barbara Hepworth. But his
work at the *Burlington Magazine*, and his proximity to the group of
artists in Hampstead, led to a habit of attending exhibitions and visiting studios that kept him in intimate touch for thirty years with the
changing features of the artistic scene and with the personalities and
achievements of its figures.

He was not merely a spectator and an observer. His inclination,
as a critic, to formulate a theoretical basis for artistic practices attracted him towards artists who themselves tended to justify their

practice philosophically. This was an important element in his interest in Kandinsky and later in the Surrealists, and early in 1933, when
a number of artists he admired formed themselves into a group called
Unit One, he welcomed the statement of their spokesman, Paul Nash,
with its rejection of naturalism and its insistence on 'Design ... considered as a structural pursuit; imagination, explored apart from literature or metaphysics'. The leading figures in the group were the
artists who became his neighbours at Parkhill Road, and when they
issued an enlarged manifesto in volume form, calling for vitality
rather than beauty as a criterion for the artist, Read wrote the preface. Two years later, in 1936, when avant-garde British artists entered
into a temporary and unstable affiance with the disciples of André
Breton, and the Surrealist Exhibition created a mild scandal in artistic London, Read not only took an active part in organizing the
events, but edited and introduced *Surrealism*, a volume of manifestos
in which he and Hugh Sykes Davies joined with the leaders of the
French movement, Breton, Eluard and Georges Hugnet. His introduction was a passionate statement of commitment in which he identified surrealism as a logical extension of romanticism, and declared
his rejection of authoritarian social doctrines and of academic (or
'classical') artistic doctrines, which he identified with each other.

> There is a principle of life, of creation, of liberation, and that is the
> romantic spirit; there is a principle of order, of control and of repression,
> and that is the classical spirit. Naturally there is some purpose in the lat-
> ter principle—the instincts are curbed in the interest of some particular
> ideal or set of values; but on analysis it always resolves into the defence
> of some particular structure of society, the perpetuation of the rule of
> some particular class.

Read's definitions of romanticism and classicism and his attitudes
towards them fluctuated constantly, and it is significant that in the
introduction to *Surrealism* he chooses to speak in his role as the poet,
dedicated to romanticism, rather than as the art critic, committed to
impartiality. In fact, if any real alignment as an art critic appears in
Read's writings as he moves out from the shadow of the academy, it
is a dedication to the interpretation of the contemporary whether it
can be defined as romantic or classical. Not long afterwards, when he
was asked to write in *The Listener* of his favourite work of art in a
British gallery, he chose Seurat's 'La Baignade', and in discussing it he

dilated on the factors that make it difficult for us to understand and therefore to appreciate completely a work that is not contemporary.

> I am not and cannot be in possession of all the factors necessary for the full appreciation of an 'Old Master', or of any work of art distantly removed from me in time. Only in works of art contemporary with my experience of life do I feel fully aware of all their potentialities.

But it was more than a question of understanding the artists of one's own time. For, at his most euphoric, Read argued that the artists who were his contemporaries possessed means of understanding their world which their predecessors had lacked, and he presents this understanding as an important factor in the process by which art plays its part in the broadening of the human consciousness.

> The difference in our own period [he said in an essay contributed to a symposium entitled *Circle* in 1937] is that we have become more conscious of these historical processes, *and can attack directly what other ages could only discover accidentally.* Just as surrealism makes use of, or rather proceeds on the assumption of, the knowledge embodied in psycho-analysis, so abstract art makes use of, or proceeds on the basis of, the abstract concepts of physics and dynamics, geometry and mathematics. It is not necessary for the abstract artist to have a knowledge of these sciences (nor is it necessary for the superrealist to have a knowledge of psycho-analysis); such concepts are part of our mental ambience, and the artist is precisely the individual who can make this ambience actual. He can make it actual in detached and non-utilitarian works of art; or he can make it actual in architecture and the industrial arts.

It was thus that Read saw the artists who were his contemporaries actually functioning. Those he variously called super- realists (a vastly wider concept than surrealism), or expressionists, projected through their fugitive imagery the symbolic forms that illuminated man's individual and collective inner nature, his unconscious; abstract art, and particularly the form he found most sympathetic— the constructivism of Gabo and Pevsner—departed from traditional forms, genres and even materials to create out of the offerings of the new technological society the impersonal images that would redeem its soul.

Read continued occasionally to write on artists of the European past, tracing principally the historical principles that would illuminate the work of modern artists, yet from the mid Thirties all but an infinitesimally small proportion of his writing on painting and sculpture, as well as his work in such organizations as the Industrial Design Unit and the Institute of Contemporary Arts, was dedicated to artists of the modern movement which, for Read, began with Cézanne and Seurat. He did not lose his admiration for the great romantic painters of the past like Turner and Delacroix, or for such splendid precursors of abstract art as Piero della Francesca, but when he left the modern period it was usually to seek parallels for the innovations of contemporary artists outside the European traditions, so that scattered through collections like *A Coat of Many Colours* and *The Tenth Muse* one encounters pieces on primitive art, Etruscan art and Chinese art. Read did not regard himself as expert in any of these fields, but in observing traditions which had not followed the classic canons of European art he found much that helped to illuminate the work of his contemporaries which, more than the art of any other period in human history, can be called eclectic, though, as Read was careful to point out in *Contemporary British Art*, its eclecticism has never been the dominant characteristic.

We are prepared to admit with Kipling that 'East is East and West is West, and never the twain shall meet'; but this observation might have been made with equal justice of the north and the south. We cannot escape our mental climates, for they are in a literal sense the creation of our prevailing winds and the chemistry of our soils. It is inconceivable that English art should be *decisively* influenced by Indian art, or French art, by African art. In saying this I am fully conscious of such cross currents as the influence of Negro sculpture on Picasso (though Picasso himself refuses to attach any special importance to this influence), or the influence of Mexican sculpture on Henry Moore. Such influences are like injections of a drug: they act as a temporary stimulus and restore the body to health. I do not deny their necessity or deprecate their usefulness. But they are shocks which should be absorbed into the main bloodstream: they should not persist as a habit or a fashion.

Read's special preferences in the arts can be gauged by considering the artists on whom he chose to write at length and in depth. There are full-scale books on Henry Moore and Hans Arp. There are collections of paintings with lengthy introductions published at various times between 1934 and 1959 on Moore and Paul Nash, on Ben Nicholson and Lynn Chadwick, on Klee and Kandinsky and Gauguin. There is also a considerable essay on Picasso which first appeared in 1934 as part of a symposium entitled *Great Contemporaries*. A long piece on the constructivist art of Gabo and Pevsner was published for the first time in *The Philosophy of Modern Art*, a mosaic collection of essays issued in 1952, which also reproduced the already mentioned essays on Moore, Nash, Nicholson, Klee, Gauguin and Picasso, as well as the introduction to *Surrealism* ('Surrealism and the Romantic Principle') and a group of partly philosophical and partly historical essays on contemporary painting before and after World War II. The volume might indeed be described as philosophic in mood, since it poses the dialectic movement between freedom and order which Read detects in all artistic manifestations, but it does not present the fully developed system of aesthetic philosophy that emerged from Read's later works in the field.

It will be seen that the list of individual artists on whom Read wrote specific volumes or long essays corresponds fairly closely to the list at the beginning of this chapter of those whom—in a rare moment of confidence—he named as having his personal preference. It is true that on some of these artists Read never wrote at length Seurat, Juan Gris and Léger in particular. Also—though one chapter of *Art Now* deals with Picasso, Kandinsky and Klee as the three important seminal painters of the modern era—Read wrote less on Picasso than one might have expected. This was partly due to the fact that Picasso attracted a disproportionate amount of attention from art critics in general, so that Read felt it was more important to press the claims of artists less publicized in his time, like Gabo and Kandinsky. But one also has the feeling that he was overawed by Picasso's immense energy and bewildered by his protean changefulness, and this in spite of the fact that Picasso exemplified more abundantly than any other contemporary artist Read's thesis that abstraction, realism and all their variants can alternate within the work of the same artist. Read's instinct—the instinct of the author of *The Innocent Eye* and *The Green Child*—led him away from such a many-sided vigour as Picasso's towards the contained intensity. There is one especially significant essay which begins *A Coat of Many Colours*. It is entitled 'The Greatest Work of Art in the World', and its episodic framework is provided by a visit to Arezzo. Naturally, one expects that the 'greatest work' will be one of Piero della Francesca's splendid frescoes in Arezzo itself or perhaps his masterpiece at Borgo San Sepolcro. It is neither, but a tiny Etruscan bronze head of a Negro boy—no more than two inches high—which Read saw in a jumbled case in the Florence Archaeological Museum. Perhaps there was a touch of whimsicality in this choice of a totally unknown work—certainly the photograph that accompanies the article suggests charm and spontaneity but hardly greatness—yet one's sense of being made the victim of a rather perverse jest vanishes when Read disclaims the wish to give any apocalyptic significance to the experience of discovering the little head and goes on to say:

> As a matter of fact, the little bust had merely jumped into its place as a ready symbol for an attitude which is innate: I have a characteristic preference for the miniature—for the epitome, the episode, the epigram. ... Art must be intimate if it is to be a personal possession. It belongs to a private world.

Here I suggest we have the clue to Read's particular devotion to Kandinsky and Klee. If one is seeking an epitome of the abstract movement in art, surely it can be found most clearly in the work of Kandinsky, in his theoretical writings on abstraction in art as much as in the precision of his artistic methods and the extraordinary coherence of his work. For Read, Kandinsky epitomized at the beginning of the movement all that was essential in abstract art, and in particular the belief 'that there exists a psychic or spiritual reality that can only be apprehended and communicated by means of a visual language, the elements of which are non-figurative plastic symbols'. Beyond Kandinsky lay the constructivists, with their desire 'to escape from the internal necessities of our individual existence and to create a pure art, free from human tragedy, impersonal and universal'. And here, in the crystalline works of Gabo, where transparent wings of perspex and elusive webs of cord transform all our conceptions of the role of space in sculpture, Read sees the epitome of a new realism beyond abstraction, for the constructivist has created his own 'new and logically consistent reality', and 'the images which the artist projects to make this reality concrete, the constructions of his imagination and his hands, are the only forms of art which can properly be called realistic'. Within this constructivist paradox is neatly synthesized the dual movement of modern art.

In Paul Klee, Read found a fellow devotee of the miniature, and in his essay on him he emphasizes precisely these features of Klee's work, his 'little discoveries', his desire, as Klee himself expressed it, 'to work out for myself a tiny, formal motive, one that my pencil will be able to hold without any technique'. But that pencil, as Read remarks, 'moves and the line dreams', and what he is really discovering in Klee is not the extraordinary half-calligraphic style, but a symbolizing power even greater than that of Gauguin, and all the more intense because Klee—like the sculptor who made the Etruscan bronze head—worked in miniature. 'Great poetry does not need big print nor does great painting need acres of canvas,' as Read said in his essay on Klee in 1948. 'It is the still small voice that is the most penetrating.' A decade later, in *A Concise History of Modern Painting*, he went further in his claims for Klee's importance; his 'insistence, at one and the same time, on the subjective sources and the objective means of art' have made Klee 'the most significant artist of our epoch'.

Yet, while Read is ready to grant pre-eminence, in painting at least, to the continental masters of the modern movement, it is—with the one remarkable exception of Hans Arp—of British artists, his contemporaries and for the most part his friends, that he writes with most intimacy and understanding. The long essay on Paul Nash which he put together out of three separate articles and included in *The Philosophy of Modern Art*, and the biographical-critical study of Henry Moore, which he published in 1964 as a volume in the World of Art series, are the best of his studies of these fellow countrymen, though the long passage on Graham Sutherland in the 1964 edition of *Contemporary British Art* follows them closely.

We find an excellent oblique explanation of this inclination towards British artists in the last sentences of *Contemporary British Art*. Read, of course, is talking of the painters and sculptors whose work he had discussed, but when we read the passage with attention we realize that what he here applies to the process of creation can equally be applied to the process of critical understanding.

The history of art shows that the art of any particular region always tends to revert to a regional norm—to a mode of sensibility and style of expression determined, we must assume, by ethnic and geographic factors. There is no need to base a philosophy, much less a religion, on such simple materialistic premises. Art cannot be confined within frontiers—

it lives only if continually subjected to foreign invasions, to migrations and transplantations. But if art's vitality comes from the cross-breeding of styles, its strength comes from stability, from roots that grow deep into a native soil. The typical style of northern Europe alternates between abstraction and expressionism. We may for a time successfully absorb the style of southern Europe, and we have had idealistic and naturalistic artists of great talent. But our natural talent lies elsewhere in those styles which spring from introspective and personalistic moods. Such styles are in both the critical and historical sense romantic by nature; the genius of our greatest poets was always romantic. In that sense the general trend of contemporary art may be interpreted as a return to our romantic tradition.

If our talent lies 'in those styles which spring from introspective and personalistic moods', so, by implication, must our natural taste, and in Read's case this is certainly true, leading him to some insights which are patently accurate and to others which now seem distorted by partiality.

For example, one feels no doubt at all of the justice of Read's admiration for Henry Moore, though it was based on deeply personal foundations. Moore came from Yorkshire, and responded deeply to the landscape of moors and dales, and the first biographical chapter of Read's *Henry Moore* (1959) is a restrained yet intense account of the sculptor's childhood and its setting, an account enriched by the fact that Read is obviously comparing Moore's experience constantly with his own. Later, during the years from 1933 to 1939, which for both of them were richly productive, Read was Moore's neighbour and observed many of his finest works developing from the plaster maquette to the ultimate form in stone, bronze or wood. He watched Moore at work, saw how he responded to the will of the material, its natural formal propensities, and how he derived from one great Mexican sculpture, the Mayan reclining figure of the god Chac Mol, a series of variations at once intensely personal and intensely English in their romantic evocation of myths all the more potent because they were not articulated.

Read also listened to Moore's explanations of his works. Moore always claimed that his aim was not beauty (which Read himself always regarded as a classicist ideal) but vitality. For Moore was in no strict sense an abstractionist; if his work is not representational, it is certainly figurative in the sense that it derives from images drawn

out of the natural world and endowed with symbolic resonances. For
Read, Moore is the equal in sculpture of Picasso and Klee in painting;
he represents at its heights 'the new revelation' which comes from the
willingness 'to seek below the level of consciousness for those archetypal forms that represent life in its deepest recesses and most powerful manifestations'. I do not think a better summary of Moore's
achievement has yet been written than that contained in the closing
sentences of *Henry Moore*, where Read emphasizes that Moore's
power, the source of his true greatness, lies not merely in his originality, but even more in the strength of his true traditionalism.

> Beauty is no mystery: it can be represented by geometrical formulas, by
> calculated proportions. But the vital process is intangible, and can be
> represented only by symbolic forms—forms symbolic of the racial expe-
> riences that have left an impression on our mental constitution—the
> archetypal patterns of birth and death, of social conflict and tragic
> drama.
>
> Such archetypes were, of course, represented in the art of the past,
> and we have seen how Moore's archetypal motives, the Reclining Figure,
> the Mother and Child, the King and Queen, are echoes of the most pow-
> erful creations of the art of earlier ages. Some of these works, in prehis-
> toric art, in tribal art, in the art of Sumer or Egypt, do not differ in their
> essential forms from Henry Moore's archetypal figures, and from this
> point of view it could be maintained that Moore is more traditional than
> the average academic artist. His originality does not lie in his motives,
> nor even in the aesthetic significance of his forms—in these respects he is
> a traditionalist. His originality is rather a consequence of his having
> extended the whole concept of tradition—of having reforged the links in
> the Great Chain of Being that had been broken by a materialistic concep-
> tion of life and art.

Read ends by emphasizing that, by whatever historical or scientific criteria the critic interprets Moore's work, the artist's actual
process remains 'unprogrammatic ... almost naive'.

> He is a maker of images—or, as I prefer to call them because they have
> material existence—of icons, and he is impelled to make these icons by
> his sense of the forms that are vital to the life of mankind.

From 1934, when he wrote his first essay on Moore, down to the end of his life, Read was the ardent advocate of his fellow Yorkshire-man's work. Moore's stature remains, in the 1970's, as massive as ever; he towers above his fellow artists as the last great representa-tive—Picasso alone excepted—of the modern movement which emerged in the early years of the century. And if he no longer needs Read for an advocate, as Turner ceased to need Ruskin, this is only a sign that Read's judgement, like Ruskin's, was as true as it was gen-erous.

The case of Paul Nash is somewhat different. Here also there were personal reasons for Read to become interested in Nash's work, which he first saw on returning from the front in 1918 after the retreat on the Somme, and which he recognized as a successful ren-dering into visual form of experiences he himself had been trying to express in prose and verse. There followed the later associations of living as neighbours, of collaboration in Unit One, and of working together to justify Surrealism to a British public. Read was attracted by Nash's 'obstinate Englishness', and especially by his intense feel-ing for the landscape of southern England, which resembled his own feeling for the Yorkshire dales. In Nash he detected a special faith in the *'genius loci'*, and recognized that this implied 'a particular kind of sensibility, an awareness of "atmosphere"'.

These observations are true; at his best Nash was an intensely lyrical artist of a kind peculiarly English. But in late years it has become evident that he was not so pre-eminent in this role as Read's faithful enthusiasm suggested. Yet, as Read pointed out of Baude-laire, an occasional excess of enthusiasm does not discredit the essen-tial truth of a good critic's judgement, and Paul Nash has his assured place, if it is not so high as Read suggested, in the tradition that includes Cotman and the Cromes and Girtin. Perhaps the real mis-take was to hail him as a representative of the modern movement, when in his best work he was a belated representative of the English landscape tradition.

One of the striking developments of Read's last years was the ten-dency for sculpture to replace painting as the main focus of his inter-est in the visual arts. In 1956 he published *The Art of Sculpture*, a lavishly illustrated elaboration of a series of lectures he had delivered at the National Gallery of Art in Washington. It traces historically the evolution of sculpture from a relief carving dependent on its background to a three-dimensional mass standing autonomously in space as a kind of magnification of the amulet which needs neither

base nor wall for its independent existence. *The Art of Sculpture* is
one of the few books in which Read takes in the whole history of an
art from its primitive beginnings through the Classical and Renaissance development of the cult of beauty, to the varied currents of our
own day, finding fulfilment on the one hand in a realization of all the
artistic implications of mass, and on the other—in the work of the
constructivists—in a defining of space in which mass has been dissolved and negated. If the book has a flaw, it is one shared with many
of Read's works; a kind of messianic dialecticism which sees modern
art as better than past art in the sense that it represents an extension
of consciousness, and which in this way imparts to the reader's mind
an almost Hegelian sense of predestined progression.

The Art of Sculpture was followed in 1964 by Read's *Concise
History of Modern Sculpture*. It is not hard to determine the reasons
for the change in the direction of Read's interests which these books
and his studies of Moore and Arp represent. First, I suggest, Read
was attracted to sculpture because it was the art in which British
artists excelled in the years after World War I. Much as he admired
the work of painters like Sutherland, Nicholson and Bacon, he found
surer satisfaction in that of Moore and Barbara Hepworth, and later
of Lynn Chadwick, Ken Armitage and Reg Butler. As abstract im-
pressionism turned academic, and action painting declined into Pop
Art, he found reason for a growing disillusionment with current
trends in painting. Sculpture, it seemed to him, showed a more obstinate vitality, though even here he was moved in the end to protest
against a facile desire for novelty, a tendency to make works of art
into objects of 'horror and hatred' instead of contemplation.

An even more important reason for Read's turning towards
sculpture may be found, however, in his return to Yorkshire, to the
dale country whose beauties are essentially three-dimensional, contained in the soft contours of the land and the fractured cubes of the
decaying stone buildings. With his physical return there was also a
return in memory to the childhood world of *The Innocent Eye;* in
that world Read first became aware of the joys of creativity, and that
early creativity was essentially sculptural, as the child watched the
visiting smith creating his artifacts with fire, and himself, in the sad-
dleroom, made lead shot, 'gleaming silver bullets'.

In these two shrines I first experienced the joy of making things.
Everywhere around me the earth was stirring with growth and the beasts

were propagating their kind. But these wonders passed unobserved by
my childish mind, unrecorded in memory. They depended on forces
beyond our control, beyond my conception. But fire was real, and so was
the skill with which we shaped hard metals to our design and desire.

It is not surprising that such a child, grown up, should become fascinated with the art of sculpture, particularly when its practitioners
themselves turned their designs and desires to the shaping of hard
metals.

6

Read's last work on the visual arts was the volume he wrote on Hans
Arp for the World of Art series; it is a remarkably sensitive study of a
versatile and lyrical artist, adept in many media, who attained little
popular fame and yet remains one of the most suggestive and satisfying of all twentieth-century artificers.

At first sight one is puzzled why Read should have chosen Arp as
one of the two individual artists on whom he chose to write whole
books. Yet the more one reads his *Arp*, the more comprehensible the
choice becomes. Arp was not English, but he was perhaps the most
stateless of all modern European artists born into the curious border-
land of Alsace at the end of the nineteenth century; speaking French
and German as native languages, yet feeling no special loyalty to
either land; coming to maturity as an artist in Switzerland, and divid-
ing his final years between a studio in Meudon near Paris and another in Italian-speaking Ticino.

But there was more to the attraction that Read felt towards Arp
than the latter's lack of national identity or even their shared attachment to Surrealism (which for Arp was a natural consequence of his
membership of the original Dada movement). Arp resembled Read
in character; he had the same gentleness and reserve, and sometimes,
in photographs of Arp, one recognizes an expression of private joy
that would sometimes rest on Read's face. Arp was a particularly
pure artist, and few sculptures created in our century have shown
such intense dedication to formal integrity as his. Yet he refused to
call himself an abstract artist; he used the word *concrete* to describe
his sculptures and collages, and he insisted that all his work had its
origins in an apprehension of natural forms. He was also a fine poet.

And, with the strength of mind that characterizes some shy men, he refused to allow himself to be distracted from his work by the demands of the outside world, but continued it to the end of his life, bowing to such tragic necessities as war, yet refusing to be deflected from the path of creation into any other way. It is almost as if writing an epitaph on the self who might have been, that Read, at the end of his own life, says of Arp: 'He found his direction early in his life; he chose a narrow path and never deviated from it.'

One is faced by the kind of classic distinction which is expressed admirably in Buddhism by the concept of Hinayana and Mahayana, the lesser and the greater vehicles. The Hinayanist—Arp in this case—chooses the direct way to personal fulfilment. The Mahayanist—and Read perfectly fits the description—is willing to postpone personal fulfilment (or salvation) for the sake of all living beings (or, in our terms, in the interests of social fulfilment through the liberating forces of art). In Buddhism one observes that the Hinayanist, serene in his pursuit of personal nirvana, never envies the Mahayanist; the Mahayanist, whose attitude in the western world seems the nobler, often envies the Hinayanist whose way to salvation seems the more direct. There is no need for us to evaluate the respective achievements of Hans Arp and Herbert Read; let us merely profit from the recognition that they complemented each other. Were it possible for two such personalities to coalesce, the perfect artist might be produced. But in fact the dialectic, as Proudhon maintained, is a continuing process, and while thesis and antithesis are real, the synthesis is all illusion.

6

Art and the World

Like Shelley, but unlike most of the other libertarian philosophers, Herbert Read combined his anarchism with a devotion to the doctrines of Plato. It was not, however, the élitist structure of the commonwealth envisaged in *The Republic* that appealed to him, but rather Plato's conception of an aesthetic foundation for the political life, of a discipline based on the harmonious training and control of the life of the senses. Thus the most profound of Read's works in the philosophy of the arts, *The Forms of Things Unknown*, ends in a chapter devoted to the problem of peace which developments in modem technology have made so much more urgent than it was ever before. 'I have resorted to Plato,' Read concludes, 'not for a mystical doctrine, but for a practical solution to the problem of peace; and we have found, not moral exhortations, but the outline of a precise discipline, a discipline that is a reconciliation of Strife and Love, of what Tolstoy called the mutually exclusive and separately incomprehensible conceptions of freedom and inevitability; and the image of such a reconciliation is this "flower of peace, the Rose that cannot wither".'

Plato is a complex and sometimes ambiguous philosopher, and it would be easy to extract from his dialogues the outline of an attitude towards the arts, towards education, towards political organization, that runs counter to Read's essential philosophy, for the authoritarian element in Plato is undeniable. But in the present context the significance of Read's interest in Plato lies in the fact that he found in the Greek philosopher's writings a paradigm for the reconciliation he was seeking between the varying aspects of his own view of existence.

The chapters of *Annals of Innocence and Experience* in which Read describes his mental life as a youth in Leeds suggest that, like so many half-educated young men of his time and place, he was concerned with a variety of discrete interests, all followed passionately, but not organized into a philosophic structure more complex than that found by the obvious analogies between revolutionary ideas in politics and modernist ideas in the arts. As time goes on, a structure does begin to emerge; the pattern of analogy is replaced by an organic relationship in which Read's anarchism, his preoccupation with education, his critical attitudes, his aesthetic philosophy, appear as aspects of a consistent view of existence in which the central core is the creative impulse. Art becomes the clue to political and ethical problems, for all, Read argues, can be embraced within a philosophy that finds in the harmonies created by the artist, and in the images revealed by him, keys to a way of life that ideology can never encompass because, unlike the work of the artist, it operates on the most superficial levels of consciousness and has no access to those depths of the unconscious where one must seek out the great collective archetypes which unite mankind. Read's claims for art go even wider; if it provides us with the only thread that can guide us in the labyrinth of an alarming world, this is because in the steady evolution of human consciousness the forms of art, concrete and sensual, have preceded and inspired the development of ideas. 'Without the creative arts', he says categorically in *The Forms of Things Unknown*, 'there would have been no advance in myth or ritual, in language or meaning, in morality or metaphysics.'

It is against such high claims that one has to consider the books Read devoted to the consideration of the role of art in human society: *Art and Industry, Art and Society, To Hell with Culture, The Grass Roots of Art, Icon and Idea, The Forms of Things Unknown, The Origins of Form in Art* and *Art and Alienation*. They reveal Read's thought operating in a wider range than that of the critic and historian of art. He now appears as a philosopher of art; and as a moral philosopher in the sense that he finds in art the clues to a comprehensive view of existence and a corresponding ethical standpoint. These books provide that bridge that links Read the critic with Read the anarchist and educator who will be the subject of later chapters.

Before discussing individually the books I have just cited, it is necessary to consider certain underlying assumptions which distinguish Read's view of the evolution of the human consciousness and of human society from that presented by anthropologists and biologists who sustain currently orthodox views on the nature of man's development.

To begin with, Read does not accept evolution as a random process. His conception of it is frankly teleological; he sees it as inspired by a creative urge that propels mankind along a way of deepening consciousness. Here is evident the influence of Henri Bergson, whose writings Read acknowledges as basic tools for an aesthetic philosopher as distinct from a critic of the arts. In *The Contrary Experience* he tells how Bergson wielded 'a decisive influence, not merely on the direction of my intellectual growth, but also on its quality'. Bergson saved him from the mental impasse he had reached when the loss of religious faith

> ... had left me with little more than a mechanistic interpretation of the universe, a bleak rationalism which was not consistent with my romantic temperament. Bergson, keeping within the world of scientific fact—indeed, drawing all his evidence from that world offered an interpretation of the universe that was neither mechanistic nor finalist—that provided a way out of the closed system of predestined fact. He showed that the system contains a principle of change: that simply to exist is to change: that to change is to mature, and that to mature is to create ever new elements in the universe.

Forty years after his introduction to Bergson's philosophy of Creative Evolution, Read could still, when he published *Icon and Idea* in 1955, 'acknowledge the inspiration I continue to receive from the only metaphysics that is based on biological science—the metaphysics of Henri Bergson. I rely, in particular, on his definition of such necessary terms as consciousness and intuition'.

If Read found such orthodox evolutionary concepts as 'natural selection' of little use in explaining the emergence of art, and preferred the Bergsonian concept of a shaping urge to creativity, he continued to insist that the basis of his philosophy, since it was rooted like the art it studied in the senses, could not be other than biological. Yet here he departed in another direction from currently accepted ideas by adopting the Jungian concept of the collective unconscious, with all that it implies in evolutionary terms, including the heterodox notion of the inheritance of acquired characteristics. For Jung explains the existence of archetypal symbols in dreams and art by assuming that repeated or powerful impressions can actually change the physical constitution of the brain, and that such physical changes are inherited and give rise to the recurrent symbols which inhabit the collective unconscious and are part of the experience of all men. Read accepts this Jungian hypothesis, and therefore adds to the Bergsonian concept of Creative Evolution, rejected by modern biologists, a view of mankind united by a common biologically influenced consciousness, rejected by the existentialists. Thus, though he claims to base his aesthetics on biology, and to be philosophically a kind of existentialist, he is in both respects heterodox.

In Read's mature writings on aesthetic philosophy there emerges the familiar image of the cycle. In *The Forms of Things Unknown* the view which Read applies to individual lives in *The Green Child* and *The Contrary Experience* is expanded to comprehend the idea of civilizations moving in cycles, which he finds in Yeats and in Plato alike, and which he uses—and not entirely metaphorically—to present the idea that though we may seem culturally—and by implication morally and politically—to be living in a declining civilization, unseen forces may already be swinging the process upwards to a renewed age of social integration and cultural vigour.

The circular pattern can indeed contract so far as to view the poem or other artifact as a *closed* form, like a mandala, and to see 'the experience of art' as a 'circular process which may be set in motion at any point, the possible points being image, feeling, percept, idea, material, or even the handling of tools'. But it can expand into a cosmic image as when, in the culminating pages of *The Forms of Things Unknown*, Read relates the spiritual needs of the world to 'the artist's capacity to create images of wholeness, symbols of love and reconciliation'; it is now Homer's description in the *Iliad* of the great shield which Hephaestus wrought for Achilles that he takes as his prime example. The shield, of course, is a great mandala, 'round, to indicate the roundness of the world, and within it three circles, to represent the Earth, the Sea, and the Heavens', and around the circumference of the shield, in Homer's words Englished by Chapman,

> He wrought the ocean's curled violence,
> Arming his work as with a christall wall.

'It is', Read remarks, 'the uroboric snake, the primordial ocean ringing the world, the source of creation and of wisdom, familiar to us in the myths of Egypt and Babylon. It is the Great Round whose signif-

icance Erich Neumann has elucidated for us: The Archetypal Feminine, "which is and contains the universe".'

We are not to assume that Read wishes us to accept conceptually
the cyclic forms which occur so frequently in his works and which
shape them. At these points he is talking as a poet, and accepting the
symbolic insights offered by other poets in their role as creators of
myth.

> I accept Plato's cosmic ages, and I accept Nietzsche's eternal recurrence
> and Yeats' cycles or gyres, as convenient myths to explain inconvenient
> experiences. They indicate that the human imagination is always more
> resourceful than the human intellect: that art has the capacity, and the
> audacity, to transcend history. They indicate more than this, for the vital
> function of the imagination is not to escape from reality but to make it
> viable.

The presence of such cyclic symbolism can play an important role
in reconciling one of the principal difficulties we encounter when
Read sets out to explore the role of the arts in the record of human
development. For though it is possible to map out a steady growth of
the areas of human consciousness, and thus to indicate a forward
movement of creative evolution proceeding by a kind of zigzag
dialectical course, it is not possible to do the same for the aesthetic
faculty, which may change in aspect from age to age, but which since
the palaeolithic cave painters shows no increase in either its power or
its function in human life. Therefore, as Read says in *Icon and Idea*,
'Our axiom in art history should be: *always expect a constant aesthetic factor; look for the external forces that transform it.*' Thus the
role of the aesthetic faculty in human history can best be suggested by
the image of the circle whose surface changes endlessly like a kaleidoscope but whose form is constant. It is this constancy in the aesthetic faculty, rooted in the collective unconsciousness, that makes it
so vital a factor in the ever-evolving pattern of human development.

2

There is little evidence in Read's surviving early writings that he had
thought at all deeply on the social nature of art, or that he had con-

ceived the possibility of elaborating an aesthetic philosophy (embracing ethical values), before he became occupationally involved in the visual and tactile arts by joining the staff of the Victoria and Albert Museum in 1923. From this point, however, the line of development is clear and strong. Read's first book which considered in depth the social role for the arts was *Art and Industry* in 1934; under the stimulus of political passions in the Thirties he wrote *Art and Society*, which endeavoured to create a sociological setting for art and to reconcile it with ideologies of revolution. During the 1940's, in *To Hell with Culture* and *The Grass Roots of Art* he was already considering art as an agent of social transformation and harmonization. In this decade he also developed the concept of art as an educative force. But only in the 1950's was he ready to proceed, after decades of studying anthropology, sociology, psychology and the other sciences and half sciences that border on the field of aesthetics, to consider, in *Icon and Idea*, the role of the artist in the evolution of human consciousness and hence of human society, and, in *The Forms of Things Unknown*, the promise which art may hold for curing the psychic ills whose symptoms in our age are social disorder and the threat of nuclear destruction. Though Read wrote later essays enlarging on these themes, the essential shape of his philosophy of the role of art in human society and human destiny had been completed by the end of the 1950's; *The Forms of Things Unknown* was published in 1960, but the essays and lectures which comprised it had been written over the preceding decade from 1951 onwards.

'Art', as Read never ceased to insist, 'does not exist unless it is concrete; a symbol only functions if it is precise, of definite form.' Whatever origins he might find in the unconscious for the original aesthetic impulse, whatever role he might give the resultant form in terms of metaphysical enlightenment and social harmonization, he never lost sight of the created object in all its physicality, working not through the intellect but through the senses.

This knowledge he held as a conviction born of experience, for it was strengthened daily during his period at the Victoria and Albert Museum by the fact that he was concerned not with paintings and sculptures, where the ideological element is often emphatic and obvious, but with pottery and glass, where the original utilitarian purpose is evident, and where forms originate in function. A painter can project an idea or imitate a natural scene so that the mind is led away from the essential concreteness of his work; this is rarely possible in making a pot or a glass vessel, which, even if we do not use it for its original purpose, we still appreciate visually and tactilely with a directness little impeded by extraneous elements.

As Read has told us, his experience led him to reject the idea of a hierarchy of the arts, with painting and sculpture elevated above ceramics and the so-called applied arts. The aesthetic quality of the form, its vitality or harmony, was—he realized—of prime importance; the material and treatment, the elements of personality and period, were the variables that determine the form's external aspect and together constitute style—the style of the age, the style of the artist.

Approaching the arts by way of utilitarian objects, Read came close to the essential roots of art in human evolution, for he was led to consider the relationship between the development of functional perfection and the emergence of the consciousness of form. Thirty years after the end of his service at the Victoria and Albert, in a lecture delivered in 1960 at Ascona on 'The Origins of Form in the Plastic Arts' (and collected in *The Origins of Form in Art)*, he pointed out that '*Form* in art is the shape imparted to an artifact by human intention and action'; he then traced the development of the consciousness of form as 'an evolutionary sequence that passes through three stages: (1) conception of the object as a tool; (2) making and refinement of the tool to a point of maximum efficiency; (3) refinement of the tool beyond the point of maximum efficiency towards a conception of form-in-itself'. At this point, in the 'refinement of the functional form in the direction of free or symbolic form', art emerges as an originative force in human life, and begins to give visible form to feelings that the intellect will later conceptualize.

The philosophic elaboration and description of this process belongs to a later period of Read's life than his museum service; at that time he was more deeply concerned with the implications of his work in fields of art whose social relevance was emphasized by their utilitarian element. A pot, more often than not, was the product, not of an artist romantically conceived as the creator of individual and autonomous objects of contemplation, but of a craftsman working in an industry that produces articles for daily use, a worker involved on a basic level in the social and economic functioning of his world. During the early 1920's, Read and Bernard Rackham had already shown in *English Pottery* a deep interest in the connection in ceramic forms between industrial processes and aesthetic quality. At the

end of the decade, in *Staffordshire Pottery Figures*, Read himself discusses a kind of ceramic sculpture made for common people by pot-
ters who were 'mostly humble men who worked in obscurity and
without a thought of possible fame'; he goes on to make a comparison between porcelain and pottery figures which reveals his conception of an ideal relationship between industry, art and the life of
the people.

> The porcelain figure was destined to grace the mantelpieces of the aris-
> tocracy and rich bourgeoisie; the pottery figure was never meant to be
> more than a cheerful ornament in a farm-house or a labourer's cottage.
> The potter who made the figure was himself a peasant with a simple
> mind and a simple sense of humour. But because of this simple sense he
> often strays unconsciously into a realm of purer forms. He blunders into
> beauty, and though beauty can never be reduced to a definition, we know
> that it is the simplicity and sincerity of the potter's vision which has
> caused the miracle. All true peasant art is of this type; and if a more exact
> parallel is wanted in an age where 'peasant' is an obsolete or sentimental
> category, we can find the same qualities in the French painter, Henri
> Rousseau 'Le Douanier', a man of much the same social standing as these
> Staffordshire potters and a genius whose sense of beauty was equally
> unaffected by academic influence.

Here the first outline of Read's aesthetic philosophy begins to
emerge. From the fugitive beauties of figures made for cottage man-
telpieces to the view of art as a means to educate men into life of
peace and social justice may seem a great leap, but in relating popular art to the life of the people Read first began to consider what the
presence or absence of an aesthetic quality in things of everyday life
might mean to a civilization and the people who inhabit it. Henceforward this problem would never be absent from his thoughts, for,
even when he was defending the most esoteric types of modern art, it
was with the knowledge that a culture in which the artist is isolated
from the people is a culture spiritually moribund.

In deciding that a vital relationship between art and industry is
essential to social health, Read accepted the influence of Ruskin and
Morris, with both of whom he shared a social idealism that rejected
capitalist economics as well as the authoritarian political structure of
modern society. With Morris his political sympathy was even more
close than with Ruskin, for Morris when he dreamt of the socialist
Utopia was an anarchist without admitting it. Read admired Morris

as a whole man and as 'a practical genius, carrying things into action, embodying beauty in things of use, giving organization to opinion'. He also agreed with him that the relationship between harmony in art and harmony in society was more than analogical; it was organic. Art was necessary for the life of society, and each man was potentially an artist; like Morris, Read believed that 'the necessary faculties exist in every human being, and only need a right ordering of society to educate them and make them adequate'.

In *Art and Industry* Read first explores these ideas in the context of the modern world. He supplements the arguments of Morris by those of Marx (for unlike many other anarchists Read never denied that, like Plato, Marx was visited by genuine insights that sometimes ran counter to his habitually authoritarian attitude). 'The greatest problem of the age is the problem of alienation; the separation of man from nature, of the growing child from the use and development of his physical sensations,' he says. 'The greatest agent of this process of alienation, as Marx was the first to recognize a hundred years ago, is the machine'. Like Marx, and unlike Morris, Read recognized that, as he said in *The Annals of Innocence and Experience*:

> We must not scrap our machinery, but perfect and control it; we must not assume that art and machinery are mutually exclusive, but experiment until we discover a machine art. Always we must go forward with the instruments which evolution or invention have placed in our hands, and if only we had intelligence enough to establish our principles and sensibility enough to express them, then a new art might develop in a new world. We have now lived long enough to be aware of the first signs of such an art.

This is the theme Read develops in *Art and Industry*, and the 'new art' which he envisages as reconciling the 'opposition of organic vitality to mathematical law' is Abstract Art.

Art and Industry is, as Read himself says, 'schematic rather than chronological'; it is a Read mosaic, a diptych in which the first part discusses the theoretical aspects of the relationship between art and industry and the second becomes a kind of handbook in which the author suggests how his views may be applied practically in the various industrial arts.

> The whole purpose of art in industry [he says in relating these practical considerations to his aesthetic philosophy] is to reconcile the necessary

qualities of an object (material, working and function) with incidental
qualities of beauty. That these incidental qualities are no less necessary to
the biological process of life is a philosophical assumption which this
book takes for granted.

Read opens *Art and Industry* by pointing out that 'industrial
design, as a separate branch of the art, was originally a British conception'. Here he is not referring to William Morris, but to the Prince
Consort and the organizers of the Great Exhibition of 1851, who
realized that the factory process had destroyed some indefinable
quality that survived in the craft work of the eighteenth century.
Where the men of the Great Exhibition made their mistake, Read
suggests, was in believing that art can be *applied*, as ornament, to the
products of industry. His whole argument is based on the contention
that art must enter from the beginning and inspire the whole design,
and that ornamentation must arise organically from the conjunction
of design and material; it can never be added or superimposed without violating the aesthetic integrity of the object.

Essential to Read's position—so essential that he mounts his
attack in the opening pages of *Art and Industry*—is a denial of the
theories of barren functionalism current among architects and industrial designers at the beginning of the 1930's:

> We may therefore conclude [he declares] that the organic principle is
> basic to all our activities, that we design in relation to bodily functions,
> and that functionalism of any other kind should rather be called utilitar-
> ian, which Morris defined as 'the reckless waste of life in the pursuit of
> the means of life'.

He continues a few pages later:

> Functionalism in industry, to conform with which we have invented
> vocationalism in education, is the exact contrary of humanism. Its final
> effect is to eliminate the human element from production, that is, from
> work—and to achieve complete automatism.

And he concludes:

> We must realize that between functional thinking and imaginative think-
> ing there can be no compromise. One mode of thought is based on the

principle of causality and its method is logical; the other is based on symbolic discourse and its method is creative. One relies on the accumulation of knowledge; the other is an extension of consciousness.

It is important to note how strongly Read stressed his opposition to functionalism in design, since this emphasis makes quite clear the deep division that has existed between modernist trends in art and literature and their spokesmen such as Read, and, on the other side, the uncritical defenders of technological progress. The division between the two trends has always been sharp and definite, and Read in particular has emphasized the difference between the conceptual bases of technological thinking and the intuitive bases of artistic thinking. Because man is a feeling as well as a thinking being, it is important that aesthetic standards should apply not merely to the pictures a well-to-do collector can afford to hang on his wall, but also to the manufactured articles which the ordinary man will use and make, for it is in the whole cycle of existence, in the factory as well as in the home, that man's life must regain aesthetic significance.

> To give material or plastic expression to his inner feelings is a necessity; it is one of the facts that distinguish man from the animals, and wherever we find man, we find some kind of plastic expression. Art is a biological necessity.

But if art is to enter industry and therefore more completely enter life, there must be an integration between design for use and design for aesthetic pleasure. The attempt, for example, to superimpose on ceramics as applied ornamentation the forms proper to painting is worse than useless. But, Read declares, there is a kind of art that can be applied with understanding to the products of industry; this is *abstract art*. At this point he makes a distinction parallel to those he has made in the past between romantic and classic, organic and abstract art. Now he talks of 'humanistic art, which is concerned with the expression in plastic form of human ideals or emotions, and *abstract* art, or nonfigurative art, which has no concern beyond making objects whose plastic form appeals to the aesthetic sensibility'.

Industry's utilitarian need for clean, economical shapes accords more closely with the purely aesthetic aims of abstract art than with the ideological overtones of humanistic art, and Read sees the possibility that on at least two levels abstract art can be adapted to the design of machine-made objects. One type of 'rational' abstract art can be applied with almost mathematical exactitude to standardized production, but Read also claims that even the abstraction that springs from 'an intuitive apprehension of form' can inspire industrial design, and that, indeed, there are 'endless possibilities implicit in industrial art'.

In spite of such euphoric anticipations, and of his own direct activity in encouraging the elevation of this branch of art after he became director of the Industrial Design Unit in 1943, Read was forced to admit in later editions of *Art and Industry* that the promise he had seen in the Thirties had not been fulfilled and that after World War II caution rather than foresight dominated the world of industrial design. Now he saw the solution in education the emergence of inspired designs through a general system of education based on aesthetic principles, on the cultivation of the senses as well as the intelligence. He continued to believe that nothing made by man was not amenable to the gentle discipline of art. For:

> It follows, I think, that we must enlarge our concept of the work of art. The things we use in modern life are infinitely more numerous and more complex than ever before. When such things come into our life—such things as typewriters, petrol pumps, refrigerators, vacuum cleaners— our first impulse is to put them in a category altogether distinct from objects such as dishes and candlesticks, which we have grown accustomed to regard as fit objects for aesthetic form. But once these objects too were intruders into a world of simpler utensils, or of no utensils at all. And just as they have been assimilated to the traditions of good form and design, so these new and complicated tools and utensils must equally be regarded as material for the application of the principles of design. For those principles are ubiquitous; there is absolutely nothing we make or use which cannot submit to the discipline of form, and its accompanying grace or harmony.

3

The consciousness that it is more than mere mental obtuseness, more than aesthetic insensitivity, that prevents in our time the remarriage of art and industry, is present throughout *Art and Industry*, though its expression is muted, since this is a work intended to inform and persuade mainly on the aesthetic level. Revolutionary in that Read argues that we cannot make a Morris-like return to the past (for 'The economic law ... compels the human spirit to adapt itself to new conditions, and to be ever creating new forms'), it retains some of the caution of Read's civil service persona when it comes to suggesting the general social changes that may be necessary before every man can enjoy not merely the relief of living in a world where the things he uses are made beautifully by machines, but also the delights of individual creation.

> If the necessary adjustments can be made in the monetary system so that the capacity to consume bears a relation of approximate equality to the power of production; if the age of plenty, already potential, can be realised in fact: then the increase in leisure will undoubtedly lead to a development of man's innate desire to create an art expressive of his individuality humanistic art, as we have called it. Such art will bear to abstract machine art the kind of relation that a landscape painting bears to the architecture of a functional building; the relation of an arbitrary phenomenon to a logical or necessary one. But if we are not to relapse into the nineteenth century muddle again, there will be no confusion between the two types of art.

In *Art and Society*, which he described thirty years after its original publication in 1936 as 'a contribution to the problems then being urgently discussed in the wake of the Russian Revolution', Read turns to the consideration of the kind of art that can be classed as 'an arbitrary phenomenon', and of the society in which the artist operates. By the time Read first delivered, at Liverpool University during the winter from 1935 to 1936, the lectures that constitute *Art and Society*, he had become politically vocal, had already published in 1935 his first revolutionary pamphlet, *Essential Communism*, and was about to become with André Breton's blessing a member of the Surrealist movement, with its open advocacy of social revolution. Once again, as in his youth, he openly called himself an anarchist, though he also accepted the title of socialist, and acknowledged Marx at least as a critic of existing society. Yet he stood apart from Marxist orthodoxy in refusing to consider art a by-product of social life or of ideological necessity.

According to his own definition, art 'is like a spark springing, at the right moment, between two opposite poles, one of which is the individual, the other the society. The individual expression is a socially valid symbol or myth.' Art therefore is socially significant, and Read implicitly dissociates himself from the extreme aestheticist attitude expressed in the Wildeian slogan, 'Art for Art's sake'. Art makes its contribution as 'one of the original elements which go to form a society', and it 'has necessary relations with politics, with religion, and with all other modes of reacting to our human destiny. But as a mode of reaction it is distinct and contributes in its own right to that process of integration which we call a civilization or a culture.'

Art, Read further asserts in seeking to establish its identity and its value in a social context, is 'a mode of knowledge, and the world of art is a system of knowledge as valuable to man as the world of philosophy or the world of science'. It opens to us 'a whole aspect of the world which is only accessible to instinct and intuition'. It is a 'language', fully equipped 'to convey a meaning—by which I do not mean a message'. And because it is a language with different functions from the denotative language of speech and writing, it can only be harmed by the attempt to make it subordinate to political doctrines or philosophic points of view; artists themselves cannot 'be disciplined without disastrous effects on their creative energy'. What art has to give, in other words, society must accept on art's own terms. But this is not the same as saying that art is unaffected by its relationship with society; the effects of that relationship inevitably affect its *style*, even if they do not change the fundamental character of its *forms*.

Read sets out to present in *Art and Society* a general introduction to the problems of art in its social context. It is partly historical and partly schematic in its arrangement, with the meaning weaving through a series of chapters which proceed from 'Art and Magic' through 'Art and Mysticism' to 'Art and Religion' and thence to 'Secular Art', following a more or less chronological pattern. Then, reaching the modem age, it breaks into studies of 'Art and the Unconscious' and 'Art and Education', and finally, in 'Art in Transition', considers the social implications of the various currents of the modem movement. More than most of Read's works, *Art and Society* distils the aroma of its period, not only in its innovative introduction of anthropological and psychological concepts now familiar but then novel even to critics, but also in its immersion in arguments that bring to mind the atmosphere of controversy which permeated the artistic world of the Thirties, when Surrealism and Socialist Realism, both claiming to be forms of art fit for a revolutionary society, competed for the attention of the intellectual Left. By temperament as well as by conviction, Read took his stand on the side of the Surrealists, but in doing so he enlarged their doctrine, under the name of superrealism, to embrace a whole area of symbolic art that at other times he would have named *romantic*.

As in all of Read's discussions of the aesthetic philosophy, *Art and Society* presents art as a unity, a function manifest in men of all races and going back to the dawning, in the palaeolithic age, of a consciousness we may call human. From the beginning, even among the cave painters of the Pyrenees and the Dordogne, he sees art as an independent activity, having its separate origin, and only later associated with a magic that may itself have developed through the images by which art suggested correspondences between human artifacts and the natural world. The values of palaeolithic art, he insists, 'are not those of verisimilitude, but of vitality, vividness, and emotive power, which are precisely aesthetic qualities'. These, one must add, are qualities Read discovers in certain currents of art down to his own age. Indeed, so ancient does he consider the central strains of artistic expression that he finds, no later than the New Stone Age, three basic types of art in existence: the organic, vitalist art of the early stone-age hunters; the 'disinterested ornamental art' of a geometric type 'arising out of and during the course of technical processes of the neolithic farmers'; and a 'purposive art' of geometric origin but 'determined by symbolic ends'—specifically the spiritual requirements of a community. Read points out that these types of early art still exist—or did in the Thirties when he was writing—among primitive peoples isolated from the influences of civilization, and that in fact they represent traditions that have continued and developed through human history.

Man emerges from the chaotic darkness of prehistory; his consciousness evolves out of fear and loneliness and desire; he forms tribes and societies and adopts various modes of economic production, and in the process his soul is swept by those alternations of superstition and joy, of love and hate, of intellectual confidence and humble faith, which transform his life, making and unmaking dynasties and nations and civilizations. But throughout all this welter of forces and contradiction of aims the aesthetic impulse, like the sexual impulse, is essentially constant. It has these different aspects, hedonistic, purposive and expressive—and sometimes one and sometimes another will dominate a whole epoch. But all these aspects relate to one reality. For the essential nature of art is not given to it by a civilization or a religion, but by an indefeasible faculty of man himself—a certain disposition of sensation and intuition which impels him to shape things into forms or symbols which are aesthetic to the degree that they take on harmonious proportion and rhythm.

Of the existence of a stubbornly enduring aesthetic impulse in man there can be no doubt; it is impossible to explain otherwise the emergence of artistic activities in so many times and countries, and their persistence even in civilizations like our own where material and moral conditions are fundamentally hostile. But to define that impulse in the logical and denotative terms art itself avoids is difficult, and Read is perhaps most successful when he approaches the matter obliquely by describing how the aesthetic impulse functions to widen man's consciousness. For, as he remarks, 'in its essentials art has little or nothing to do with the intelligence. It is an exercise or activity of the senses, elemental as the primary emotions of love, hate and fear.' Since in its earlier manifestations art tended to be associated with magic, with animism, with pre-rationalistic religion, Read spends a considerable time discussing the relations that exist between these various aspects of human consciousness, and he concludes that 'neither magic nor mysticism are effective causes of art' but that they 'may be the appropriate *occasions*, saving the artist from that self-consciousness and introspective analysis which ... spell the death of art'.

But if neither magic nor religion creates art, art can make itself useful to them, and an important stage in the relationship between art and religion emerges at the point when man moves out of the pre-logical stage which Lévi-Strauss—whose significance as an anthropologist Read recognized early—proclaimed to be characteristic of primitive, tribal man, the stage when 'art could not be clearly separated from nature ... the image of an animal was as real as the animal itself ...' Once man is 'caught up in the process of logical thought, the work of art becomes an intermediary between the world of natural phenomena and the world of spiritual presences. It becomes either a symbol to express a mental or emotional state, or a representation or imitation of a natural object. In either case it is a vehicle which conveys information, a means of communication.' And it is at this point that there enters the danger of art becoming subordinated to religious or later to political dogma.

Yet 'art, like murder, will out'. And in spite of the universality of the aesthetic impulse itself, and of the origin of forms in a collective unconscious that is shared by men irrespective of race or period, art as a concrete phenomenon takes the impress of its environment; like religion, it 'adapts itself to the prevailing ethos—that emanation of the soil and weather which is the characteristic spirit of a community'. Hence the importance of the *genius loci* which, as Worringer argued, inclines men of the north towards abstract and men of the south towards humanist forms of expression. But there is a further involution in the pattern that in art unites the universal, the local and the individual, for it is in the last of these terms that the uniqueness and durability of the work of art exist:

> The survival value of a work of art—the qualities in it which survive the ideas and aspirations of a particular age to appeal to the aesthetic faculties of succeeding ages—these are to be regarded as primarily the creation of individuals endowed with exceptional skill or sensibility.

In the end, it is not as a classic Greek or an ancient Egyptian, as a Christian, a Buddhist or a primitive animist, that the artist succeeds, but as an independent person using his skills to produce concrete objects whose forms express his intuitions of universal truths.

At this point we come to the difference between the artist as a social being, following objective goals, and the artist as a private being, following subjective impulses. For the two aspects can and do exist in the same individual, and it is in attempting to assess the realities of the relationship that Read leads us to the vital difference—in terms of understanding the process of artistic creation—between 'concepts which are sought and concepts which are found'. It is the difference between the logician and the seer. For, as Read argues:

> ... we shall never discover the secret of art, the very condition of its origin and life, unless we learn to distinguish between mental processes which are the deliberate act of a conscious will, and mental processes which normally take place below the level of consciousness and only occasionally, and precisely on the occasion; which constitutes the artist's

inspiration, emerge to the surface of awareness and are given plastic expression. That is the conclusion to which we are driven by our examination of the history of art.

It is true, Read concedes, that the artist is inevitably 'a unit of a necessary social organization' and that without the conditions provided by the existence of a culture he 'cannot arrive even at the threshold of his potentialities'.

But having reached that threshold, he must be allowed to proceed alone, as an individual. For he can cross that threshold only within his own self. Across the threshold is the subliminal self; a self which is more than the conscious entity of the ego, limited as that is by all the restrictions and conventions of the compromise we call civilization; a self which is in fact another order of reality, profounder and more extensive than any known to our daily perceptions. It is just because the artist can cross that threshold into that more extensive realm and bring back some knowledge of its meaning that he is supreme among his fellow-men.

The idea of the artist as 'supreme among his fellow-men' seems an arrogant expression of élitism, and, indeed, Read accepted frankly the contemporary fact that art was the preserve of a minority who express in their works the truths the majority needs but is likely to reject. But he regarded it as an unnecessary condition. Doubtless in history—and in prehistory to the best of our knowledge—the artist has always been regarded as an exceptional being, only because society has never been harmonious.

In any natural order of society [Read insists] *all* social activities would be aesthetic. Rhythm and harmony would pervade all that we do and all that we make: in this sense every man would be an artist of some kind and no art would be despised merely because it was mechanic or utilitarian.

In other words, art in the present is inevitably aristocratic, but aristocratic values can be universalized. That, surely, is the whole message of anarchism. Read emphasizes it by demanding, in the Nietzschean terms of his youth, 'a transvaluation of all values', and an acceptance of the need for 'educating the instincts instead of suppressing them'.

In an unnatural society, however, 'the artist is always to be regarded as the psychotic'; he is the man who finds it impossible to accept the ambient world of values and resolves his frustrations by means of creativity rather than through mental sickness. The realization of this fact leads Read once again towards psychoanalysis as 'the key to most of the unsolved problems of art'. In approaching this question in *Art and Society* he shows himself very much a man of the Thirties, for it is not to Jung, whose work he already knew and was later to accept so widely, that he now turned, but to Freud, whose essential rationalism is in fact ill equipped to deal with the psychology of the artist. Thus there is a curiously dated tone to Read's argument when he attempts to explain the activities of the artist by a rather orthodox application of the doctrine of the Oedipus complex; one encounters an almost mechanical schematism to his attempt to find correspondences between various phases of the work of art and the various levels in the Freudian cosmology of the mind. Of the former he says (and the italics are his own):

> It derives its energy, its irrationality and its mysterious power from the id, which is to be regarded as the source of what we usually call inspiration. It is given formal synthesis and unity by the ego; and finally it may be assimilated to those ideologies or spiritual aspirations which are the peculiar creation of the super-ego.

Later Read would find this Freudian scheme inadequate, yet his recognition of the general validity of the psychoanalytic method led to his acceptance of Jung's less rationalistic approach, even though there were points—e.g. in his modification of the theory of psychological types and in his stress on the importance of child art—on which he eventually failed to agree even with the Master of Zurich. Even in 1936, if one can judge from the remarks which Read makes when he is considering the question of education in *Art and Society*, he was already prepared for the acceptance of the central Jungian hypothesis of the collective unconscious without yet attaching Jung's name to it. Discussing 'the deeper layers of the ego and in the id', he remarks:

> If we consider that this region, this cauldron, into which the artist is able to peer is a region of timeless entities, then we seem to have some explanation of the source of vital energy which is transmitted to the artist's

creative impulse, and at least the suggestion of an explanation of the universal appeal of what the artist is inspired to express. For what is timeless is by the same token universal.

The hypothesis of the collective unconscious merely serves to deepen and elucidate this view of the sources of aesthetic values. Freudian and Jungian ideas thus appear, so far as Read's theories are concerned, merely as successive contributions to a synthetic theory of the nature and uses of art.

It is in discussing the uses of art that Read parts company with Marxist orthodoxy, though he remains selectively Marxist. He accepts Marx's view of society as a totality; he admires 'that second characteristic of the Marxian dialectic—its capacity to pass from the static to the dynamic, from a system of logic to a mode of action'. But he differs from most exponents of Marxism in seeing art as a separate dialectical process, not merely a 'reflection of such a process'. Art must be accepted not as an *aid to thought*, which Communist propagandists tend to consider it, but as itself a *mode of thought*. Long afterwards, in the preface to the 1963 edition of *To Hell with Culture*, Read would say:

> Personally I can travel a long way with the Marxists in their analysis of the social origin of the forms and uses of art. What neither the Marxists nor their opponents can explain by their doctrinaire methods is the phenomenon of genius in art: they cannot explain the nature of the artist nor even the conditions that determine his eccentric existence.

Such a view has inevitably lead Read to reject Socialist Realism and to reach a conclusion that could only be repugnant to the orthodox dialectical materialist:

> The necessity for the future, then, is a reintegration of art as an independent mode of apprehension and expression; as the sensuous correlative, equal and opposite, of intellectual abstraction.

As a believer in the teleological urge of creative evolution, as a writer sensitive to the mood of his age, Read in the 1930's could hardly be expected to end his study of art and society on a note of pessimism. It was only age and the disillusion of waiting for the development of an aesthetic ethos that led him eventually to such a stoical attitude.

Now he combined a faith in Freud with a faith in the probability of the social revolution, to end on a mood of conditional optimism:

> That general release from fear and depression which is promised by the technique of modern psychology no less than by the growing determination to win for humanity the benefits of modern methods of production will recreate the conditions of a great art. This, at least, is a possible faith to oppose to all who would leave us in despair and cynicism, without pleasure, without joy, without that highest and subtlest ecstasy of which the human mind is capable—the ecstasy of art, of poetry, the creation of a world of imaginative reality.

Read was writing before the Spanish Civil War, before World War II, before Hiroshima, before the effects of an unbridled technological revolution had become evident. Such events would eventually weaken his confidence in the possibility of a world inspired and harmonized by the universalization of aesthetic values; they never destroyed his faith in the aesthetic philosophy as the only teaching that stood a chance of creating such a world.

4

Read's full development of the aesthetic philosophy came only in the 1950's with the writing of *Icon and Idea* and *The Forms of Things Unknown*. The intervening publications in which he considered the relationships between art and society were occasional works conditioned by the circumstances under which he wrote them. In its original form, *To Hell with Culture* was a pamphlet composed hastily in the middle of a war as part of the Democratic Order series published by Read's own firm of Routledge. *The Grass Roots of Art*, bearing the sub-title 'Lectures on the Social Aspects of Art in an Industrial Age', was a byproduct of his practical work at the Industrial Design Unit rather than a pendant to *Art and Industry*. The lectures that formed it were originally delivered at Yale University in 1946, and the first version of *The Grass Roots* appeared in the following year; an expanded version, with two additional lectures, was printed in 1953.

The deliberately provocative title, *To Hell with Culture*, does not mean that Read agreed with the remark once attributed to Hermann

Göring: 'When I hear anyone talk of Culture, I reach for my re-volver.' It is to be taken rather in the spirit of the Dadaist campaigns against 'art' which were inspired by a hatred of pretence rather than by a hatred of art itself. As his later works show, he did not reject the idea of a culture in the sense of a total society, harmonized and inspired by aesthetic values; in fact he elevated it as the opposite of a mere civilization. He objected, rather, to the way in which the modern world reduced culture to a commodity. A culture detached from the society in which it existed was to him a symptom of the self-consciousness that brings the death of art. This is what he meant when he said that 'Culture belongs to the past: the future will not be conscious of its culture.' But such a future will come into being only when the community that seeks to create it obeys the law: 'There is an order in Nature, and the order of Society should be a reflection of it.'

As Read sketches out the functioning of a society in which culture is unnoticed because it is part of the mental air, we become aware of a sideways diversion in the course of his thought which will be cor-rected in his later books. In *Art and Industry* he attacked the func-tionalists. In *To Hell with Culture*, perhaps under the influence of Eric Gill, then his neighbour in Buckinghamshire, he himself came to preach a kind of functionalism.

> If an object [he says] is made of appropriate materials to an appropriate design and perfectly fulfils its function, then we need not worry any more about its aesthetic value; it is *automatically* a work of art.

He continues shortly afterwards:

> Fitness for function is the modern definition of the eternal quality we call beauty, and this fitness for function is the inevitable result of an economy directed to use and not to profit.

Comparing such passages with the anti-functionalist statements quoted earlier from *Art and Industry*, it seems clear either that Read is deliberately cultivating the Proudhon-like provocation implied by his title, *To Hell with Culture*, in the hope of shocking people into a sense of the need for a society thoroughly inspired by aesthetic val-ues, or that he is developing the idea, adumbrated in *Art and Indus-try*, of 'design in relation to bodily functions', according to 'the organic principle', as the one admissible form of functionalism.

Read reinforces his cry of 'To hell with culture!' with that of 'To hell with the artist!' ; here again the influence of Gill, that obstinate aesthetic leveller, seems to emerge as he declares: '*Art as a separate profession is merely a consequence of culture as a separate entity.* In a natural society there will be no precious or privileged beings called artists: there will only be workers.'

Clearly, this is a Utopian vision, not far removed from that embodied in Morris's *News from Nowhere*, and Read qualifies it by allowing into his ideal commonwealth an artistic elite in disguise when he admits: 'There are certain types of genius which are always in advance of the general level of sensibility—even the general level of professional sensibility.' He does not discount the possibility that in a natural society these men will exist and will be frustrated. But the real basis of the natural society as he *sees* it at this point lies in arousing the latent sensibility of the ordinary worker by restoring meaning to his daily work and allowing him to create his own culture. For it is at the level of what we now call the crafts that art must begin its socially regenerative function, since

> until a society can produce beautiful pots and pans as naturally as it grows potatoes, it will be incapable of those higher forms of art which in the past have taken the form of temples and cathedrals, epics and dramas.

In such a society art can fulfil its aspirations towards the impersonal, for 'when every man is the artist, who shall claim to be the superman?'

Yet even here—for Read—the possibility lingers that, while it is only in a 'democratic' (read 'anarchist') society that the artist will at the same time address humanity in general and his particular society, there will always be exceptions that do not fit into the democratic pattern.

Such types of art he calls 'archetypal'; they are 'beyond daily reality, supersocial and in a sense superhuman'. This recognition preserves the continuity of theoretical development that in other ways *To Hell with Culture* appears to abandon. For it is in the 'archetypal' that Read will shortly be finding the meaning of all significant art, a meaning that, even if not superhuman, will certainly be supersocial in the sense that it speaks universally, to all men who wish to hear.

Much of *The Grass Roots of Art* repeats and recapitulates Read's arguments about the social functions of art in *Art and Industry* and *Art and Society;* much of it is an application of his political ideas to the world of art, as in the opening essay ('The Roots of the Artist') when he speaks of the ideal environments for creativity as 'communities of a comfortable size, where intimacy is possible and a personality can have free scope and a friendly audience', and declares:

> I am afraid of the internationalizing tendencies of our age of anonymous powers that would obliterate frontiers, expedite communications, standardize living. I am in favour of all that makes for diversity, variety, the reciprocity of individual units.

Much also has reference to education, and appears to have been written under the impetus which Read generated in the writing of *Education Through Art;* the dominant ideas in this context will find a better place when we consider the development of his educational philosophy.

But there remain interesting aspects of *The Grass Roots of Art,* and among them a curious example of the dialectical progression of Read's thought, provided by the fact that in the second essay ('Society and Culture') Read does invert the definition of culture in his preceding pamphlet and describes it favourably but rather indefinitely as evincing spontaneity, variety and freedom, and manifesting itself through 'certain tangible assets', including great works in the various arts. More than that, 'culture' is 'a biological phenomenon', linked with Read's conception of creative evolution; for, he insists, 'the process itself is vital, is spontaneous, is a *generation* of new forms of life'.

What militates against the development of a true culture of this kind in the modern world is the alienation which, both Ruskin and Marx contend, the machine has precipitated. Read accepts Ruskin's values, but he argues that a place must be found for them 'in the world of facts which has developed inevitably from the economics of machine production'. That world of facts can become tolerable only if we create 'a new social order' and also 'a new way of life', for which Read offers a series of basic requirements:

> 1. *The reconstruction of our physical environment to secure the most favourable framework for a vital culture.*
> 2. *A social system without wide diversity of personal wealth.*
> 3. *An industrial system that gives the worker a direct responsibility for the quality of his work.*

4. *An educational system that preserves and matures the innate artistic sensibility of man.*

These requirements bring one close to the schematic vision of the free society which, as we shall see, Read worked out earlier in the Forties on a more directly political level in *The Politics of the Unpolitical*. But a paradox existed, as Read was well aware, for if a 'new social order' was necessary for the development of a genuine culture and the universalization of art, how could it be obtained? Not by ordinary political means, nor even by a revolution, which merely rearranges the pattern of power. Read was brought back, when he came to consider this question in dealing with Tolstoy's views on art, to the point on the circle where he had begun. He agrees with Tolstoy that 'The only change that permanently affects the structure of society is a chemical change—a change of consciousness, a change of heart.' But he asks how it can be affected. Tolstoy declares by the pure gospel of Christ, using art as its vehicle. But Read believes that if it is used as a vehicle art loses its intrinsic power, which is no less than the power to change human consciousness.

> I believe that art can change the chemical constitution of the social crystal—it is my fundamental belief. But art can only work within its own aesthetic limits. What are such limits? They are, one might say, the limits of the physical universe; they are the laws of proportion and rhythm and harmony which ensure grace and vitality in movement, and beauty in structure—physical, material entities. But civilization is a physical thing—can only be changed by physical means. Spiritual changes will follow on physical changes. It was the belief of Plato, and it is my belief, that the only way in which we can bring about a moral improvement in society is by first effecting an aesthetic improvement. Man is seduced to the perceptions of goodness, by habits of grace. Beauty of action, beauty of environment, and, above all, the creative experience of beauty, lead inevitably to a sense of nobility, a perception of character.

Nowhere is Read's sense of the symbiotic relationship between society and art more admirably shown. The perfect, self-effacing culture in which all men are artists depends on a chemical change in the crystal of society, but only by the action of artists can that change take place. And here, asserting his faith in the power of art to work historic changes in the consciousness of man, Read prepares the way for his most important works in aesthetic philosophy.

Before passing on to those works—*Icon and Idea* and *The Forms of Things Unknown*—let us linger briefly on the last page of the essay ('The Irrelevance of Realism' in *The Grass Roots of Art)* which I have just been discussing; it contains a definition of art as an active and creative process which serves as an eloquent introduction to the ideas Read will develop in his last and most fruitful decades:

> Art [he says] is an affirmation, not of reality, but of man's ability to cre-
> ate something beyond reality. Reality, as Sartre has said, is never beauti-
> ful. Beauty belongs to the realm of the imagination, and involves a denial
> of the world as it actually exists. We might say that art is the creation of
> values by which we judge reality—values that represent all that is posi-
> tive and expansive, of all that is formative and definitive, of clarity and
> concentration and unity. Its principles are not moral, are not even spiri-
> tual; they are harmonic, and therefore physical. But as such they are par-
> adigms of all intellectual beauty; the patterns of all noble habit. There is
> no perception of beautiful action—no ideal of equity or love—that is not
> first evolved in its material perfection in a work of art. Art discovers
> beauty, for our benefit, for our emulation, for our consolation. All moral
> impulses, all feelings of goodness, all grace and truth, are but shadows
> cast from the dance of life; shadows cast, as Shelley said in his great
> poem, by the light of Intellectual Beauty.

From this statement it is only a short step to the main theme of *Icon and Idea* which Read—duly acknowledging his debts to Con-rad Fiedler and Ernst Cassirer—declares to be the attempt to 'estab-lish for the symbols of art a claim to priority which is historical'. He proceeds from Fiedler's mid-nineteenth-century insight: 'In the cre-ation of art, man engages in a struggle with nature not for his physi-cal but for his mental existence.' In accepting Fiedler's argument, Read goes beyond the existentialist thinkers with whom he has so much in common, for, where they regard art as a means by which man can define himself in a world which his knowledge does not allow him to regard as more than absurd, he sees art over the ages as 'the means by which man was able step by step to comprehend the nature of things'. For Read the universe is never in reality absurd: it only appears so in so far as we fail to understand it.

There are, Read admits, two ways of considering art. It can be dismissed as a kind of game by which man fills his time until death. It also can be seen as a system of revelation, and this is Read's choice. In one of his political pamphlets, *The Philosophy of Anarchism*, he made an unexpected but eloquent plea for religion as a vital factor in human society. 'I am not a revivalist,' he argued when he wrote that pamphlet in 1940. 'I have no religion to recommend and none to believe in. I merely affirm, on the evidence of the history of civilizations, that a religion is a necessary element in any organic society.' Read never did accept a religion in the literal sense, though he respected the faiths of others and at times envied them, but there is a messianic tone to his treatment in the 1950's of art as a means of approaching an understanding of existence and of evolving the vision of a harmonious society. One may justly regard his approach as the surrogate religion of a man of deep spiritual feeling. The kind of inner harmonization necessary for the creation of a peaceful and productive society which his contemporary Aldous Huxley found in the meditative practices of the mystics, Read found in the artist's concrete projections of universal truths, and in this sense what he preached in *Icon and Idea* and in *The Forms of Things Unknown* was a mysticism for the agnostic.

The process of art differs of course from that which writers like Huxley have attributed to the mystical experience in that it never involves an insight both immediate and total.

> Art has never been an attempt to grasp reality as a whole—that is beyond human capacity [says Read in implied dismissal of the claims of the mystics to have seen the universe in an instant] ... rather it has been the piece-meal recognition and patient fixation of what is significant in human experience.

And in this way his aesthetic equivalent of a religion is linked firmly to the biological reality of human development, provided, of course, we regard the latter in the teleological sense implied in 'the only metaphysics that is based on biological science—the metaphysics of Henri Bergson'. However Read's speculation may soar in its consideration of the high role of art in human destiny, it is, like the soaring of the falcon, a flight that has its origin and end on earth, in the physical reality of human existence.

Since Read sees art and its functions as so closely linked with the progress of man through a course of steadily expanding consciousness, it is appropriate that *Icon and Idea* should assume a quasi-historical form as he examines the course of human development according to the slogan, 'Before the word was the image.' He sees the earliest art as 'a response to vital needs', as a means of acquiring the synchronicity that enables men to work out the correspondences between events and thus to give not only meaning to their individual lives but also a teleological purpose to the life of the race. Endowed by the demands of their hunters' lives with an intense eidetic faculty, primitive men were led almost compulsively to make their naturalistic drawings of the animals which they needed to kill in order to survive; Read argues that it was only when the images had been given form that the associations on which magic is based began to take shape within the human mind. Art is a sensual act; magic is a conceptual act. Through history Read seeks to establish the primacy of the sensual in every development of human thought, so that each renaissance, each dawning culture, begins as an aesthetic event and only at a later stage undergoes a conceptual metamorphosis that makes it a stage in the intellectual development of a civilization.

Since the palaeolithic days of the cave-painters, Read insists, art has retained its essential characteristics, and above all its role as 'a key to survival'.

> However much it may have been smothered in false idealism and intellectual sophistication, it is still the activity by means of which our sensation is kept alert, our imagination kept vivid, our power of reasoning kept keen.

But in spite of the essential uniformity in the origins and effects of all forms of art, Read realizes that as a result of the evolution which took place between the palaeolithic and neolithic eras, and which developed fully only during the humanizing phase of classic Greek antiquity, the traditions of art have been divided. Thus the very definition of 'aesthetic' can be held to embrace 'two very different psychological processes'. One is directed towards the projection of *vitality*, drawn either from the external world or from the recesses of the artist's own mind; the other aims at 'discovering the still centre, the balance and harmony of *beauty*'. The greatest artists combine the Dionysian ideal of vitality and the Apollonian ideal of beauty, and it is in this combination that the influence of a work of art is most potent and most enduring. But *vitality* is not only the first-manifested but also the essential quality of art, the source to which *beauty* must always return for renewal, which is why classical art—dedicated so completely to the ideal of harmonious beauty—can never for long exist as a living style in its pure form.

Much of *Icon and Idea* is an elaboration, supported by the author's subsequent reading, of the discussion regarding the development of art that appears in *Art and Society*, but the approach is refined and also extended. Here, for example, he first argues that, while palaeolithic man probably had no real aesthetic sense at all, neolithic man, by developing a geometric and therefore ultimately an abstract art, evolved for the first time an awareness '*of form itself*, form as an imagined and articulated entity, as a product of constructive effect'. And the sense of form, with the act of composition as its inevitable manifestation, represents a major expansion of human consciousness.

Out of the neolithic discovery of form and composition arise in turn the Greek sense of unity and serenity, the classic laws of harmony and proportion, and at this point, after art has done its work, begins the development of philosophy in its metaphysical and ethical aspects. But beyond the world of intellectual harmony lay that numinous and mysterious world, that transcendental realm outside the world of immediate sensation, of which man in his tribal stage of development was perpetually conscious. Here again, Read claims, art played the primal role, and art and religion were for long indistinguishable.

> The image of the god was not 'projected by the rite'; the rite was the image, and the image was both work of art and god. Only after centuries of development did that dissociation of action and sensibility take place which led to the rationalization of religion and the intellectualization of art.

So, through art, emerged both Greek idealism and Christian transcendentalism, and each tradition, in making itself independent, sought to dominate art and so became its enemy. In that process lies the whole significance of iconoclastic movements, which were less matters of conflicting religious dogmas than of the effort of the rationalizing intellect to escape from man's dependence on the senses (exemplified in art) for his understanding of the natural world which, however much he may rebel against it, is his only certain reality.

Always, in considering such matters as the growth of magic, or the link between transcendental religion and the development of the dome as an aesthetic form defining space, one returns constantly to what Read calls 'the underlying thesis, that first there was a shape or an image, then an idea', for our first response to the unknown is to make it evident to the senses, 'visibly and haptically', and here the very compression of the work of art, its concentration in the image, makes it 'more real to the senses than the incalculable and incomprehensible sky'. If reality is 'a construct of the senses', the work of art is its most felicitous expression.

Beside the world of art, the world of reality expressed through the senses and apprehended through the feelings, there appears eventually a 'system of harmony ... divorced from the world of sensuous experience and given a prior existence in another world—a world of essence'. Read, like the existentialists, rejects this mental world. For it leads to the development of a reflective culture detached from the life of the senses, and hence to 'a certain corruption of consciousness which is the real explanation of social decadence'.

Throughout this process, and especially as Read brings us to the modern movement in art, the stress is on a perpetual return, through the instrumentality of the artist, to the fact that the essential base of consciousness lies in existence, in sensual experience, in perception translated by the processes of art into significant form. For the artist seeks, 'not a theory of reality or of the nature of being, but just the reality that he himself can perceive, standing in a particular place at a moment of time, the purity and singleness of an act of vision'. The other world tempts the artist to debase his forms into clichés of design which illustrate 'intellectual concepts and religious dogmas', or represent and imitate actuality. But the meaning of rebellion in art is the constant rejection of illustration, of representation, of imitation, and the attempt to achieve 'not the illusion of the real, but the reality of consciousness itself—subjective reality'.

This attempt characterizes the modern movement in art, whether it assumes the aspect of expressionism or abstractionism, of superrealism or constructivism. It represents a further advance in consciousness as the artist penetrates ahead of the psychoanalyst the mysterious depths of the unconscious. Exploring this aspect of mod-

ern art, Read is led to that curious genre, the self- portrait, in the past
often a mere mask—a constructed persona—but among artists like
Klee a means of extraordinary revelation.

> The self, the artist is now telling us, has little or nothing to do with the
> conventional mask I present to the world; it can be adequately represent-
> ed only by signs or symbols which have a formal equivalent to an inner
> world of feeling most of which is submerged below the level of con-
> sciousness.

The great advance of the modern artist is indeed to make what at one
point Read calls 'the final decisive step', the attempt 'to represent a
purely subjective world, the contents of which might be held to have
some correspondence to the true dimensions of the self'.

But is that really the 'final decisive step'? For in tapping the realms
below consciousness the artist is reaching 'that secret place where
primeval power nurtures all evolution', a definition which included
Jung's collective unconscious and perhaps something more. And
here we come to the possibility that the images which the artist creates out of subjective experience may in their effect be objective, and
embody 'values that are impersonal or absolute'.

At this point Read quotes with approval Cassirer's argument that
art does not merely create a form to signify a feeling, but that it
wields a 'constructive power in the framing of our human universe'.
And here with no need to follow the fascinating elaborations of
Read's argument we arrive at an understanding of the dual functions
of art in the modern age: the personal exploration by symbolic means
of the frontiers of the self, which is the task of superrealist art in all
its forms, and the development of a communal art that will once
again 'lift a dome over the heads of a wondering congregation'. The
promise of the latter development Read sees in constructivism,
which aims at the 'creation of new images, images of a possible new
world, a world in which a new style in art will bring about a new style
of life'.

In art, Read concludes, lies our hope of escaping from 'the dead
rain of matter', for it is art that, as he claims in words that echo from
his own youth, transfuses our minds 'by a sense of glory' and lifts us
above 'a brutal sense of nullity'. But this, he warns, does not mean
that art can be separated from life, for we can possess its gifts only 'in

so far as we are all, in our degree of capacity, natures in immediate contact with the growth and form of the visible world'.

It is evident that during the 1950's Read lived in an emotional world precariously balanced between a consciousness of the growing threats to the quality and even the existence of human life, posed by unrestrained technological development, and an increasingly urgent feeling that only in the insights of contemporary artists appeared any chance of awakening humanity to such dangers. As the decade progressed, it became increasingly evident that whatever collective understanding art could generate was perilously weak in comparison with the forces of negation and disintegration; this explains the increasingly pessimistic tone that clouds his writings on the aesthetic philosophy towards the end of the decade, and the emergence during the 1960's of something approaching despair as he realizes that the new movements in painting, and particularly Pop Art, are themselves infected by the disintegration from which society as a whole is suffering.

And so *The Forms of Things Unknown*, though in shape it is a series of lectures, mainly on problems of aesthetics—delivered to predominantly academic audiences—on another level is a continuation of *Icon and Idea in* an even more urgent tone, a tone that at times rises towards the shrillness of revivalist propaganda (as when Read begins by declaring 'I strive to reanimate the only philosophy that can save us') and at times is clouded by a sense of almost apocalyptic doom. But the millenarian passion that displays itself spasmodically throughout the book does not detract from Read's other very serious purpose, to continue his investigation of the nature of the aesthetic faculty and of its origins in man's efforts to place himself in a meaningful relationship with the universe.

Much of the early part of *The Forms of Things Unknown* is devoted to establishing the idea that it is not in a vague or mystical way that art can be regarded as a process of indefinitely expanding the human consciousness. Read argues that art is in fact a parallel cognitive system to science.

> The fundamental purpose of the artist is the same as that of the scientist: to state a fact. And the fundamental purpose of attending to works of art is not to enjoy values, but as in science to establish truth.

And art establishes truth and survives precisely by its concreteness, its physicality.

What is verifiable is a perceptible form which communicates a notion of being, a man-made piece of reality.

And since philosophy, too, is not a disembodied energy, but has meaning only as a human activity, 'a free choice of facts in a world of facts', art has as great claims as science to be the basis of a philosophy, for it extends the existing world, enlarges it with new facts, with elements that give continuity to the human experience.

In stating his aesthetic philosophy, Read poses as central to it the question: 'Is it possible that life acquires meaning only to the extent that man is creative?' Merely to pose such a question in such a context is to answer implicitly in the affirmative, and the rest of *The Forms of Things Unknown* is concerned with establishing the significance of human creativity, and the uniqueness of art as a mode of discourse giving access 'to areas of knowledge that are closed to other types of discourse'. The argument is densely loaded with quotations, for Read draws widely on the insights and opinions of other aestheticians, of anthropologists and of psychologists, especially Jung, on whose teaching regarding the collective unconscious Read relies perhaps more heavily in this than in any other of his books.

The Jungian doctrine leads Read to consider the extent to which 'the artist is merely a medium, a channel, for forces that are impersonal', that 'convert the personal into the supra-personal', and are embodied in the myths or archetypes which emerge through the artist's unconscious but are to be conceived as 'unifying forces'. In this context he implies that the spontaneity of which the Romantics talk is not an exercise of individual caprice, but rather an opening of the mind so that the artist may apprehend intuitively 'the artistically valid symbols … which rise … from the depths of the unconscious'. And here Read comes in another way to that classic dilemma of the anarchist, the existence of freedom in a situation where biological necessity reigns. He solves it thus:

> The forms of art are only significant in so far as they are archetypal, and in that sense predetermined; and only vital in so far as they are *transformed* by the sensibility of the artist and in that sense free.

Vitality, in other words, is synonymous with freedom; the actual work of art is a libertarian act. But it is also an act of creative evolution in so far as it represents 'the exercise of an expanding consciousness', of 'an increasing apprehension of the nature of being'.

> In the growth of that apprehensive faculty, art has been the essential
> means, the instrument for refining the apprehending sensibility. Without
> the creative arts there would have been no advance in myth or ritual, in
> language or meaning, in morality or metaphysics.

Here, of course, is the answer to Read's rhetorical question. Only art
enables us to apprehend meaning in life, and art is by very definition
creative. Thus, in the process of a series of essays in which he has considered art as a unique cognitive process and a unique mode of discourse, or language, Read has really reinforced the conclusions
about the importance of art in the development of human consciousness which he had already sketched out in more historical form in
Icon and Idea.

He expands his field in chapters on 'The Poetic Consciousness',
'The Creative Experience in Poetry' and other related subjects, to
bring the literary arts into the field of his aesthetic philosophy. And
he ends with a group of essays in which he seeks to establish a creative humanism which will give a coherent conception of human
existence, 'and an affirmation, as firm as the empirical facts will
allow, of any values that give significance to our daily activities'. This
brings him inevitably to the moral problems of our age, and these he
finds not in the fact of suffering through intensity of conscience or
commitment, but rather in the question 'why people who have no
personal convictions of any kind allow themselves to suffer from
indefinite or undefined causes, drifting like shoals of fish into invisi-
ble nets. The problem is mass-suffering, mute and absurd; in one
word—inhumanism.' The tragedy is that of a society without organic unity; but to achieve organic unity a culture is necessary, and 'there
is no culture unless an intimate relationship, on the level of instinct,
exists between a people and its poets'. Yet, even if artists are 'essential to a civilization', they do not create it; if they can provide an
image of reconciliation, they cannot compel its use. 'The great artist
... by transcending personal feelings discovers symbols for the universal archetypes of the psyche', and so presents truths which are
salutary for the community, but he will not be heard except in a society attuned to receive his message. And Read ends his book by
returning to Tolstoy and Plato and considering the harmonizing disciplines which must be reinstituted if men are to become responsive

to the reconciling processes of the aesthetic life. 'The creative imagination, conceived actively', is indeed 'the only effective instrument of peace'. But it is solely, as Read recognizes, by education that the creative imagination can be made generally active. His views on education, and on the anarchism which with education forms the active ingredient of his aesthetic philosophy, are the subject of the following chapters.

Essentially, in terms of general concepts, there is little in *The Forms of Things Unknown* that Read has not in some sense adumbrated in his earlier books. By the time he reaches his middle years a writer has usually developed his essential attitude towards life, has charted the fundamental tenets of his philosophy, and is likely then to engage, as Read did in the books from *Art and Society* to *The Forms of Things Unknown*, in a process of refinement and deepening. Read was not in the beginning, and never became, a systematic philosopher, and this enabled him to carry out constant variations on his thoughts, to test their differing aspects, to modify them perpetually, without his central principles or insights ever being imperilled. He has been accused of contradiction, of inconsistency, but the twists of thought one encounters in his writings can best be understood as the workings of a flexible and resolutely open mind. For even if a logical scheme is not discernible in Read's philosophic writings, any more than it is in the writings of men like Nietzsche or Proudhon whom he admired, one is never in any doubt of the nature of his explorations, of the look and feel of the terrain of human consciousness he is mapping before our minds' eyes, of the truths he is defending, of the principles he deduces from the practices of art, or of the side on which he is fighting. I doubt if one can ask more of a poet who has turned metaphysician.

7

The World Renewed

I

'I have never been an active politician, merely a sympathizing intellectual,' said Herbert Read in 1940, and the statement is generally true of his whole career as a social and political philosopher. Yet I do not think the title 'philosophic anarchist', which has so often been applied to him, is really justified. It suggests the detached thinker who conceives an ideal ungoverned commonwealth, but does not concern himself with the means by which that society might come into being. Read was deeply concerned with the means that, through art and education, could make men receptive to the great political and social changes needed to create a libertarian world. He was also, on occasion, willing to take other action. But he certainly did not become involved in the day-to-day business of politics—even anarchist politics. This was mainly because he held strongly the anarchist idea that the struggle for freedom must be initiated by the worker within his own occupational group, and Read's vocation was that of the poet and the critic of art and literature. He believed the freedom of the arts was linked intimately with general freedom; he believed that the artist should take his part in the struggle to bring about a society that fostered rather than frustrated creativity ('Deep down [he said] my attitude is a protest against the fate that has made me a poet in an industrial age'); he believed also that the artist has a function as mediator between the individual and society; these were the paths he mainly followed when he spoke in political terms. To stand as a representative of the workers, or even as a preacher to them, would have seemed to him presumptuous. 'Intellectuals writing for proletarians will not do,' he wrote to me in 1949. 'It is merely another form of *la trahison des clercs*.'

It is important to remember these facts in order to avoid the error of seeing Read either as an anarchist philosopher primarily, or merely as an impresario of the arts who considered the anarchist kind of society the best in which the arts could flourish. He believed that the connections between art and the revolutionary impulse were intimate and vital.

> It is not that art is incompatible with revolution far from it [he declared in *To Hell with Culture*]. Nor do I suggest that art has no specific part to play in a revolutionary struggle ... Art as I have defined it is so intimately linked to the vital forces of life that it carries society towards ever new manifestations of that life. Art, in its full and free subjective action, is the one essentially revolutionary force with which man is endowed. Art *is* revolutionary and art can best serve revolution by remaining true to itself.

The last clause of that quotation—'art can best serve revolution by remaining true to itself'—is essential to Read's aesthetic philosophy and no less to his anarchist social vision. The free society and the universalization of aesthetic values are two facets of the same process of social harmonization which Read advocates, but this does not mean that their role is interchangeable, as Read made clear in a polemic on socialist realism which he conducted with the Communist critic Alick West during the late 1930's. The following paragraph from his article, which was later collected in *A Coat of Many Colours*, summarizes effectively Read's conviction that the expression of political theories or moral judgements is not in itself part of the poet's function, which is nevertheless in no way incompatible with political statements on unpoetic—or to enlarge the reference— unartistic occasions.

> The basis of the poet's activity is sympathy—an intuitive understanding and projection of himself into the object of his contemplation. Intellectual attitudes, moral prejudices, political judgments—all alike destroy the operation of these universal sympathetic faculties. I believe no statement I have ever made has done me more harm than a note I added to one of my poems—*The End of a War*: 'It is not my business as a poet to condemn war ... Judgment may follow, but should never precede or become embroiled in the act of poetry.' In spite of the anger it has aroused, I still stick to that statement. No one can hate war more strongly than I do, and my hatred of war springs from the experience. And on other occasions, which were not poetic, I have expressed this hatred in no uncertain terms.

During the 1940's, I was able to observe directly, from working closely with him, the voluntary limitations of Read's engagement in anarchism, and his inclination to remain aloof, even among anarchists, from anything that resembled political organization. He did not aspire to be a leader. 'Power corrupts even the intellect,' he once said. But he had no intention, either, of being caught in the net of group orthodoxy.

When I first met Read, I was publishing in Cambridge a little magazine called *Now*. Having come through pacifism to what still seems to me the logical end of non-violent anarchism, I asked Read for a contribution. He sent me a brief essay on Paul Klee, who had died the year before, and not long afterwards, in the early summer, he came to Cambridge to do some research for *Education Through Art* at the Fitzwilliam Library. He sent me a postcard giving me his telephone number, and we met at the Copper Kettle on King's Parade.

Read was almost fifty, but he looked younger; he had, indeed, a face that gave little hint of his age, rather like the faces of some Tibetans I have since known, though there was nothing oriental about the cast of his features, but rather an elfin quality, so that I have often thought that in Read the genes of some ancient and wise race of the Yorkshire fells were manifesting themselves. He wore the black pork-pie hat and the bow-tie that were then almost a customary uniform with him, and his expression had a defensiveness that created a curious first impression of anonymity. From that first meeting—as from so many others—I remember the silences, the tentative approaches, the warmth in the eyes.

Though I knew Read for another quarter of a century, and during certain periods saw him often, I never really made up my mind whether he was an excessively shy man, or whether, as he would assert, it was his Yorkshire phlegm and taciturnity that made the silences so long and yet so living. He seemed to deploy them as a kind of strategy in conversation, and I cannot remember that they ever impeded the free flow of ideas. Read was not an accomplished monologist, as Orwell was, and though he could recite anecdotes that portrayed some other person with concise accuracy (I remember from that first meeting a description of Henry Miller that has coloured my impressions of him ever since) he said surprisingly little about himself, and particularly about his past, which was unusual in a writer, and surprising in a man whose autobiographical essays were among his best work. In later years, when he travelled often, he came back with little to tell that had a personal flavour. On his return from his first visit to the United States after World War II, for example, he came to see me and talked mostly about supermarkets, which he had seen for the first time, and which interested him because people took what they wanted from the shelves; it seemed to him that, if only the cash desks at the entrances could be removed, the supermarket would be the perfect model for free anarchist communist distribution as envisaged by Kropotkin in *The Conquest of Bread*.

I remember with so much vividness that first meeting in Cambridge, sipping Earl Grey tea and eating scones and Tiptree's Little Scarlet among the academic wives of a generation past, because the direction of our conversation—literary journals, poetry, anarchism—tended to chart out the areas of interest we shared in later years. From Read's reputation I had imagined him an active anarchist militant, committed in the same way as some of my acquaintances like Randall Swingler and Charles Madge were then committed to the Communist Party; I thought he would be actively working with the group that had inherited Freedom Press (Kropotkin's foundation) and published an anarchist fortnightly called *War Commentary*. I was bewildered when he answered my questions rather vaguely. I assumed he must be an initiate following a politic line with an untested stranger. But he told me the name of the tall, dark and extraordinarily beautiful girl I had seen at anarchist meetings in London; she was Marie Louise Berneri, daughter of the Italian anarchist leader Camillo Berneri whom the Communists had murdered in 1937 in the streets of Barcelona. When I went to live in London two months later I met Marie Louise in the little shop which the anarchists ran off Red Lion Square, and that meeting transformed my libertarianism from a passive to an active belief.

It also demonstrated to me that Read's vagueness in talking about the anarchist movement arose not from a desire to conceal, but rather from deliberate ignorance. He chose to stand apart, with a poet's freedom, from a group of middle-class intellectuals whose proletarian aspirations he distrusted. He believed that anarchism was a doctrine which each man must relate to his own experience, and his experience was that of the artist; his political beliefs were linked inextricably with his view of the relationship between art and society.

At that time the militant anarchists in Britain had a double organization. The Freedom Press group was a circle of intellectuals, some of them personal friends of Read, who operated openly and were concerned mainly with publication; the leading figures were Marie Louise Berneri, her husband Vernon Richards, whose father had been a close friend of Malatesta, and John Hewetson, a physician who had reached anarchism by way of the Forward Movement in the Peace Pledge Union. This group was part of a larger, secret organization, the Anarchist Federation of Great Britain, which balanced the grandiosity of its title by the thinness of its ranks. I was eventually admitted to both groups, but Read never belonged to either, partly from his own choice, but partly because, like Kropotkin before him, he supported Britain's participation in World War II as an unpleasant inevitability, though like Orwell he did so with the view that it 'would inevitably lead to revolution that it would be neither won nor lost without a social upheaval'; except for a small Jewish group in the East End of London, the other anarchists opposed it with an extremity that in some ways affected their attitude to Read, as I learnt early in our relationship.

After our meeting in Cambridge, Read gave me for publication in *Now* his article, 'The Paradox of Anarchism'. I found he had offered it to Freedom Press—which had already published two of his libertarian essays in pamphlet form—and its editorial committee had rejected it because they disagreed with part—and only part—of the argument. Most of the essay consisted of an unexceptionable exposition of anarchism, but it ended with a specific reference to Germany and what should be done to that country in what seemed—at the end of 1941—the uncertain eventuality of an Allied victory. In Read's view Germany as then constituted would remain a permanent danger because of the immoderate worship of the national state that had infected all classes. None of the solutions that had lingered in the minds of politicians since the Treaty of Versailles seemed likely to prevent a resurgence of national feeling such as had taken the Nazis to power in the 1930's, and Read saw the only solution in the practical application of anarchist doctrines by the destruction of the German state.

> This can be done in stages [he suggested], first by the restoration of independence to the provinces whose union made the German state possible, and then by the devolution within these separate provinces of all economic power to trade unions and other voluntary organizations.

This proposal offended the anarchist doctrinaries of Freedom Press because (a) it suggested that an anarchist society could be achieved gradually instead of by means of the apocalyptic act of revolutionary destruction which was an article of faith among them, and (b) it implied that the German state could be destroyed by other states which might then succumb to Germany's example of peaceful and constructive anarchism. Personally I thought the proposal rather unrealistic, since I believed that in the event of an Allied victory the triumphant powers would be more likely to stamp out than to foster any inclination towards anarchism in a defeated Germany, but I thought it was a point of view that should be made public, and I printed the piece in *Now* and vainly tried to persuade Freedom Press to distribute that issue. I was too naively enthusiastic at the time to allow the incident to prevent my later joining the Freedom Press group, though on reflection long afterwards I realized that it contained within it all the divergences between free intelligence and fanatical minds, that explained Read's disinclination to join any existing anarchist group. But the incident cemented my personal association with Read, and when *Now* became an openly anarchist review he was its most frequent contributor; he wrote long essays for eight out of its twelve issues.

In 1943 or 1944—I cannot now remember the exact date—the Anarchist Federation decided to come into the open; once the pressure of clandestinity was removed, it immediately broke apart, the anarcho-syndicalist faction (which included a few real workers) retaining the title—a hollow victory, since the intellectuals kept the printing press, the stocks of literature, the paper licence (vital in wartime) and the Freedom Bookshop. A new organization of 'pure anarchists' led by the Freedom Press intellectuals was formed in 1945, with a London Group and a Federation of Anarchist Groups; the dominant theoretical influence was Kropotkin, though Malatesta's example was revered, and room was given for the notions of such strange prophets as Wilhelm Reich and even the Marquis de Sade. Read took a close but temporary interest in these developments. He attended at least one of the organizational meetings, and in August he wrote me from a summer villa at Braemar ('a Victorian house with all its period equipment amusing but exhausting, a relic of the slave age') : 'I am glad to hear that the London Group is taking shape. I would like to see a copy of the programme.' I think he hoped it would be a true guild of anarchist intellectuals, which he could have joined, but the old pseudo-proletarian line prevailed, and he held aloof, as did Alex Comfort. I joined for a while, and withdrew in 1948; my reasons, discussed elsewhere, have no place in this book.

If Read evaded involvement, he did not avoid action. As he wrote in 'The Contrary Experience', a poem of this period,

> But even as you wait
> like Arjuna in his chariot
> the ancient wisdom whispers:
> Life in action.

He saw anarchism specifically as 'an activist philosophy', and in his own way—in fact in a variety of ways—he followed the advice of Krishna in the Bhagavad Gita, to which his poem refers. He wrote *Poetry and Anarchism* and *Essential Communism;* he prepared pamphlets to be published by Freedom Press *(The Philosophy of Anarchism* and *Existentialism, Marxism and Anarchism) ;* he edited and introduced a selection of Kropotkin's writings; he wrote for *Freedom,* the propagandist organ of the post-war anarchist movement, and more often for *Now;* he occasionally appeared at Conway Hall or Memorial Hall to address public meetings organized by anarchists, pacifists or civil libertarians.

1945 marked the beginning of the period when Read's political activity reached its peak. In that year four members of the Freedom Press group were arrested on charges of seditious behaviour under the notorious wartime Regulation 39A, which gave the authorities a virtually free hand in suppressing anti-war publications and punishing their publishers. Read spent a great deal of time and energy on their defence, and in the process rendered himself open to retaliation by the authorities, though in fact this never eventuated. He and I drafted together a letter which we persuaded a group of writers to sign, denouncing the arbitrariness of the first raids carried out on the Freedom Press by Special Branch agents. Stephen Spender, T. S. Eliot and E. M. Forster were among the signatories. Spender was censured by the Foreign Office, for which he was then working, and refused to sign any more such protests. Forster rather fussily insisted on altering a few words in the letter after Eliot had signed it. Eliot was angry that we had allowed Forster to interfere with anything he had signed, but stood by the protest, a fact which I am always happy to quote against those who describe him as a reactionary.

Read also became chairman of the committee which was set up to conduct the defence of the four anarchists; he made speeches for them, wrote articles on the case and a pamphlet—*Freedom: Is it a Crime?*—raised money. Three of the accused, Vernon Richards, John Hewetson and Philip Sansom, were found guilty and went to prison; Marie Louise Berneri was acquitted, and she and I edited *Freedom* until the other editors were released early the following year.

The defence committee set up for the trial was continued as a semi-permanent organization, the Freedom Defence Committee, to take up the cases of other people arrested under oppressive wartime regulations, to secure an end to conscription and an amnesty for deserters, and to protest against police violation of civil rights. Read remained its chairman until the committee came to an end in 1949, and the fact that he was willing to be an active member of such a group and not to join an actual anarchist group dedicated to propaganda, is significant of his attitude towards organization. The Freedom Defence Committee was an *ad hoc* body which committed its members to action with a limited objective over a limited period of time, and it was action that fitted Read's vocation as a writer; to join an anarchist organization would have involved sweeping ideological commitments and implied a willingness to make his writing serve partisan ends rather than the free development of ideas. Similar considerations moved other unaffiliated left-wing writers who served on the committee —George Orwell as Vice-Chairman, Julian Symons as a member of the working committee, and I as treasurer and later as secretary. Read and Orwell, libertarians of different shades who shared the inability to live happily with organized political groups, and who were both disillusioned by the failure of the war to precipitate radical social changes, were much closer than their differing life-styles and ways of writing might suggest. 'His personality, which remains so vivid after all these years, often rises like some ghost to admonish me,' Read wrote to me in 1966 after I had published my book on Orwell, *The Crystal Spirit*. 'I suppose I have felt nearer to him than to any other English writer of our time, and though there were some aspects of his character that irritated me—his proletarian pose in dress, etc., his insensitivity to his physical environment, his comparatively narrow range of interests—yet who was, in general, nearer in ideals and even in eccentricities?'

2

To me, when I met Read in 1942, anarchism was new and dazzling.
To Read, who held it as almost a lifetime faith, it was already a familiar doctrine to which he had been converted in his own youth nearly
thirty years before. 'Actually', he insists in *The Contrary Experience*,
'there was an unfailing continuity in my political interests and political opinions. I would not like to claim that they show an unfailing
consistency, but the general principles which I found congenial as a
young man are the basic principles of the only political philosophy I
still find congenial.'

The continuity was not quite so unbroken as Read suggests, for
as a bank clerk at the age of fifteen he followed the traditions of his
class of Yorkshire farmers by becoming a fanatical Tory: 'I worshipped my King with a blind emotional devotion, and even managed to make a hero out of Lord Salisbury.' He also read all of
Disraeli's novels and these—with their doctrine of the Two
Nations—appear to have had the effect of disturbing rather than
confirming his conservatism. What Disraeli revealed to him in fiction
was reinforced by what he saw as he went to and fro in Leeds on Savings Bank business:

> The fundamental contrasts between town and country, industry and
> agriculture, wealth and poverty, were forced upon me by my daily expe-
> riences in Leeds. (*The Contrary Experience*.)

Yet he remained true to his ancestry by finding the opposing pole of
peasant politics to Toryism: anarchism.

> In spite of my intellectual pretensions, I am by birth and tradition a
> peasant [he said in *Poetry and Anarchism*]. I remain essentially a peasant.
> I despise this foul industrial epoch—not only the plutocracy which it has
> raised to power, but also the industrial proletariat which it has drained
> from the land and proliferated in hovels of indifferent brick. The class in
> the community for which I feel a natural sympathy is the agricultural
> class, including the genuine remnants of a landed aristocracy. This per-
> haps explains my early attraction to Bakunin, Kropotkin and Tolstoy,
> who were also of the land, aristocrats and peasants.

'Proudhon, Tolstoy and Kropotkin were the predilections of my youth,' Read remarks elsewhere. But it was in fact a now forgotten political tract that precipitated Read's acceptance of anarchism as a lifelong faith.

> I date my conversion to the reading of a pamphlet by Edward Carpenter with the title *Non-Governmental Society*, which took place in 1911 or 1912, and immediately opened up to me a whole new range of thought—not only the works of professed anarchists such as Kropotkin, Bakunin and Proudhon, but also those of Nietzsche, Ibsen and Tolstoy which directly or indirectly supported the anarchist philosophy, and those of Marx and Shaw which directly attacked it. I use the word 'conversion' to describe the experience because it was undoubtedly quasi-religious; I was at the same time slipping away from the Christian faith I had acquired from a pious family background. (*The Cult of Sincerity.*)

Here, right at the beginning, by his early twenties, one has all the important influences that shaped Read's lifetime political philosophy, with two unmentioned exceptions. One of these is Max Stirner, whose *The Ego and his Own* was and remained an abrasive presence in Read's mind.

> To say that it had a great influence on me would not be correct, for influences are absorbed and become part of one's mind. This book refused to be digested to use our vivid English metaphor: it stuck in the gizzard. (*The Forms of Things Unknown.*)

And, sticking there, it saved Read from accepting collectivist solutions too complacently and from taking freedom for granted as an easy matter to define or to achieve. The second unnamed influence was that of Sorel, whose *Reflections on Violence* Read acquired as soon as Hulme's translation appeared in 1916.

> Few books have impressed me so deeply and so permanently. It worked on me in a surer way than Nietzsche had done. It appealed to something more fundamental than my intellect—namely to my temperament and instincts—and again opened up endless new perspectives. It was from Sorel, if I remember rightly, that I passed to Bergson, and certainly to Proudhon. But his main function, in my case, was to supply to socialism the imaginative quality that I found lacking in Marx. (*The Contrary Experience.*)

Sorel's most durable influence on Read was probably to introduce
him to the uses of political mythology, and thus to enable him to
accept philosophically that, even if the free society of the anarchists
showed little possibility of coming into existence, it could still serve
its purpose as an exemplary myth, so that, in his last writings on
anarchism, Read could say, with Sorelian sangfroid:

> My understanding of the history of culture has convinced me that the
> ideal society is a point on a receding horizon. Nevertheless we must
> engage with passion in the immediate strife—such is the nature of things
> and if defeat is inevitable (as it is) we are not excused. (*The Cult of Sin-
> cerity*.)

Read's was a pattern of influence not unusual in the early twentieth century among the literary young; Joyce in Dublin and Kafka in
Prague were studying roughly the same writers at the same period.
But Read remained permanently and profoundly under their influence; the others did not.

At first he called himself a 'Socialist' and, in his early radical speculations, Marxist and anarchist attitudes were intermingled; he even
believed—as he did not in later years—that nationalization of the
means of production might be the prelude to the dissolution of the
state. In a note written in 1914, and quoted in *The Contrary Experience*, he says:

> For the present, both Collectivism and Syndicalism have their respective
> duties. The role of Collectivism is the expropriation of Capital. This is to
> be brought about by the nationalization of industry. But Collectivists are
> wrong in regarding nationalization as an end in itself; it is only a means.
> For whilst the Collectivist state is evolving, Syndicalism will be playing
> its role—i.e. it will be developing the economic, industrial and educa-
> tional functions of the Trade Unions. Trade Unions are, I am convinced,
> the units upon which the future society will be built. They must be organ-
> ized and extended so as to be powerful enough to demand, and fit
> enough to undertake, the control of industry when it has been national-
> ized by the state. ... By a devolution of power, a decentralization of con-
> trol, and, above all, by a development in the social conscience of the
> nation, the ideals of today will become the realities of tomorrow.

Read was always to respect the doctrines of anarcho-syndicalism, and to regard the natural organization of society as one based on workers' control of industry; it was his trust in the state as a mechanism for achieving any social good that rapidly dissolved under the impact of his wartime experiences. A little later, early in 1915, he wrote his first political essay, 'An Economic Interpretation of Morality'; it was never published, but the handwritten manuscript has survived.

Like most socialists and anarchists in 1914 Read had been a theoretical pacifist, yet at the same time he was a member of the O.T.C. at Leeds University. When he found himself thrust incontinently into the war, and realized that the international working class was unprepared to halt the militarists by a universal general strike, he made the Nietzschean best of a bad job, and set out to meet what he saw as a challenge. As late as May 1917, when he had reached the front but had not yet experienced war's full horrors, he could still write of it in 'A War Diary' as 'an adventure'.

Eight months later he had again become a pacifist, and this time with the conviction of experience. He remarked that 'the means of war has become more portentous than the aim' and that among the soldiers there had been 'an immense growth of pacifist opinion'. And during 1917 and 1918, while he was writing articles for the *New Age* and *The Guildsman* supporting both Syndicalism and Guild Socialism (the continental and the British variants of the doctrine of the control of production by producers), he was experiencing a cumulative revulsion against static social orders and against the state in particular. In January 1917 he wrote:

> I've a theory that all the evil things in the world are static, passive and possessive; and that all good things are dynamic, creative. Life is dynamic; death is static. And as life is dynamic, passive remedies of society are false. Hence the folly of having cut and dried Utopias as ultimate aims: by the time you get to them, life has left them behind. Hence the folly of basing society on possessive institutions (such as property and marriage, as a rule). Our institutions should appeal to our creative impulses; what a man *does* and not what he *has*.

In April 1918:

> I don't think I'm ready to discuss the change that is taking place in my 'political sentiment'. It is a revolt of the individual against the association

which involves him in activities which do not interest him: a jumping to
the ultimate anarchy which I have already seen as the ideal of all who
value beauty and intensity of life. 'A beautiful anarchy'—that is my cry.

In May 1918:

> But simply because we are united with a callous inhuman association
> called a State and because a State is ruled by politicians whose aim (and
> under the circumstances their duty) is to support the life and sovereignty
> of this monster, life and hope are denied and sacrificed.

In a positive as well as a negative way, Read's anarchist tendencies
were intensified during the war, for he found—as Orwell was later to
find during the Spanish Civil war—a comradeship in the trenches of
a kind he had never before known, 'a feeling of unanimity aroused by
common stresses, common dangers', and so, in this unlikely setting,
his convictions of the validity of the anarchist doctrine of mutual aid
seemed to be justified by experience. He had also a hope that, in the
event, was doomed to disillusion, for early in 1918 he had written in
one of his letters:

> As soon as peace is declared the one and only hope is in International
> Socialism. If it does not *recreate* the world, then International Capitalism
> will *restore* it.

Looking back in 1962, when he completed *The Contrary Experience*, over the period after 1918, Read felt that 'the no-man's-years
between the wars' had been 'largely futile, spent unprofitably by me
and my kind', mainly, he believed, because of forces outside their
power to change—'blind forces of economic drift and political inep-
titude with the walls of faith and reason turning to air behind us'. At
the same time, he adds that, 'in spite of a disillusion at once personal
and universal, I persisted in a simple faith in the natural goodness of
men', and it was in the latter half of the inter-war period that he
began to develop his theories of the interrelationship of art and anarchism, and to write the series of essays and books that contain his
socio-political arguments.

The years from 1919 to 1931 were in these respects a time of
enforced silence. There are points in Read's career when he surprises
the observer—as he surprised many of his friends—by acting with an

inconsistency that seems to exceed even the licence to impulsiveness he allowed himself as a proclaimed romantic. A pacifist, he fought in World War I. After declaring in *Poetry and Anarchism* (1938) that 'anarchism naturally implies pacifism', he came out in 1939 in support of Britain's participation in World War II. In 1953 he bent the knee to receive a knighthood, and set off an international storm among anarchists in which so far as I can remember—Augustus John and I were alone among his comrades in defending the right of a libertarian to make his own choices, even in his relations with the State.

1919 was another such time; after considering such strange careers for a professed anarchist as a permanent commission in the army and professional politics, Read decided that 'the political situation offered no basis for allegiance or enthusiasm', and finally chose the civil service; he felt he would have more time and energy there to devote to writing. He served first at the Ministry of Labour under Arthur Greenwood, who had taught him economics at Leeds, and then for several years in the Treasury, where he acquired a lifelong loathing for bureaucrats, before he moved on to the Victoria and Albert Museum. But even at the Museum he was still a civil servant, inhibited by governmental rules from expressing publicly any opinion that might suggest political partisanship. He was liberated in 1931 when he went to the University of Edinburgh, but for twelve years civil service rules had prevented him from publishing anything expressing his radical views, and even when he was free it was some years before, in 1938, he expounded his libertarian philosophy at length in *Poetry and Anarchism*, though, three years before, he had at least sketched it out in the brief pamphlet *Essential Communism*.

Essential Communism appeared in the same year 1935 as *The Green Child*, which was written with at least an oblique political intent. Read tells us that in this novel he 'described symbolically' how 'the realization of a rational blue-print leads to the death of a society'.

The hopes generated by the Russian Revolution died hard and slowly during the 1930's even among the many radicals who were in no way orthodox Marxists, as Read's example showed.

> From 1917 onwards and for as long as I could preserve the illusion [he confesses in *Poetry and Anarchism*], communism as established in Russia seemed to promise the social liberty of my ideals. So long as Lenin and Stalin promised a definite 'withering away of the State', I was prepared

to stifle my doubts and prolong my faith. But when, five, ten, fifteen, and then twenty years passed, with the liberty of the individual receding at every stage, a break became inevitable.

The suicide in 1930 of the poet Mayakovsky, hounded by the Stalinist bureaucrats, stirred Read's first doubts. By 1936, when he wrote the introduction to *Surrealism*, he complained that 'even Communism, the creed of liberty and fraternity, has made the exigencies of a transitional epoch the excuse for an unnecessary and stupid form of aesthetic intolerance'. Two more or less simultaneous events in 1936 left Read with the conviction that he had no alternative but to break openly with Marxist communism and declare just as openly for anarchism. These were the Moscow Trials, and the outbreak of the Civil War in Spain, where anarchism emerged from the shadows Marxism had cast over it in the rest of Europe since 1917, and attempted, in a land at conflict, to lay the foundations of a libertarian society, in the village communes of Andalusia and the socialized factories of Barcelona.

Between 1936 and 1939 Read wrote articles for *Spain and the World*, the anarchist paper of the time, served on committees to aid refugees, addressed meetings, and wrote two of the best poems about the Civil War, the compassionate and angry 'Bombing Casualties in Spain' and 'Song for the Spanish Anarchists', in which is condensed his whole vision of the organic strength of a free and natural society where the individual is defined by what he *does*, and where men *have* in common.

3

With minor exceptions, Read's socio-political writings appeared between 1938 and 1954; the most important had seen first publication by the end of 1943. One can perhaps fairly assume that Read's impulse to write on anarchism began to fail as the 'sense of glory' associated with the early days of the Spanish civil war faded in his mind. However, in his last decade, in recollective mood, he wrote several essays that touched on his libertarian beliefs and in particular one that summed up the political reflections of a lifetime: 'My Anarchism', which appeared in *Encounter* in the January before his death and was later collected in the posthumously published volume, *The Cult of Sincerity*.

A confusion exists, in the publication history of Read's anarchist writings, similar to that which we have already observed in connection with his essays in literary criticism, owing to the various combinations in which he issued and reissued them. *Poetry and Anarchism* (1938), *The Philosophy of Anarchism* (1940) and *Existentialism, Marxism and Anarchism* (1950) all appeared first as separate volumes, or at least as pamphlets, while 'The Paradox of Anarchism', printed first in *Now* (1942), was later collected in *A Coat of Many Colours* (1945). *Essential Communism*, his earliest published statement of political views, apart from the fugitive articles in the *New Age* and *The Guildsman*, appeared first as a pamphlet in 1935, but later formed a chapter of *Poetry and Anarchism*. All these eventually came together with a new introductory essay, 'Revolution and Reason', in *Anarchy and Order* (1954). 'Chains of Freedom' appeared first in *Now* (1947), later in an expanded version in *Existentialism, Marxism and Anarchism*, and in an even fuller version in *Anarchy and Order*. *To Hell with Culture* appeared separately as a small pamphlet in 1941, and in 1943 it was included—revised—as a chapter in *The Politics of the Unpolitical*; a new volume in 1963, comprising most of *The Politics of the Unpolitical*, plus a few essays mainly concerning problems of the arts, was entitled *To Hell with Culture*. As I go on to discuss the leading themes of Read's socio-political philosophy, I shall do my best to avoid confusion by giving each book or pamphlet the title under which it was published originally.

The opening lines of 'Song for the Spanish Anarchists' contain the image that most concisely expresses Read's view of the nature of a free society:

> The golden lemon is not made
> but grows on a green tree ...

The free society cannot be developed according to a plan; it must grow according to nature. Its ideal condition is 'the same as the ideal condition of any living body—a state of dynamic tension'; it must allow itself to be 'stirred into the vibrations and emanations of organic growth'. Hence its condition is the reverse of Utopian rigidity. It should allow men to live 'in harmony with natural law'—a phrase which Read is careful to point out should not be interpreted literally (thereby reducing mankind to the level of animal life'), but analogically so that we envisage 'exactly the same kind of relationship as we have discovered between nature and art'.

The laws that govern such a society's development may follow reason, but they are not in the narrow sense rational, and perhaps it is from this distinction that one can begin the examination of Read's attitudes towards society and its political development. He calls himself a materialist; he declares that we must 'admit the universalism of truth and submit our life to the rule of reason'. The life of reason he sees as 'a practical ideal, extending to wider and wider circles of humanity, and promising an earthly paradise never to be attained only because each stage towards its realization creates its superior level'. (*The Politics of the Unpolitical.*) But he says also that reason is much more than rationality or mechanistic logic.

> Reason should rather connote the widest evidence of the senses, and of all processes and instincts developed in the long history of man. It is the sum total of awareness, ordained and ordered to some specific end or object of attention. (*Reason and Romanticism.*)

In Read's view, a society that tried to exist on a purely rational basis 'would probably die of a kind of communal accidie'. We are involved inevitably in 'certain intangible and imponderable elements which we call emotion and instinct'; and, while adhering to no religion, Read grants that 'a religion is a necessary element in any organic society' and that a new religion might even develop out of anarchism. For 'if ... religion is the life of contemplation, the fruit of pure meditation, spiritual joy, then it cannot help but prosper in a society free from poverty, pride and envy'.

Indeed, even anarchism at its most rational is not without its metaphysical element, for such a doctrine cannot exist without recognizing certain absolute values.

> Let us but ask what we mean by the word 'justice'. It is not something we can measure by an economic scale; it is not even egalitarianism. It is a sense of values, of human values, and our only clue to those values is our intuition of an absolute and metaphysical quality—justice. (*A Coat of Many Colours.*)

Freedom and anarchism are synonymous, but anarchism is not nihilism, and freedom is not licence. On the contrary, Read insists, it is part of natural law, intimately linked with the phenomenon of evolution. 'Freedom is not an essence only available to the sensibility of men; it is germinatively at work in all living beings as spontaneity and autoplasticity.' (*Anarchy and Order.*) But just as society gains life from its dialectical opposition to the individual, so freedom is made real by its dialectical opposition to existence and its necessities.

> And so with the individual and the community; complete freedom means inevitable decadence. The mind must feel an opposition—must be tamped with hard realities if it is to have any lasting power. (*The Politics of the Unpolitical.*)

Thus Max Stirner's egoism is rejected by Read in favour of the anarchist-communism of Kropotkin, or at least of his own adaptation of that doctrine.

> In all that concerns the planning of economic life, the building up of a rational mode of living in a social community, there can be no question of absolute liberty. For, so long as we live in a community, in all practical affairs the greatest good of the greatest number is also the greatest good of the individual. (*Poetry and Anarchism.*)

The 'duty to create a world of freedom' which he accepted seemed to Read far removed from the 'freedom to do as you like' which is the characteristic excuse of the capitalist and the imperialist. Freedom as he saw it was 'a positive condition specifically, freedom to create, freedom to become what one *is*'. He had thought deeply on the relationship between the concepts of *liberty* and *freedom*, and much of 'Chains of Freedom' was devoted to refining his definitions of these words. 'A man *is* free: he is given his liberty,' he says at one point, where he describes freedom as a personal attribute and liberty as a civil right. And later he expands the definitions.

> Liberty is one of the conscious values of a civilization. It is conceived and cultivated, defined and protected: it can also be abrogated, denied, perverted.
> But freedom is the *unconscious* creation of a culture ... It is a pulse, a living breath of which we are scarcely aware until it ceases.

But freedom implies the willingness to surrender that is necessary for the common good—for example 'to put all our property into the common fund'—and here Read is using the word *property* in a special

way, meaning 'the talents and skill of a person' which are 'his contribution to the commonwealth'. Thus he is a communist in the libertarian sense, implying not an imposed economic order, but 'a
spontaneous association of individuals for mutual aid'.

Indeed, Read is so opposed to the more antisocial concepts of
'freedom' that he is even willing to use that word shunned by most
anarchists—government—though he quickly makes clear that he
means some form of control quite different from the processes of the
State as we know it.

> Government—that is to say, control of the individual in the interests of
> the community, is inevitable if two or more men combine for a common
> purpose; government is the embodiment of that purpose. But govern-
> ment in this sense is far removed from the conception of an autonomous
> state. (*Poetry and Anarchism.*)

In choosing his political forms, Read rejects both authoritar-
ianism (including communist as well as fascist totalitarianism) and
democracy as history has known it (though not democracy as its
more intellectually pure theorists have conceived it). A single passage
of dismissal is enough to express his rejection of the authoritarians.

> The authoritarian believes in discipline as a means; the libertarian in dis-
> cipline as an end, as a state of mind. The authoritarian issues instruc-
> tions; the libertarian encourages self-education. The one tolerates a
> subjective anarchy below the smooth surface of his rule; the other has no
> need of rule because he has achieved a subjective harmony reflected in
> personal integrity and social unity. (*Anarchy and Order.*)

It is at this point that Read makes his break with the general stream
of socialism as it is commonly understood (the italics indicate his
own emphasis on what he regards as the vital distinction):

> *The tendency of modern socialism is to establish a vast system of statu-
> tory law against which there exists no plea in equity. The object of anar-
> chism, on the other hand, is to extend the principle of equity until it
> altogether supersedes statutory law.*

There is of course no essential difference between ideal democracy and anarchy, and neither has in fact been tried. The democracy

that has been tried has failed because it is tied to the notions of universal suffrage and majority rule. The theory of majority rule and the concentration of power in central parliaments have between them imposed on democracy the tendency to seek continually 'some form of centralized control', and hence to increase the power of the state; they result in a 'partitive' version of equality, which is 'a denial of brotherhood, of communion, of true communism'. As for universal suffrage, Read condemns it as emphatically as Proudhon ever did.

> It is a myth, a quite illusory delegation of power … a fiction of consent where in fact no liberty of choice exists. (*Poetry and Anarchism.*)

The myth of universal suffrage allows even communists and fascists to claim that they are democrats: 'They all obtain popular consent by the manipulation of mass psychology.' What else, Read implies, do parliamentary politicians do?

The ideal democracy is another matter, and, as one sees by the three conditions which Read lays down for its fulfilment, it is, in his mind, not different essentially from anarchism.

> The first condition is that *all production is for use, and not for profit.*
> The second condition is that *each should give according to his ability and each receive according to his needs.*
> The third condition is that the workers in *each industry should collectively own and control that industry.* (*Politics of the Unpolitical.*)

These conditions represent Read's view of necessary organization as functional and economic rather than political and social, and of equality as dependent on community.

> For the essential is not to make all incomes equal—the ideal of the average democratic socialist—but to abolish all incomes and *hold all things in common* … It is essential to stress the radical nature of this distinction between equal partition, and community ownership. It is the distinction between false communism and true communism, between the totalitarian conception of the State as a controlled herd, and the libertarian conception of society as a brotherhood. Once this conception is fully realized, the ambiguities of the doctrine of equality disappear: the concept of equality is dissolved in the concept of community. (*Anarchy of Order.*)

This brings us to the classic anarchist position: the denunciation of the State, the proclamation that societies must be built, like houses, from the ground up. For a culture 'grows out of the soil, out of the people, out of their daily life and work. It is a spontaneous expression of their joy in life, their joy in work, and if this joy does not exist, the culture will not exist.' (*Politics of the Unpolitical*.)

Like all anarchists, Read is reluctant to create elaborate plans for the ideal society. Warnings against such presumptuousness are scattered through his writings. 'The Utopia fades the moment we try to actualize it.' 'It is foolish to indulge in anything but relatively short-term policies for the human race.' 'It is always a mistake to build *a priori* constitutions. The main thing is to establish your principles: the principles of equality, of individual freedom, of workers' control.' 'I believe that the only idea of society which is capable of generating the integrity of the person is the negation of the idea of society.'

Decentralization and arbitration instead of normal legal procedures are the main additions that Read makes to these simple requirements on the rare occasions when he draws a sketch plan for the future, as in the early 1940's he did in *The Politics of the Unpolitical*. There he listed as follows the features of his plan for a 'natural society'.

    I.   The liberty of the person.
    II.   The integrity of the family.
    III. The reward of qualifications.
    IV. The self-government of the guilds.
    V.   The abolition of parliament and centralized government.
    VI. The institution of arbitrament.
   VII. The delegation of authority.
  VIII. The humanization of industry.

Read differs from most anarchists other than Proudhon in the stress he lays on the family as the basic natural social unit. It is 'the integral unit', 'the most effective unit' because it is the smallest, and it is the basis on which can be built the next unit upwards, the parish, 'the local association of men in continuous dwellings'.

Such local associations may form their courts, and these courts are sufficient to administer a common law based on common sense. (*A Coat of Many Colours*.)

Next in importance comes the guild, which anarchists with a different background from Read's early connection with Guild Socialism and the *New Age* might call the syndicate: 'the association of men and women according to their calling or practical function'. With 'political power' distributed among families and parishes ('human tangible units'), with economic power vested in the guilds and workshops, with financial power 'altogether excluded from society', with 'productive labour' recognized as 'the basic reality and honoured as such', the organizational shell of Read's vision of the free society is complete. It is based on regionalism, on the sense that 'if we can make politics local, we can make them real', on the knowledge that the creative communities of the past were never too large for all their members to feel they were 'contributing to the common glory'.

So far it is little different from other anarchist sketches of the future. One finds the same ideas more forcefully expressed by Proudhon and more elaborately by Kropotkin. What most distinguishes Read's anarchism from that of past theoreticians, and brings it closer to the socialism of William Morris, is the stress he places on the role of the arts—on (as we have seen) the artist as mediator, and (as we shall consider more fully in the following chapter) on art itself as the vehicle of a revolutionary form of education. In my view this particular emphasis is much more important than the other novel feature of Read's anarchist writings, the wide use of psychoanalytical concepts and terminology, which in this context mainly serve to replace the somewhat outdated scientism of Kropotkin and Reclus, who used evolutionary concepts in much the same way as Read used psychoanalytical ones, to prove that anarchism was given support—and hence credibility—by the most contemporary scientific developments. However illuminating Read's borrowings from Freud, Jung *et al.* may have been in his aesthetic criticism and philosophizing, I doubt if they have greatly strengthened his case for anarchism, though he has drawn out of them a few entertaining aphorisms, e.g. 'I would define the anarchist as the man who, in his manhood, dares to resist the authority of his father.' (A definition I am inclined to dispute; I have known many anarchists with gentle fathers and domineering, hated mothers.)

The place of art in Read's view of the ideal anarchist society becomes clear as soon as we move away from his plans for its organizational functioning, and sense the kind of life he would like to see lived in the future, the quality he would like it to radiate. Needless to

say it is the rural world of a self-proclaimed peasant, rather like that
of Morris's *News from Nowhere* without its earnest laboriousness,
for while Read often denounces the factory system he realizes that
'industrialism must be endured'. As we have seen, he even goes
beyond that realization to search for means by which the machine
will not merely perform the unpleasant tasks, a role Morris eventually allowed it, but will also produce beautiful objects, which Morris
would never admit to be possible. At the same time, Read is aware
that no civilization or people can lose touch with things, can abandon organic processes, can forget the feel of wood and clay and metal
worked with the hands, and still remain healthy. Therefore he wishes to use machinery to simplify existence, to end pointless labours, so
that when men leave the 'inhuman' cities they will find 'a world of
electric power and mechanical plenty where man can once more
return to the land, not as a peasant, but as a lord'. For 'there is no
need to become primitive in order to secure the essentials of democratic liberty'.

In such a world there will be no real distinction between work
and leisure, for 'the enjoyment of life' involves 'an undifferentiated
performance of mental and manual functions; things done and
things made in response to a natural impulse or desire'. (*Anarchy and
Order.*) Men and women will have no difficulty in sorting themselves
out 'so that every man and woman is doing the job for which he or
she seems naturally qualified', and play will resume its true place in
human life, for

> ... it was *play* rather than work which enabled man to evolve his higher
> faculties—everything we mean by the word 'culture' ... Play is freedom,
> is disinterestedness, and it is only by virtue of disinterested free activity
> that man has created his cultural values. Perhaps it is this theory of all
> work and no play that has made the Marxist such a very dull boy. (*Anar-
> chy and Order.*)

Of play, of course, art is the highest form (though it is also a great
deal more), and Read sees for the artist a high role in the hypotheti-
cal free society of the future. For he is, Read insists,

> ... the man who mediates between our individual consciousness and the
> collective unconsciousness, and thus ensures social reintegration. It is
> only in the degree that this mediation is successful that a true democracy
> is possible. (*Poetry and Anarchism.*)

It was in accordance with his view that a man must approach life by way of his vocation that Read wrote almost all his works on anarchism from the viewpoint of the artist or the poet, and, conversely, that his anarchist views often found their way into works that were not political in their general orientation. In this he resembled and may have been more influenced than he admitted by Oscar Wilde, whose *Soul of Man Under Socialism* anticipated *Poetry and Anarchism* in presenting a libertarian society as the best environment for the nurture of the arts. But in stressing the interests and the role of the artist Read did not express an élitist point of view. He might hope that artists would be, in the Shelleyan phrase that he approved, 'the unacknowledged legislators of the world', he might give the arts a unique role in the development and extension of human consciousness, but he did not see artists eventually as a guiding minority like Plato's Guardians or the Samurai who would govern the Wellsian ideal society of *A Modern Utopia*. For he felt that the development of a free society was not only conducive to, but even dependent on, the universalization of art, in the sense that aesthetic standards would apply to all the products of human work and by this token all men would become in their various ways artists. As the aim of work changes from profit to use, so will the life-view of the worker change.

> The worker has as much latent sensibility as any human being, but that sensibility can only be awakened when meaning is restored to his daily work and he is allowed to create his own culture. (*Politics of the Unpolitical.*)

Then we shall realize that 'every man is a special kind of artist,' for 'art is skill: a man does something so well that he is entitled to be called an artist'.

So art is brought down from the isolation to which bourgeois cultures have condemned it, and becomes a matter of everyday activity. This does not mean that *art* has progressed; but it does mean that *civilization* has progressed, because it has admitted the aesthetic impulse as a vital force in its life and its relationships. The artistic Utopia is a peculiarly English vision, a local contribution to the socialist and anarchist tradition, and Read, developing the insights of the Pre-Raphaelites and Ruskin, of Morris and Wilde, presents it in a more elaborate manner than any of his predecessors.

What applies to the man applies also to the child, who is a potential artist from the beginning, and in whom a system of education through art can—in Read's view—develop existing inner harmonies which will prepare him more felicitously for social initiation than any rival system. Read sees such a system of education as a potent agent of social liberation; it can be argued that his *Education Through Art* (which he himself described as 'deeply anarchist in its orientation') was in fact his most original contribution to anarchist theory and also to the strategy of the social revolution; I shall examine that possibility in the next chapter.

Yet, for long periods, Read also held to more orthodoxly anarchist views of change by physical means. In a general sense he regarded revolt as a necessary and regenerative element in human society. 'Freedom is not a state of rest, of least resistance. It is a state of action, of projection, of self-realization.' But such natural and spontaneous revolt was different from the kind of rebellion which Read deemed specifically necessary in the unregenerate present. Poverty must be abolished, the class-divided society brought to an end; at the very least the most monstrous injustices of the social order must be ended, and 'if we do not revolt ... we are either morally insensitive or criminally selfish.' (*Anarchy and Order.*)

During the late 1930's Read envisaged revolt in activist terms. 'Naturally the abolition of poverty and the consequent establishment of a classless society is not going to be accomplished without a struggle,' he said in *Poetry and Anarchism* (1938). 'Certain people have to be dispossessed of their autocratic power and of their illegitimate profits.' And two years later, in *The Philosophy of Anarchism*, he argued that 'an insurrection is necessary for the simple reason that when it comes to the point, even your man of good will, if he is on the top, will not sacrifice his personal advantages to the general good'.

Read did not however think in terms of violent action. He insisted that anarchist rebellion must be non-violent, that the example of Gandhi must be followed, with its need for 'immense sacrifice and angelic discipline', and the only insurrectionary strategy he discussed at any length was the general strike, 'the natural weapon of the working classes', which he believed had never been used to full effect. Though he saw himself as a rebel, an insurrectionist, he did not admit to being, at least in the political sense, a revolutionary. As early as 1940 he accepted the validity of Max Stirner's distinction between *revolution* and *insurrection*, and later, when Camus made in *The Rebel* his even sharper distinction between *revolution* (a totalitarian act) and *rebellion* (a libertarian act), Read adopted it.

Revolutions, as has often been remarked, change nothing; or rather, they merely substitute one set of masters for another set. Social groups acquire new names, but retain their former inequality of status. Rebellions or insurrections, on the other hand, being guided by instinct rather than reason, being passionate and spontaneous rather than cool and calculated, act like shock therapy on the body of society, and there is a chance that they may change the chemical composition of the societal crystal. ... (Rebellion) eludes the world of power—that is the point, for it is always power that crystallizes into a structure of injustice.

Before the aftermath of World War II renewed and deepened the doubts Read had experienced at the time of the Treaty of Versailles, his attitude was, like that of many other political idealists of the 1930's, coloured by an optimism, a feeling that only human greed and stupidity prevent what is really an easy solution to social ills, which is hard to duplicate in the world of the 1970's. Typical is the following passage that in 1938 appeared in *Poetry and Anarchism*.

The problem, in its broad outlines, is simple enough. On the one side we have mankind, needing for its sustenance and enjoyment a certain quantity of goods; on the other side we have the same mankind, equipped with certain tools, machines, and factories, exploiting the natural resources of the earth. There is every reason to believe that with modem mechanical power and modern methods of production, there is or could be a sufficiency of goods to satisfy all reasonable needs. It is only necessary to organize an efficient system of distribution or exchange.

Clearly at this period Read was as little conscious as most of his contemporaries of the acceleration of problems that would in later decades make immensely more complicated any rational organization of production or distribution: problems of growing population, of shrinking natural resources, of industrial pollution, of the benefits of science turning into menaces as deadly diseases were conquered and millions were freed to enjoy longer lives of hunger: all the Malthusian spectres which a generation ago we imagined had been exorcized for ever.

Ironically, it was not until long after the period of his main anarchist writings—not indeed until the early 1960's (his own late sixties)—that Read, at a time when his thoughts were increasingly clouded with pessimism, finally moved for the first time in his life

into practical activism. He then became involved in the passive resistance tactics of the Campaign for Nuclear Disarmament and the
Committee of 100, of which he was a member. He sat down beside
Bertrand Russell in the roadway of Whitehall, not to usher in anarchy, but to protest, with more conviction than hope, against the
destructive aspects of the existing unfree society. Later he resigned
from the Committee of 100 after protesting against its adoption of
aggressive tactics incompatible with the Gandhian strategy of Satya-
graha which in his last years he regarded as the only truly anarchist
way of struggle.

Read's later years were marked by a steady loss of the hope of seeing a better world in his time, or even of foreseeing one for his children. He seized comfort where he could, and sometimes in unlikely
places; I find a letter he wrote to me in November 1959, with a post-
script on his recent trip to China: 'China—very exciting! The communes as near to our kind of anarchism as anything that is likely to
happen.'

But he soon realized that even here his optimism had been mis-
placed, and it was with a flickering confidence in the future that he
performed in 1962 the symbolic act of putting his autobiographical
writings together in the final form of *The Contrary Experience*.

Nihilism—nothingness, despair, and the nervous hilarity that goes with
them—remains the universal state of mind [he wrote then] . From such
an abyss the soul of man does not rise in a decade or two. If a human
world survives the atomic holocaust—and it is now difficult to see how
such a holocaust is to be avoided—it will only be because man has first
overcome his nihilism. A few prophets have already pointed the way—
Gandhi, Buber, Simone Weil, C. G. Jung—but the people are also few
who pay heed to them. Spiritually the world is now one desert, and
prophets are not honoured in it. But physically it still has a beautiful face,
and if we could once more learn to live with nature, if we could return
like prodigal children to the contemplation of its beauty, there might be
an end to our alienation and fear, a return to those virtues of delight
which Blake called Mercy, Pity, Peace and Love.

He had come to regard the technological revolution as 'a disaster
that is likely to end in the extermination of humanity', and he debat-
ed fervently with C. P. Snow on this point. Yet at the same time he did

not abandon his conviction of the rightness or reasonableness of the anarchist vision, though he was even more conscious that it represented less a realizable vision than a direction point on the horizon and that its virtue lay largely in its planlessness, its anti-Utopian character. The main thing was not to lose interest, not to let the will slacken, and in 'My Anarchism', written in the last months of his life, he still insisted that

> There is nothing in the anarchist philosophy to justify indifference, complacency, or anything but a pragmatic activity patiently and consistently directed to a revolutionary end.

Yet his view of the means of achieving that end had changed considerably, as he moved, like Kropotkin in his later years, towards accepting the possibility that one might proceed gradually to the anarchist goal. In his introduction to *Anarchy and Order*, written in the early 1960's, he had called for an abandonment of the 'rhetoric of revolt'.

> Our ideas must be solid as ever, and our strategy must be realistic. But revolutionary realism, for an anarchist in an age of atom bombs, is pacific: the bomb is now the symbol, not of anarchy, but of totalitarian power.

If the anarchist could no longer effectively maintain the stance of revolt, it was patently ridiculous, Read believed, for him to attempt to 'contract out' individually from the prevailing society; this would merely reduce his power of changing it. He made an illuminating defence of his own position when he replied to Edward Dahlberg's passionate accusations of inconsistency.

> What kind of an anarchist am I? My own kind, no doubt. I do not believe that I shall bring the anarchist ideal one step nearer by joining an artificial commune, accepting the standard of life of savages, or wearing a loincloth in a sub-arctic climate. I do not believe that I shall bring that ideal any nearer realization by selling all I possess and giving the proceeds to the poor. I believe I can best serve that ideal by cultivating my small-holding of seven acres, by establishing a sense of community in this village, by living at peace with my neighbours, by creating what Gill called a cell of good living.

Read, in fact, tended to see anarchism more and more as a way of life that might be established before any general social transformation took place, and in 'My Anarchism' he blended libertarian and Jungian goals by suggesting that 'none of its critics has considered anarchism as a long-term process of individuation, accomplished by general education and personal discipline'. In this context the most interesting of all Read's speculations on the development of a libertarian consciousness parallel to an existing authoritarian and capitalist order is perhaps to be found outside his strictly anarchist writings, in the final chapter of *The Grass Roots of Art*, which was originally delivered under the title of 'Towards a Duplex Civilization' as the last of his series of lectures at Yale in 1946.

In this paper, which introduces the preoccupations that dominate Read's later social thinking, he sees the managerial revolution and the corporate state, in either monopolist or totalitarian form, as virtually inevitable for the immediate future, and admits that he does not look forward to it with 'any personal pleasure'. But he feels that under monopoly civilization there will be 'more amenities ... than in the totalitarian state', and he envisages a strategy, largely based on his earlier ideas on industrial art, in which an endeavour to introduce good standards of design in industry would parallel a kind of underground movement, assisted by an aesthetic education of the senses, to produce a private leisure-time art 'standing over against the public art of the factories'. He sees a small beginning of that in existing craft cults, but calls for a universalization of this tendency 'as the only preventive of a vast neurosis which will overcome a wholly mechanized and rationalized civilization', and as the means of keeping in man's consciousness the realities of the natural world.

> Only a people serving an apprenticeship to nature can be trusted with machines. Only such a people will so contrive and control those machines that their products are an enhancement of biological needs and not a denial of them. Only such a people will be secure from the debilitating effects of mass production and mass unemployment (miscalled leisure'). Only such a people with sensations still vivid and intelligence ever active, can hope to form a stable and integrated society in the industrial world of the future.

Today such ideas have been taken over by to a great extent the so-called 'counter-culture' which, ironically, does not recognize Read as one of its prophets. But in the late 1940's, and even in the 1950's and 1960's, they were as the emanations of a voice crying in the wilderness, and little heeded by the audiences of academics and dilettanti whom Read addressed. The mood they suggested was one of resignation, with a little hope: a melancholy but not an unusual end for an anarchist. One cannot help contrasting the mood of such passages with that in which *The Philosophy of Anarchism* was brought to an end in the clear-eyed and still optimistic Thirties.

> Faith in the fundamental goodness of man; humility in the presence of natural laws; reason and mutual aid—these are the qualities that can save us. But they must be unified and vitalized by an insurrectionary passion, a flame in which all virtues are tempered and clarified, and brought to their most effective strength.

It is such words that evoke for me the Read I knew. Though in many ways his life was curiously bourgeois, his anarchism had fostered—or perhaps merely refined—a limpidity of nature and outlook such as I have always imagined Kropotkin possessed. Read's occasional lapses into the Tory conformity of his youth one has to balance against the times when he took public stands, particularly in the defence of other people, that might have cost him a great deal materially and in terms of his career. It was after all to Read, and no one else, that George Orwell wrote in 1939 when he thought of setting up an underground press in the event of wartime censorship, and it was in the attic of his house at Beaconsfield that Read allowed a cache of anarchist pamphlets to be hidden for safe keeping during the crisis of the Freedom Press raids of 1945. One lamented at times his inconsistency, but never doubted his sincerity. Whatever romantic fantasy leaping from his Yorkshire childhood induced him to become Sir Herbert, I know that Queen Elizabeth II never dubbed a gentler or more errant knight.

When one tries to sum up his achievements as a social and political writer (and if one leaves out *The Green Child* and the poems of war and anarchism), these seem perhaps less than those in his other fields. He gave a new and attractive expression, a luminous clarification, to the few and simple truths that comprise the anarchist doctrine. He investigated more thoroughly than any of his predecessors the relationship between freedom, art and the artist. He was largely responsible for the libertarian attitudes that dominated so much

English and American poetry during the 1940's. But one cannot say that in any of these fields—except in his work on education through art which we have yet to examine—he was a great originator. His anarchist writings in fact attract one and project most light when they are seen in the context of his entire achievement, in relation to his verse, to his writings on education and revolutionary art, on industry and romantic poetry; then one sees his world-view complete, with the love of freedom its inspiring spirit.

8

Redemptive Education

Of all Read's many books the most influential was undoubtedly *Education Through Art*. Its reputation spread far beyond the cognoscenti of arts and letters who were Read's special audience; it reached and influenced many of the very people he had hoped to convert—the teachers and the instructors in colleges of education. Its influence led to the foundation in Britain of the Society for Education through Art, and a few years later, in 1951, to the establishment under UNESCO auspices of an International Society for Education through Art. Yet the success of *Education Through Art* was largely one of esteem, and to that extent transitory; today one does not hear so much talk among educators as one did a decade ago of the fresh ideas and insights that Read—an outsider—had brought into the field of educational method. This fate is at least in part due to the fact that the ideas Read advanced have been absorbed into educational theory, and have invisibly and often indirectly modified teaching methods and curricula in many parts of the world, while the book itself has receded into the background stance of an educational classic.

At the same time, the total revolution in educational philosophy which Read envisaged has not taken place; education in the arts has been improved, but art itself has not become a central guiding force in education as a whole, and in consequence contemporary schools are no more successful than their predecessors in what Read regarded as the vital task of education, the harmonization of society through the fostering of the natural instinct for order.

What Read wrote as a scenario for revolution had in fact been taken as a text for reform. He was aware of this, and in 'My Anarchism', the essay which in the last year of his life assessed so much of his past, he remarked that few people had realized 'how deeply anarchist in its orientation a work such as *Education Through Art* is and was intended to be', and added that it was 'of course humiliating to have to confess that its success has been in spite of this fact'.

Those who were aware of Read's political inclinations had never any doubt of the anarchist orientation of *Education Through Art*, though few even among them appear to have understood that this book, so scholarly in its presentation and so uninflammatory in its tone of writing, was perhaps Read's most originative contribution, not only to libertarian theory, but also to the strategy of the revolution. For, like the anarcho-syndicalists, Read had devised a method which, if it were successful, would provide not only the model for a free society, but also the means by which that society could be prepared for and in part achieved.

To stress the anarchist quality and intent of *Education Through Art* is not to minimize its importance in giving a practical shape to Read's aesthetic philosophy. It is merely to preserve the balance of a critical view that sees all of Read's works (including *The Green Child* and his poems) as manifestations of a unified activist philosophy developing out of the consciousness that, as Read remarked in one of the later editions of *Art and Industry*,

> The problem of good and bad art, of a right and wrong system of education, of a just and unjust social structure, is in the end one and the same problem.

Anarchists before Read, like the authoritarians who were their political rivals, had always been aware of the importance of education to the achievement of their final aims. They had criticized the authoritarian features of existing schools, and had realized how vital for their own type of society was a form of education that would virtually change the human character as we know it by removing the pattern of constraint and inhibition which characterizes traditional ways of teaching and learning.

But most nineteenth-century anarchists were men in an apocalyptic hurry, convinced that the authoritarian structures of the State and the capitalist order could actually be overthrown in their lifetimes by determined insurrectionary action, and for this reason few of them paid much attention to educational methods; they did not regard them as part of revolutionary tactics but believed society should freely evolve them once it had been liberated. This attitude was one aspect of their resolute anti- Utopianism, of their distrust of social patterns by which the present might constrain the free men of the future.

William Godwin, who never succumbed to the insurrectionary illusion, alone anticipated Read by recognizing the revolutionary potentialities of a libertarian educational system. In *Political Justice* he forecast with impressive accuracy the uses which dictatorial governments would make of a system of national education that in his day was only a possibility for the future, and in *The Enquirer* he sketched out a method of training based on an equal relationship between teacher and student, and on the creation of an atmosphere in which the student's initiative would be stimulated so that he would learn by desire. Between Godwin and Read, however, the copious literature of anarchism is surprisingly lacking in original thought on education. Celebrated libertarian educators like Francisco Ferrer seem—at least by present-day standards—singularly cautious in both ideas and practice, and the few anarchist schools established, mainly in France, by the end of the nineteenth century were more concerned with injecting revolutionary propaganda into their pupils and thus breeding little anarchists than with seeking the kind of training that would lead to personal integration and hence to social harmony.

Even among the celebrated modern progressive educators, like John Dewey, Edmund Holmes and A. S. Neill, who went beyond the doctrinaire anarchists in their theoretical and experimental approaches in the direction of a free education, Read felt the lack of a valid inspiring purpose. It was not enough merely to free the students from constraint; there must be some more positive principle at work if children were to be properly equipped to change not only their lives, but also their society. The difficulty, Read suggested, lay in the fact that, while all progressive educators agreed 'that in a democratic society the purpose of education should be to foster individual growth', few of them in fact understood the actual nature of growth.

> It is usually regarded as a process of gradual physical enlargement, of maturation, accompanied by a corresponding development of various mental faculties such as thought and understanding.

If such a view were correct, then education would be a simple matter of lifting constraints so as to allow natural development to take place. But Read had seen too many maladjusted children emerging from so-called progressive schools as a result of such an undirected approach, and so he adopted a strongly critical view of the simplistic theory of gradual maturation.

> We shall see that this is a wholly inadequate view of what is, in effect, a very complicated adjustment of the subjective feelings and emotions to the objective world, and that the quality of thought and understanding, and all the variations of personality and character, depend to a large extent on the success or precision of this adjustment. It will be my purpose to show that the most important function of education is concerned with this psychological 'orientation', and that for this reason the education of the aesthetic sensibility is of fundamental importance.

Read goes on to state that by this he does not mean the haphazard and rudimentary training in the arts that has formed a part of traditional educational practice. What he intends is to make use of 'all modes of self expression'—visual, verbal and aural—in the service of

> an integral approach to reality which should be called *aesthetic* education—the education of those senses upon which consciousness, and ultimately the intelligence and judgment of the human individual, are based. It is only in so far as these senses are brought into harmonious and habitual relationship with the external world that an integrated personality is built up. Without such integration we get, not only the psychologically unbalanced types familiar to the psychiatrist, but what is even more disastrous from the point of view of the general good, those arbitrary systems of thought, dogmatic or rationalistic in origin, which seek in despite of the natural facts to impose a logical or an intellectual pattern on the world of organic life.

Read's sense of the importance of education, and of art in education, persisted after the writing of *Education Through Art* in 1942 and its publication in 1943 ; it became an enduring belief that took on quasi-religious implications, so that more than twenty years afterwards, when he wrote 'The Truth of a Few Simple Ideas' for the *Saturday Review of Literature* and discussed what faith was possible for those who—drawn to religion—find themselves waiting for a grace that does not come, he declared:

What we need is the peace of mind that comes with self-knowledge, and self-knowledge implies the knowledge of the unconscious processes that cause fear and aggression, envy and crime. This self-knowledge may in rare cases come from inner illumination, and happy are those who are vouchsafed it. For mankind at large it must come from what we call education, ambiguous as the word is—an education that takes into account above all the symbolic needs of the unconscious—therefore, an education through art.

2

As in other fields, the history of Read's publications on education is rendered confusing by reissue, rearrangement and often retitling. They begin in 1931 with *The Place of Art in a University*, a printing of his inaugural lecture as Watson Gordon Professor of Fine Arts at the University of Edinburgh; this was eventually incorporated as an appendix in *Education Through Art*, published in 1943. In 1944 *The Education of Free Men* was issued as a pamphlet by the anarchists of Freedom Press; it reappeared in 1949 as a chapter in a volume of lectures and essays entitled *Education for Peace;* so did *Culture and Education in World Order*, published first as a pamphlet after being read as a paper at a UNESCO meeting. Finally, in 1966, all of *Education for Peace* except the title essay, which had been written to suit the political circumstances of 1948, was republished, together with a number of later essays, in a volume entitled *The Redemption of the Robot*. In addition, passages of *The Contrary Experience*, *Art and Industry* and *The Grass Roots of Art* deal in various ways with the question of an aesthetic education. However, the most important of Read's writings on the subject appear in *Education Through Art* and *The Redemption of the Robot*, and his basic doctrine is found in almost complete form—and with more documentary evidence than elsewhere—in *Education Through Art*.

When Read published the last version of that book in 1956, he remarked that *Education Through Art*, 'which I first thought of as an academic treatise has established itself as a manifesto for much needed educational reforms', and that he had been urged to simplify the text, but had found the task impossible. He was wise to reject this advice, for *Education Through Art*, with its remarkable illustrations of children's art and its formidable battery of psychoanalytical, anthropological and pedagogical authorities, remains far more convincing than the generalized and often facilely optimistic papers which succeeded it and which make up the greater part of *The Redemption of the Robot*.

On the other hand, and perhaps unfortunately, Read was led to attribute at times an almost apocalyptic role to *Education Through Art* which it never in fact assumed. As late as 1967 he could write that 'the progress of this "simple idea" in twenty years has been amazing, and I believe it may yet conquer the world'. If that conquest is indeed to take place, it seems likely to be far ahead, yet in the meantime *Education Through Art* has not merely exerted its modest influence on educational practices, but has certainly changed the character of libertarian theory by making it impossible for anarchists in the future to neglect the role of education as a powerful weapon in the advance towards a free society; a journal like *Anarchy*, founded in Britain during the later 1950's, has devoted far more of its space and attention to an intelligent discussion of the role of education in preparing a change of heart and climate than any anarchist journal published before the appearance of *Education Through Art*.

3

Always scrupulous in acknowledging his intellectual debts, Read began *Education Through Art* by pointing out that he was merely reviving and expanding in the context of a contemporary world a theory of aesthetic education which Plato had adumbrated long ago in *The Republic* and *The Laws*, and which had remained unacknowledged and unutilized by modern educators. Read's attitude towards Plato, like Shelley's, was always somewhat ambiguous, and while, in *Education Through Art*, written for a general readership, he praised him rather uncritically, in *The Education of Free Men*, written in the following year for an audience consisting mainly of anarchists and anarchist sympathizers, he was careful to point out that Plato, like Hegel, was a totalitarian, and that the Platonic insights into education had to be considered on their own merits, apart from the way Plato might have chosen to manipulate them in the interests of an authoritarian political order.

It is in *The Education of Free Men* that Read provides the best summary of Plato's theory, and I quote it at length since it suggests what, from a libertarian point of view, may be the one flaw in Read's own scheme of an aesthetic education—the possibility that it might be seized and perverted to uses for which he did not intend it.

> The claims made by Plato for an aesthetic mode of education are quite simply stated. Indeed, one cannot do better than translate Plato's own words. 'We attach such supreme importance to musical education'—he makes Socrates say in the *Republic* (III, 401–2)— 'because rhythm and harmony sink more deeply into the recesses of the soul, and take more powerful hold of it, bringing gracefulness in their train, and making a man graceful if he be rightly nurtured, but if not, the reverse.' Plato then describes, in what we call considerable psychological detail, the exact effects of rhythm and harmony on the growing mind. But he does not, as is too often assumed in the discussions of his educational theories, ascribe these qualities to music only. He says that the same qualities 'enter largely into painting and all similar workmanship, into weaving and embroidery, into architecture, as well as the whole manufacture of utensils in general, nay, into the constitution of living bodies, and of all plants; for in all these things gracefulness or ungracefulness finds place'. And he adds, for he has always the negative picture in mind, 'The absence of grace, rhythm, and harmony is closely related to an evil style and an evil character.'
>
> There is something at once so simple and so comprehensive about this theory of Plato's that really we need not go beyond it. Music, painting, the making of useful objects, the proportions of the living body and of plants, these will, if made the basis of our educational methods, instill into the child a grace and harmony which will give it, not merely a noble bearing, but also a noble character, not only a graceful body, but also a sober mind.

So far, excellent; the Platonic teaching seems to agree with Read's view, which we have already discussed, of the relationship between the forms and harmonies of nature and those of art; finding its paradigms in nature, art clearly has claims to the power of inducing harmonious feelings in men. It is when Read goes on to discuss Plato's later teachings in *The Laws* that the element of doubt must intervene. In Book II of that work Plato restates what Read calls 'his theory of education through art'.

The theory, I would maintain, is as simple as it is true [Read continues]. It is this: that the aim of education should be to associate feelings of pleasure with what is good and feelings of pain with what is evil. Now such *feelings* are aesthetic—a fact which would have been obvious to the Greeks. This word indicates a relationship which to the Greeks was very real and organic, a property of the physiological reactions which takes place in the process of perception.

Now, says Plato, there exist in the physical universe, which we experience through our senses, certain rhythms, melodies and abstract proportions which when perceived convey to the open mind a sensation of pleasure. For the moment we need not consider *why* these rhythms and proportions exist: they are simply part of the given universe. But if, says Plato, we can associate the concrete sensation of pleasure given by these rhythms and proportions with good, and the concrete sensation of pain given by the opposite qualities of disharmony and ugliness with evil; if we can do this systematically in the early years, while the infant mind is still open to such influences, then we shall have set up an association between natural and spontaneous feelings and graceful or noble behaviour.

Now to me the immediate associations provoked by this passage are those of Pavlovian conditioning, and of a rather unpleasant incident in Aldous Huxley's *Brave New World* in which the behaviour of children is being shaped by electric shocks which create associations of pain. Read obliquely anticipates criticism by admitting almost immediately that Plato is an authoritarian and that his 'criticism of Plato ... would charge him with abstracting from the natural process, making of it a measured pattern, and thereby destroying its quality of spontaneity, which in the human personality is the quality of spiritual freedom'. Yet he does not deal directly with Plato's inclusion of 'the concrete sensation of pain' as part of his teaching process, a factor which might easily be held to justify the standard practices of Victorian public schools in which punishment was used deliberately to further the formation of character; in this sense, Thomas Arnold might have as good a claim to one part of Plato's truth as Read to another.

Read, of course, never adopts the proposal of deliberately associating the sensation of pain with whatever is disharmonious or ugly. He proceeds instead on what he believes to be convincing evidence that the child, especially at the point when he is advancing out of

innocence towards self-consciousness, has a natural openness to aesthetic impulses, and a natural sense of form which he expresses spontaneously in his art and his play, but that during adolescence this
openness, this natural aesthetic awareness, is destroyed by a conceptual form of education and an anti-aesthetic society. Only in the rare
beings who become artists does it linger, and they, like the child, have
access to the archetypal impulses of the collective unconscious which
are common to all men and which make of art, as Read says on the
last page of *The Redemption of the Robot*, 'the only human activity
that can establish a universal order in all we do and make, in thought
and in imagination'.

When we study his evidence we understand more clearly than
ever the importance of *Education Through Art* in the cycle of Read's
works, and the reason why in the latter part of his career education
by means of art—as distinct from education *tout court*—attained
such importance as the uniting element among his many and apparently so diverse activities.

In *The Cult of Sincerity* Read tells how, because of the impossi-
bility of sending valuable British paintings abroad for exhibition, he
became involved during World War II in the task of assembling collections of children's art which the British Council could circulate in
the Allied countries; the first of these collections was exhibited in the
United States in 1941, and Read wrote the catalogue.

While visiting English schools to gather material, Read came to a
village in Cambridgeshire where he was shown a drawing which a
working-class child, aged five, had made at home. (Presumably,
though Read does not say this, she was still too young to attend
school.) She called it 'Snake round the World and a Boat'; the curious
reader will find it as Plate 1B in *Education Through Art*.

> I was deeply moved [Read remembered a quarter of a century later]
> because what this child had drawn was one of the oldest symbols in the
> world—a magic circle divided into segments and known as a mandala,
> the symbol of the self as a psychic unity, a very ancient symbol found in
> Egypt and the Far East and throughout Europe in the Middle Ages.

Read goes on to identify the child's snake with another ancient and
universal symbol, the Uroboros. The child, of course, was unconscious of what she had drawn.

I, with my more sophisticated knowledge, could recognize the drawing as a symbol that was archetypal and universal. Such knowledge on my part had been acquired largely from my reading of Jung's works, but what had been an interesting hypothesis had suddenly become an observed phenomenon, a proof. This child of five had given me something in the nature of an apocalyptic experience.

Later, Read found that the mandala—that symbol whose peculiar significance in relation to his own patterns of thought and even of living we have already observed—occurred frequently in the art of children, as it did in the art of primitive peoples, and in the symbolism of many religions. In other words, he had discovered that in all art which is unselfconscious, images and forms tend to coincide even though they represent widely different places, times and cultures; they also tend to correspond with forms found in nature, so that one can suppose a collective unconscious which is in harmony with nature but out of harmony with the world created by abstract systems and conceptual thought.

This revelation stirred a deep personal emotion in Read not merely because it suggested a way of reforming education that seemed to hold extraordinary promise as a means of liberating perception and reintegrating human life with natural rhythms and natural sociality. It moved him also because it seemed to offer the fulfilment of his inner longings, of the personal myth that had helped to shape his life; this becomes clear when he uses the very phraseology of his own memoirs of a lost and idyllic childhood to describe what he sees happening among other children, and, even more important, the kind of changed society he hopes to achieve as a result of his teachings. First, in *Education Through Art*, he makes the vicarious identification, through the children's art he has been discussing, with the memory image of childhood he had elaborated in *The Innocent Eye*.

> But when we recognize a quality in a child's drawing which we describe as 'naive', we are indicating a certain 'vision' of things which is peculiar to children, and perhaps to certain rare adults who retain the childlike faculty. I have described it elsewhere as 'the innocent eye', by which I mean an eye uninfluenced by rational or deductive thought, an eye that accepts the correlation of incompatibles, the self-sufficiency of the images which come into the mind uncalled and unchecked by observation. What the child writes, or draws, might best be described as an act of poetic intuition, and it is a mystery beyond our logical analysis.

Read is really suggesting that in childhood the aesthetic faculty is universally present, and what he wishes to attain is a society in which that universality is enjoyed by adults also; in other words the society in which every man in his own special way is an artist. The process of individuation which results from advancing maturity of conceptual thought must be balanced by a process of integration which assures that man remains open to the spontaneities of feeling that we call inspiration. This end Read again describes, in *The Redemption of the Robot*, in terms that reflect his passionate yearning for the lost paradise of childhood.

> The most simple, direct and elementary affirmation of life, of the vital principle in our being, requires that we should make the effort to restore the Age of Innocence—or, if we must express the same ideal in a different phraseology, re-establish the human organism's primary unity of motivation and behaviour.

One can relate such statements to *The Green Child*, to *The Innocent Eye*, to *Moon's Farm*, to the many writings in which Read expressed that sense of a special glory in childhood which he shared with Wordsworth and Henry Vaughan, out of whose poem 'The Retreat', with its opening lines,

> Happy those days, when I
> Shin'd in my angel infancy ...

one might take, as a fitting motto for at least one aspect of Read's inner life, the couplet:

> Some men a forward motion love,
> But I by backward steps would move ...

4

In this sense *Education Through Art* represents among Read's works the culmination of a growing preoccupation with education as an element in his own life and therefore in his philosophy of existence. There is indeed no evidence that education greatly concerned him in a theoretical sense until he began to practise it as a professor at Edinburgh, a role he appears to have accepted for its relationship to his critical interests rather than from any feeling that he had a vocation for teaching. His inaugural address at the university suggests that he had devoted proper thought to the best way of presenting the fine arts as a subject, and that he was aware of the possibility of organizing aesthetic education in such a way as to mitigate the ills of vocational and specialist training, which he nevertheless accepts as inevitable in the modern university. There is nothing one might call revolutionary in his proposals, though he makes a few statements that anticipate the aesthetic philosophy he would later elaborate. For example, he claims that in the visual and tactile arts 'you have spiritual sensibility in direct contact with matter', and that in some ill-defined way this makes such arts the only 'adequate and definite embodiment of what might be called public virtue'. He ends with a bold statement of faith that he was often afterwards to re-echo: 'in the end, art should so dominate our lives that we might say: there are no longer works of art, but art only. For art is then a way of life.'

But it is only later in the 1930's that Read begins to think deeply on education in its relation to art, considering, in writing *Art and Industry*, the problems of educating both buyers and designers of industrial products, and then, in *The Annals of Innocence and Experience*, devoting thought to the implications of his own experience in childhood as one of the educated.

His early training, through which he had learnt before the age of ten the author's basic skills of reading and writing, left so little impression on him that he does not even mention in *The Innocent Eye* the village school he attended at Nunnington, and records only vague recollections of family governesses. One may fairly assume that whatever education he then received was applied lightly by people whose lack of pedagogic training proved an advantage in the sense that it left the child mentally and emotionally unscathed. If this had not been so, his experience on entering Crossley's School at the age of ten would not have been so traumatic.

To that agonizing five years of adolescence Read devoted in *Annals of Innocence and Experience* a passage which lays the foundation for his later work on education. As schools of the time went, Crossley's was certainly better than many. It was strict, monastic, austere, reminiscent of Leigh Hunt's descriptions of Christ's Hospital; yet there is no suggestion of the psychological cruelty perpetrated in middle-class preparatory schools which George Orwell recalls in *Such, Such were the Joys*, or of the kind of brutal degeneracy that so often characterized English public-school life at the time of Read's childhood. Read admits that the masters were not tyrannical; he even describes the headmaster as a man of 'noble character and fine discrimination', to whom he owed 'my first perception of literary form and structure'. And yet it was as a result of his five years at Crossley's that Read wrote the paragraph which in germ contains the essence of all his later writings on education:

> From the age of ten or eleven to the age of fifteen or sixteen is the least genial period in the life of a boy. He has lost the innocent eye of childhood and has not yet become an experiencing nature ... It is the stage at which the sensibility of most children is irretrievably destroyed. The sense of sin or guilt is imposed on the innocent impulses, and actions lose their animal playfulness. Relations with other people become conscious instead of instinctive: the child has to begin to plot its way through a maze of unregulated paths. How it can come through this intricate process with an undimmed vision or any trace of its original freshness is still unknown: but at least we are now aware that we are involved in an educational dilemma.

Read was probably saved individually from the destruction of sensibility which he so accurately diagnoses as a general condition by the fact that what education he received from the age of fifteen was most casual; there were the evening classes in which his interest in writing poetry was first aroused by an enthusiastic instructor, and later there was his brief period at Leeds University when, bound by no scholarship obligations to a set course of study, he devoted himself mainly to the voracious plundering of the resources of a richer library than he had ever before encountered.

> Up to the age of fifteen my education had been perhaps more than usually disciplined, but from that age to the present day I have followed my own bent; the order has been of my own devising, and generally the order of my strongest inclinations. This is the kind of education which most authorities find reprehensible.

Yet, though he retained the sensibility that made him into a poet and a finely tuned critic, Read was still conscious of how much he had lost through the withering of innocent impulses, animal playfulness and instinctive relations, and the 'educational dilemma' remained strongly present in his mind. In the latter part of *Annals of Innocence and Experience* he wrote at length in 1939 on the errors of an educational system designed to build character rather than to let personality grow naturally, and his British Council assignment two years later, leading to his apocalyptic encounter with the little girl in a Cambridgeshire village, served merely as the catalyst to precipitate a task that his own past, and his desire to come to terms with the present, made daily more urgent.

5

There is much in *Education Through Art* that appeals—even though Read modestly declines any claim to be an educator—more directly to teachers than to the reader seeking the place of education in Read's wider philosophy. There is much also that has now become obsolete because it relates to an English educational system that now, a quarter of a century later, is radically changed. There are parts, on the other hand, which can still be made the subject of vigorous discussion, such as Read's daring use of psychoanalytical theories in regions of aesthetic motivation where the psychoanalysts themselves rarely dared to treat. This was particularly the case with the Jungian doctrines on which he relied so strongly despite the fact that Jung himself paid little attention to the visual arts, especially their modern manifestations, and with Swiss stolidity had refused to be moved by Read's enthusiasm for the paintings of children.

Yet *Education Through Art* remains the main guide to the practical application of Read's aesthetic philosophy. Aestheticism—that doctrine so long despised for its association with the Yellow Nineties and little better served by Clive Bell's later élitist doctrines of significant form is here transformed from an airy fantasy of art for art's sake into a utilitarian doctrine of art for life's sake, with not too heavy an emphasis on its inevitable corollary, life for art's sake. We are presented with a method that will nurture the child in his spontaneous searchings after form, whether they take the visible shape of artifacts or are manifested less obviously in the spontaneous disciplines of games, and we are presented, too, with a chart by which the vulnerable interlude of adolescence can be navigated, without the destruction of sensibility, by firmly maintaining the primacy of the aesthetic element, so that education through the intelligence never triumphs over that education through the senses which is necessary for man to live in an analogical relation with the harmonies of the natural world. All constraint must be abandoned; all moralisms that stress the concepts of good and bad must be avoided, since such concepts are merely arbitrary. And out of this denial of coercion must emerge the consequences that Read thus lists:

1. The social life developed by children among themselves gives rise to a discipline infinitely nearer to that inner accord which is the mark of adult morality than does any *imposed* system of morality. There exists a clear distinction between a morality of obedience and a morality of attachment or reciprocity, and the latter is the morality of harmonious societies.

2. The adult's relation to the child must always be that of a collaborator, never that of a master.

3. Co-operation is essential to intellectual no less than to moral development. For the laying-down of ready-made rules we must substitute the elaboration of rules through experimentation and reflection, carried out in common, and the school thus becomes a place where co-operative activities are possible. 'Autonomy is a power that can only be conquered from within and then can find scope only inside a scheme of co-operation.'

4. Absolute condemnation of the examination system, 'which helps more than all the family situations put together to reinforce the child's spontaneous egocentrism'.

5. Gradual elimination of every trace of expiation from the idea of punishment, reducing the latter to simple acts of reparation, or simple measures of reciprocity.

6. Reaffirmation of Plato's observation that in the moral as in the intellectual domain we really possess only what we have conquered ourselves.

Such a code of conduct—not in itself strikingly different from that of many free schools established before the writing of *Education Through Art*—could become fully effective, Read suggests, only if every hour of the day were dominated by the aesthetic impulses, by the consciousness of a world of things, perceived through the senses and conveying symbolically and unconsciously to the child's mind the harmonies of nature. It could take form, moreover, only within a framework of intention that had 'no other end than the basic ideals of a libertarian society; the further definition of that society becoming apparent as we progress from stage to stage, for the final stage of the educational system is not the grammar school, or the technical college, or the university, but the Society itself'.

Read foresaw the time when—as already happened for him as a professional intellectual—there would be no real distinction between work and education, since they would flow into each other, and, while *Education Through Art* is dedicated to the protection of the child's sensibility, the later essay which forms the title piece of *The Redemption of the Robot* is concerned with the salvaging of the adult whose sensibility has already been atrophied by a technological civilization. This is to be done by filling his life 'with the motives and disciplines of a creative imagination'—in other words by boldly seizing upon the leisure produced by automation to create a new and popular art in rivalry with the machine, as Read had already suggested in *The Grass Roots of Art*.

As to the ultimate consequences of such a revolution in education, we must turn to Read's more general works on anarchist theory and practice and to the works of such constructive libertarian imaginations as Kropotkin and his disciples, Patrick Geddes and Lewis Mumford. As to its immediate prospects, I can only follow again Read's own obstinately defended example of extensive quotation, and reproduce what seems to me the salient paragraph of the final chapter of *Education Through Art*, with the cautionary note that the word 'libertarian' should be substituted for the word 'democratic', which, Read later admitted, conveyed his meaning inexactly.

> The most a democratic philosopher can hope to do is to inspire a sufficient number of effective fellow-citizens with his idealism to persuade them of the truth of his ideas. The *effective* among his fellow-citizens are those who are organized into corporations or associations for a functional purpose, and in our particular case, this would mean the general body of the teachers and administrators of the educational system. If the *thought* within such a syndicate could change, a change in practice would inevitably follow; and their practice would generally react upon the whole body of the community. How quick and how effective such a gradual process can be, when it is an educational process, was clearly demonstrated by the authoritarian educational policies established in our time in Russia and Germany. Though a revolution may at first be guaranteed only by force, by means of education it can in ten years be

founded on conviction, and in twenty years it will have become an unconscious tradition. It follows that a democratic method of education is the only guarantee of a democratic revolution: indeed, to introduce a democratic method of education is the only necessary revolution.

Here Read quite clearly presents education through art as an anarchist strategy, more effective than outdated strategies of violent insurrection, and to be carried out by those who if they wished could be the most influential workers' syndicate in history, the teachers. In other words, he proposes to equip with an effective method the conception of revolution by change of heart that has haunted for centuries at least one current of the libertarian tradition, that which runs from seventeenth-century Winstanley, through Godwin and Tolstoy, to Gandhi in our own age. Neither the twenty years that Read demanded for his revolution to be complete, nor the ten that he asked for it to be assured, was to be granted. His ideas have suffered the ironic fate of being used in Mithridatic doses to prolong rather than bring an end to the old system, to the continuing educational establishment which, in accordance with Godwin's prophecy, so potently assures, despite all its changes in method, the survival of an authoritarian structure of society.

9

The Stream Returns

I

A mong the 'New Poems' which in 1965 Read included in the final version of *Collected Poems* was a piece entitled 'The Visionary Hermit', dedicated to Michael Tippett. It is not only one of Read's finest poems; it is also an autobiographical document of particular and moving significance when one relates it to Read's return to Yorkshire and to the general circumstances of his final years. It is a poem of resignation, accepting change and age, a poem that mingles a despair for the present with a conditional hope for the future. It begins with stanzas that echo the call of Krishna twenty years before in 'The Contrary Experience'.

> Action I have loved
>   and the taut rein
> the even canter
>   along the open ridge
>
> Now the pace slackens
> listlessly hangs the rein
>   over the arched neck
>   as we descend
>   into the green dale ...

The image of Read's life is before us: the restlessness made him into what the Hindus would call the *karma yogin*—the man aware of spiritual needs, longing for the meditative and the poetic life, and yet irresistibly called, as if by the voice of a god, to the life of action; then the urge slackening and the descent into the green dale that is like the underworld of *The Green Child*, except that its suggestions are not merely of serenity, but of renewal as well.

It is the green dale where, in Read's childhood, the mill of Bransdale operated like a tiny self-sufficient kingdom of industry and
abundance. Now the kingfisher flashing through the stone arches of
the deserted and decaying buildings is the only sign of present life,
though the inscriptions written in Greek on the walls by a Strickland
ancestor, and the sundial he raised, are there to witness the life that
filled this place in a happier age. One is aware of

> the silence substantial
>   the millwheel unmoving
> the granaries empty
>   the wide moors
>   an oasis enfolding
> a mill at the worlds end

This is the mill to which, as Read tells us in the last chapters of
The Contrary Experience, he sometimes thought of returning to
live—a step even farther back into time than his settling at Stonegrave—but he had found the difficulties insuperable, for 'such intentions seem to conflict with inescapable duties', and so he had kept the
place in mind as 'my spiritual hermitage, the "bright jewel" to which
I often retire in moods of despair'. Later in the same chapter he
claims that the return to Bransdale and other parts of the landscape
where he was born, brings 'the release from tensions born in exile',
'the mysterious power of reconciliation, of absolution'.

What Read projects most strongly in the poem is a sense of the
unity of his lost childhood and his present age, of a world that once
seemed limitless and eternal and now has become closed within its
mortal circle.

> The trees have not moved in their stations
>   time has become finite
> I stare at the twisted tree
>   my life

In the last part of 'The Visionary Hermit' Read tells of his rejection of 'artifice' and 'the elegant rhythm', the art of a past to which
men no longer listen, and the familiar romantic plea emerges as he
asks what has become the vital question of his last years:

> Will men listen to a new utterance
> the rhythm of the heart
> the true voice of feeling?

It is characteristic of Read, of his feeling of the rightness of things, his knowledge that through the senses rather than the intellect lies the way to truth, that he should state his ultimate vision not in conceptual or mystical terms, but in images as concrete as Blake's.

> Not until the miller returns to the mill
> and the waters grind the corn
> for farms reclaimed from the moor

> Not until the cry of the gull
> driven in from the sea
> answers in the green dale
> the human ululation

One is reminded of the 'Song for the Spanish Anarchists', in which, without reciting a single anarchist dogma, the poet implants in our inner eye a more vivid image of what anarchism really means than the whole of *Poetry and Anarchism* had done. For here, in these two verses, is compressed the sum of Read's aesthetic philosophy, with its social and economic implications. Man must reconcile again the human and the natural rhythms of existence, so that his voice can answer back to 'the cry of the gull', and this can happen only when the drift towards the mechanized society, which Read had denounced in the later chapters of *The Contrary Experience*, is reversed, when men realize the perils of an alienation from true values which the industrial and technological revolutions between them have fostered, when Kropotkin's vision of work and education, industry and agriculture, town and country, all integrated into a single organic continuum, would be realized, and the dissolution of the cities would bring life to the deserted land.

There are many strains of sorrow implied in such a poem, for reconciliation, in so far as Read achieved it by returning to the source of his life, did not come without painful recognitions. Even in the Vale of York and the dales that radiated from it, the world of childhood had not survived as Read remembered it; only the moors, never inhabited by other beings than the black-faced sheep and the wild birds and foxes, were unchanged. From the dales a way of life had departed, and its habitations had become ruins. This fact assumed in Read's mind a symbolic intensity, so that in his seventies it was in terms of a renewal of the peasant's pre-mechanical world that he saw man's only salvation. This led him to find hope in China, which he visited when the agricultural communes were being dramatically emphasized; he could be persuaded that what he saw was a 'communism swayed by a peasantry'.

Yet even here, in personal terms, his final years produced disappointment. If he could suggest to Edward Dahlberg in 1949, just after he had moved to Stonegrave, that cultivating the seven acres of land belonging to his house would be a gesture in the direction of practical anarchism, he was soon to be disillusioned, like most other intellectuals who hope to give a Tolstoyan twist to their lives. Just before Read moved to Stonegrave I had gone to Canada, and attempted on Vancouver Island to combine writing with a kind of second-hand pioneering involving the reclamation and cultivation of old farmland to which the forest had begun to return. Read was fascinated by the endeavour ('I find your experiment in living of great interest and you need not be afraid of boring me with details. *Walden* was always one of my favourite books') and I was delighted to have a responsive reader to whom I could cry out of that intellectual desert. But at the same time as Read encouraged me in what also turned out to be a disastrous venture, he admitted the failure of his own experiment. 'The economics of small holdings is, I find, very deceptive,' he wrote in the spring of 1950, and in November the same year it was obvious that he had given up the hope of reviving even in token fashion the farming tradition of his ancestors (though he still hoped that one of his sons might make the return).

Meanwhile I continue to learn bitter lessons here [he said]. Feeding stuffs, for example, are so expensive that the keeping of poultry and pigs has become an extremely extravagant hobby. To grow the food requires labour and equipment which cannot be obtained. Even the farmers, who can bring up their pullets on stubble, complain that it is a worthless sideline. Mechanization has taken command to such a degree that a smallholder must mechanize or die, and to mechanize he must cease to be a smallholder. It is very depressing, because I had had the illusion that one could still grow the basic necessities of life on five or six acres of land. Perhaps one could by becoming a whole-time slave to the land, but it is no longer to be done as a sideline.

Yet Read believed with a growing intensity in the validity of the country life that he had seen almost pass away. He could tell himself in—*The Contrary Experience*—that to succumb to the sense of the past 'is sentimental, and can be destructive of a proper sense of the present, of reality', and he could stoically admit in the same book that 'The past has vanished, and we are the last outpost of a civilization in retreat.' But he could speculate even later, in *The Cult of Sincerity*, that 'if I had my life over again I would return to the dogs and horses that waited on my father and forefathers for uncounted generations', and could add, with total seriousness and sincerity:

> Sooner or later the dogs and the horses will return, as in Edwin Muir's impressive poem; either they will return, restoring the ceremonies of innocence, or the civilization so much admired by Sir Charles Snow will blow itself up or die of dearth. It is not a question of sentimentality or nostalgia. Life is not mechanic: it is dogs and horses, roots and branches, seeds, seminal fluids, growth and form. It is these things, basically, and above these are 'the lovers and the dancers', the celebrants of a culture.

It is in the ending of the same essay (What is There Left to say?') that Read reveals the greatest sorrow of his last years. It was a sorrow like that of Tolstoy who came to know that the faith in human love as a projection of the Divine love on which he had built his view of existence had been betrayed by the failings of his own followers: perhaps even—he realized on that grotesque and tragic flight to death at Astapovo Station—by himself. It was a sorrow like that which Gandhi felt, when he realized, in the bloodsoaked villages of Bengal and Bihar during the months before Indian independence, that the people whom he had led successfully in the great non-violent action against the British had turned their violence upon each other. Read's sorrow lay in the conviction, certainly by the end of the 1950's, that the modern movement in the visual arts, in which he had placed such faith as a manifestation of values contrary to those of the contemporary technological order, had itself become infected by the sicknesses of alienation and disintegration that had already, in his view, destroyed the modern movement in poetry. As Read's essay draws to an end, he remarks that he has just received the latest issue of the *Evergreen Review*:

> an incongruously-named periodical, for it is as parched and
> crinkled as the leaf in Eugenio Montale's poem:
> > ... l'incartocciarsi della foglia
> > riarsa ...
>
> But these parched and crinkled leaves are the laurels of the beatniks and
> the drug-addicts, of the 'pop'-artists and the Californian buddhists, and
> it is towards the last phase of disintegration that the course of our
> despairing poets and painters is now set. I see no other path in Califor-
> nia, or in Paris or in London.

Read was not a pessimist, any more than he was an optimist in the ordinary facile sense. I imagine, since like Camus he did not call himself an existentialist, he would have accepted the title of Stoic; he defined his later philosophical poems, *Moon's Farm* and 'The Gold Disc', as 'stoical rather than defiant'. Certainly he never acquired religious faith, though he remained open to it.

> I cannot bear witness to the presence of God either in Buber's sense or in
> Jung's sense, and yet I am not a materialist. All my life I have found more
> sustenance in the work of those who bear witness to the reality of a liv-
> ing God than in the work of those who deny God. ... In that state of sus-
> pense, 'waiting on God', I live and shall probably die.

It was not a state of mind that would admit despair, though it could not avoid sorrow and disappointment. Read was still open in 1959 to the hope that China could offer, though later he recognized the different face to Maoism which the shifts of policy in the 1960's revealed. He could go in the last months of his life to Cuba, stirred by the challenge of a new environment, and there, disregarding the possible susceptibilities of his Castroist hosts, he could devote his last public address to a clear-minded statement on 'The problem of Internationalism in Art'. As he saw it, the problem lay in internationalism itself.

> Art is no longer the expression of a personal vision or of a subjective
> experience; it becomes an objective record of contemporary events. Such
> an art is also international in its scope and uniform in its style.

Essentially, he could see no difference in this respect between the capitalist and communist worlds; in the first, art was turned into a commodity, in the second into a means of propaganda, but both had
intensified the artist's sense of alienation. Both also had negated the
essential *universality* of art, which is something quite different from
internationalism.

> Universality is a human quality; internationalism is a political concept.
> Universality is a question of *depth*—of the depth of the artist's vision and
> sympathy. Internationalism is a question of *width*—of the extent of the
> audience to which the artist is expected to appeal.

Read does not deny the intimate links that exist between art and the
economic foundations of the society in which it is practised. Indeed,
he believes that the artist who tries to detach himself from these foundations invites defeat. But this does not mean that a political domi-
nation of art is possible.

> The danger is that we attempt to reverse the organic process in which the
> work of art originates; we begin with a social or 'mass' concept of art and
> try to impose it on the aberrant personality of the artist.

In other works of these last months of his life—such as 'The
Necessity of Art' which was published in 1969 in the UNESCO symposium, *The Arts and Man*, and 'The Limits of Permissiveness in Art'
which appeared in the *Malahat Review* commemorative issue of the
same year—Read elaborated on his concern with what he called the
'contemporary nihilism' in the arts, arguing that such movements as
Pop Art are merely disintegrative because they 'evade the central
issue in art, which is the creation of a form, the ability to "idealize
and to unite"'. Further, Read adds in 'The Limits of Permissiveness in
Art':

> Clarity, which I suggested as another essential quality in the work of art,
> is deliberately sacrificed. Again it is not a question of upholding tradi-
> tional values against revolutionary values: it is a question of communi-
> cation, of a dialogue between artist and spectator. If instead of a symbol
> of feeling we are offered a symbol of nescience, of 'not knowing', then we
> can only turn away in indifference.

He ends with these significant and true remarks, in which he marks out quite clearly the limits that revolution, even in the arts, must set for itself, and incidentally gives expression to that classicist strain which had survived under the surface of his romantic and surrealist enthusiasms.

> Contemporary nihilism in art is simply a denial of art itself, a rejection of its social function. The refusal to recognize the limits of art is the reason why as critics we must withhold our approval from all those manifestations of permissiveness characterized by incoherence, insensibility, brutality and ironic detachment. The exercise of such judgment calls for the utmost critical rectitude—for the maintenance of the supremacy of aesthetic criteria—if we are not to fall into old errors of judging art according to values that belong to another sphere of life—religious, moral, hedonistic or technological. What we seek is 'a renaissance beyond the limits of nihilism'. We cannot yet determine the outlines of such a renaissance, but we know that they must remain within the sphere of art.

But he felt at this point that such a renaissance was conditional on deep social changes.

> The art of the future? [he asked in Havana]. Our private, fragmented art will continue for many years, but its internationality will be no compensation for the loss of a universal art. In my optimistic moments I see a human race with a regenerated sensibility, using its power and vision to create a new art, an art as universal as the art of visual delight and serene form, of human measure and spiritual significance. But before this can happen we must forget the past and reform the present. There can be no great art in the future until we have achieved social unity and social justice, and until a free and joyous activity has replaced the devitalizing tyranny of the machine.

2

It is an earnest of Read's largeness of mind and of moral texture that he could admit frankly that the modern movement in art had not continued in the triumphal progress he had once foreseen; that, like other manifestations of modern life, it had largely been diverted into the lifeless channels of machine culture. At the same time, he did not admit that the modern movement had failed. Its achievements remained as artifacts in their objective and physical solidity, and the influence they would eventually have, like the artifacts from other cultures, was incalculable. The men who created them had expanded the human consciousness in an infinity of directions, and the eventual result could not be determined; certainly the movement could not be written off merely because its impetus had declined, perhaps only temporarily.

In the same way, in drawing attention to what I have called the sorrow that weighed upon Read's later years, I do not suggest that we must see the end of his life as burdened with a consciousness of failure. There is a subjective sense in which every creative man regards himself as a failure, for what is achieved will always seem somewhat less than what might have been. But in the larger, more objective sense we cannot see Read's final years as in any way less productive or significant than his earlier periods.

His last decade was one of exceptional literary industry, and while some of the books he prepared were collections and re-arrangements of formerly published material, the amount of fresh writing of a remarkable quality from the last ten years is still astonishing. There are 'Vocal Avowals' and a dozen more new poems; there are the eight essays which form the final section of *The Contrary Experience*, and the gently reflective essays on his past and his friends which formed his last book, *The Cult of Sincerity*. There is that treatise crucial in defining his aesthetic philosophy, *The Forms of Things Unknown*; there are the Concise Histories of modern painting and modern sculpture and the fine books on Henry Moore and Hans Arp. Three volumes of essays and lectures were gathered from the occasional work of this period: *Letter to a Young Painter* (1962), *The Origins of Form in Art* (1965) and *Art and Alienation* (1967). Finally, there is that curious volume *Truth is More Sacred*—in which reason strives with rage as Read disputes with the tempestuous Edward Dahlberg regarding the great literary figures of the century, from James to Lawrence and from Eliot to Joyce. It is a remarkable record of achievement in a decade whose early years were still much fragmented by travel 'Nothing will ever stop your ceaseless movement over the world, I suppose,' Eliot commented in

1963), and whose later years were largely shadowed by the mortal sickness that first attacked him in 1964, a stoically accepted threat which seems to have stimulated Read to work as hard as time and energy allowed to put his works in order before the hour of death.

Read died believing that his philosophy of life—the aesthetic philosophy—was valid, and that some day, if the world was not destroyed by technicians, mankind would come to live by it, through true education and a life in which work and art would become indistinguishable. He never denied his anarchist convictions, and though he became reconciled to thinking of the free society as a point on a distant horizon, he refused, in republishing his early libertarian writings, 'to give an air of caution to the impetuous voice of youth. Indeed, I now envy those generous feelings.' He believed in the great art of his time, and he continued to write poetry as he felt it should be written, in spite of his lack of popularity as a poet. He realized the hollowness of much of the popularity he did enjoy in his later years, and he recognized that his works most likely to survive were precisely those least noticed in his time—the poems, the autobiographies, *The Green Child*.

In a historical sense, I believe that Read will also retain a unique place as an interpreter of his time, for few writers have probed so deeply and so intelligently into the nature of our culture, and none has brought together so suggestively the insights of modern philosophers and critics, poets and artists, psychologists and social scientists, as Read did in the varied corpus of his work. In the visual arts his criticism was illuminated by a peculiar intensity of empathic understanding and an unrivalled breadth of curiosity. In literature, his criticism was limited by the personal intensity of his interests, but he remains one of the best writers on romanticism in English poetry. He was an able popularizer, and not ashamed of the role, but he also contributed profound philosophic insights into the problems of aesthetics, and if he left no system of thought the omission was as deliberate as the lack of elaborate structure in his writings. The word *deliberate*, indeed, can be applied to him in more than one sense, for it is in the studied nature of his casualness in writing, in the unsought perfection of phrase and image, that one sees his classicism and his romanticism coming together. In his writing, spontaneity was controlled by a discipline that had become unconscious, and here lay the secret of Read's charm and clarity as a writer, which alone will ensure that, like Bagehot whom he so much admired, he is likely to be read long after the immediate occasions of his writing have passed away.

I have no inclination to rank Read among the writers of his time; the last thing he would have desired would be such evaluation, for a poet, to him, was a poet true to himself, true to his vision. In this sense Read stands among his peers and contemporaries, a poet true also to his time and hence one of its authentic seers.

Bibliography

Note: Later editions are shown only when they are also revised editions.

1. BOOKS BY HERBERT READ

Ambush. London, Faber & Faber, 1930.

Anarchy and Order: Essays in Politics. London, Faber & Faber, 1945.

The Anatomy of Art. An Introduction to the Problems of Art and Aesthetics. New York, Dodd, Mead, 1932. (This book is identical with *The Meaning of Art*, London, 1931.)

Annals of Innocence and Experience. London, Faber & Faber, 1940. Revised edition, 1946.

Aristotle's Mother: An Imaginary Conversation. North Harrow, Philip Ward, 1961.

Arp. London, Thames & Hudson, 1968. New York, Praeger, 1969.

Art and Alienation: The Role of the Artist in Society. London, Thames & Hudson, 1967. New York, Horizon Press, 1967.

Art and Industry: The Principles of Industrial Design. London, Faber & Faber, 1934. Revised editions, 1944, 1953, 1956, 1966. New York, Horizon Press, 1954 (based on 1953 English edition).

Art and Society. London, Heinemann, 1937. Revised editions (Faber & Faber), 1945, 1956, 1967. New York, Macmillan, 1937.

Art and the Evolution of Man: Lecture delivered at Conway Hall, London, on April 10th, 1951. London, Freedom Press, 1951.

Art Now: An Introduction to the Theory of Modern Painting and Sculpture. London, Faber & Faber, 1933. Revised editions, 1936, 1948, 1960, 1968. New York, Harcourt Brace, 1937.

The Art of Sculpture. London, Faber & Faber, 1956. New York, Pantheon Books, 1956.

Auguries of Life and Death. Privately printed, 1919.

Ben Nicholson: Paintings, Reliefs, Drawings. (Introduced by Herbert Read.) London, Lund, Humphries, 1948.

Byron. London and New York, published for the British Council by
    Longmans, Green, 1951.

A Coat of Many Colours: Occasional Essays. London, Routledge, 1945.
    Revised edition, 1956. New York, Horizon Press, 1956.
Coleridge as Critic. London, Faber & Faber, 1949.
Collected Essays in Literary Criticism. London, Faber & Faber, 1938.
    Collected Poems, 1913–25. London, Faber & Gwyer, 1926.
Collected Poems. London, Faber & Faber, 1946. Revised editions, 1953
    1966. Norfolk, Conn., 1953. Revised edition (New York, Horizon
    Press), 1966.
A Concise History of Modern Painting. London, Thames & Hudson, 1959.
    New York, Praeger, 1959.
A Concise History of Modern Sculpture. London, Thames & Hudson,
    1964. New York, Praeger, 1964.
Contemporary British Art. Harmondsworth, Penguin Books, 1951.
    Revised editions, 1954, 1961.
The Contrary Experience: Autobiographies. London, Faber & Faber, 1963.
    New York, Horizon Press, 1963.
The Cult of Sincerity. London, Faber & Faber, 1968.
Culture and Education in World Order. New York, Museum of Modern
    Art, 1948.

Design and Tradition. Hemingford Grey, Vine Press, 1962.

Eclogues: A Book of Poems. London, C. W. Beaumont, 1919.
Education for Peace. New York, Scribner, 1949. London, Routledge &
    Kegan Paul, 1950.
The Education of Free Men. London, Freedom Press, 1944.
Education Through Art. London, Faber & Faber, 1943. Revised edition,
    1958. New York, Pantheon Books, n.d.
The End of a War. London, Faber & Faber, 1933.
*English Pottery: its Development from Early Times to the End of the
    Eighteenth Century*. (By Bernard Rackham and Herbert Edward Read.)
    London, Ernest Benn, 1924.
English Prose Style. London, G. Bell, 1928. Revised editions, 1942, 1952.
    New York, H. Holt, 1928.
English Stained Glass. London and New York, G. P. Putnam's Sons, 1926.
The English Vision: An Anthology. London, Eyre & Spottiswode, 1933.

Essential Communism. London, S. Nott, 1935.
Existentialism, Marxism and Anarchism. London, Freedom Press, 1949.

Form in Modern Poetry. London, Sliced & Ward, 1932. Revised edition, London, Vision, 1948.
The Forms of Things Unknown: Essays towards an Aesthetic Philosophy. London, Faber & Faber, 1960. New York, Horizon Press, 1960.
Freedom: Is it a crime? London, Freedom Press, 1945.
The Future of Industrial Design. London, Design & Industries Association, 1946.

Gauguin (1848–1903). London, Faber & Faber, 1949. New York, Pitman, 1951.
The Grass Roots of Art. New York, Wittenborn, 1947. London, Drummond, 1947. Revised edition, London, Faber & Faber, and New York, Wittenborn, 1955.
The Green Child: A Romance. London, Heinemann, 1935. New York, New Directions, 1948.

Henry Moore, Sculptor: an Appreciation. London, Zwemmer, 1934.
Henry Moore, A Study of His Life and Work. London, Thames & Hudson, 1965. New York, Praeger, 1966.
High Noon and Darkest Night. Middletown, Conn., Centre for Advanced Studies, Wesleyan University, 1965.

Icon and Idea: The Function of Art in the Development of Human Consciousness. London, Faber & Faber, 1955. Cambridge, Harvard University Press, 1955.
In Defence of Shelley and Other Essays. London, Heinemann, 1936.
The Innocent Eye. London, Faber & Faber, 1933.
The Innocent Eye. New York, Holt, 1947. (This volume is actually identical with the English *Annals of Innocence and Experience*.)
In Retreat. London, L. and Virginia Woolf, 1925.

Julien Benda and the New Humanism. Seattle, University of Washington, 1930.

Kandinsky (1866–1944). London, Faber & Faber, 1959. New York, G. Wittenborn, 1959.

Klee (1879–1940). London, Faber & Faber, 1948. New York, Pitman, 1949.

The Knapsack: A Pocket-Book of Prose and Verse. London, G. Routledge, 1939.

Kropotkin: Selections from his Writings. London, Freedom Press, 1942.

A *Letter to a Young Painter.* London, Thames and Hudson, 1962. New York, Horizon Press, 1962.

The London Book of English Prose. (Selected and ordered by Herbert Read and Bonamy Dobrée) London, Eyre & Spottiswoode, 1931. New York, Macmillan, 1949.

The London Book of English Verse. (Selected by Herbert Read and Bonamy Dobrée.) London, Eyre & Spottiswoode, 1949. New York, Macmillan, 1952.

Lord Byron at the Opera: A Play for Broadcasting. North Harrow, Philip Ward, 1963.

Lynn Chadwick. Amriswill, Bodensee-Verlag, 1958.

The Meaning of Art. London, Faber & Faber, 1931. Revised editions, 1936, 1951.

Moon's Farm and Poems Mostly Elegiac. London, Faber & Faber, 1955. New York, Horizon Press, 1956.

Mutations of the Phoenix. Richmond, L. and Virginia Woolf, 1923.

Naked Warriors. London, Art and Letters, 1919.

The Nature of Literature. New York, Horizon Press, 1956. (This book is identical with *Collected Essays in Literary Criticism.)*

Notes on Language aad Style by T. E. Hulme. (Edited by Herbert Read.) Seattle, University of Washington, 1929.

The Origins of Form in Art. London, Thames & Hudson, 1965. New York, Horizon Press, 1965.

The Parliament of Women: A Drama in Three Acts. Huntingdon, Vine Press, 1960.

Paul Nash. Harmondsworth, Penguin Books, 1944.

Paul Nash—Contemporary British Painters 1. London, Soho Gallery Limited, 1937.

Phases of English Poetry. London, L. and Virginia Woolf, 1928. Revised edition (Faber & Faber), 1950. New York, Harcourt Brace, 1929.

The Philosophy of Anarchism. London, Freedom Press, 1940.

The Philosophy of Modern Art: Collected Essays. London, Faber & Faber, 1952. New York, Horizon Press, 1953.

The Place of Art in a University. Edinburgh and London, Oliver & Boyd, 1931.

Poems, 1914–1934. London, Faber & Faber, 1935. New York, Harcourt Brace, 1935.

Poetry and Anarchism. London, Faber & Faber, 1938.

Poetry and Experience. London, Vision, 1967.

The Politics of the Unpolitical. London, Routledge, 1953.

The Psychopathology of Reaction in the Arts. London, Institute of Contemporary Arts [1956].

Reason and Romanticism. London, Faber & Gwyer, 1926. New York, Russell & Russell, 1963.

The Redemption of the Robot: My Encounter with Education through Art. New York, Trident Press, 1966. London, Faber & Faber, 1970.

Selected Writings: Poetry and Criticism. (With a foreword by Allen Tate.) London, Faber & Faber, 1963.

The Sense of Glory: Essays in Criticism. Cambridge, University Press, 1929. Freeport, N.Y., Books for Libraries Press, 1967.

The Significance of Children's Art. Vancouver, University of British Columbia, 1957.

Songs of Chaos. London, Elkin Mathews, 1915.

Speculations: Essays on Humanism and the Philosophy of Art by T. E. Hulme. (Edited by Herbert Read.) London, Kegan Paul, 1924. New York, Humanities Press, 1965.

Staffordshire Pottery Figures. London, Duckworth, 1929.

The Styles of European Art. (Introduced and edited by Herbert Read.) London, Thames & Hudson, 1965.

Surrealism. (Edited with an introduction by Herbert Read.) London, Faber & Faber, 1936.

The Tenth Muse: Essays in Criticism. London, Routledge & Kegan Paul, 1957. New York, Horizon Press, 1958.

Thirty-five Poems. London, Faber & Faber, 1940.

This Way Delight: A Book of Poetry for the Young. (Selected and introduced by Herbert Read.) New York, Pantheon, 1956. London, Faber & Faber, 1957.

To Hell with Culture. London, Kegan Paul, 1941.

To Hell with Culture, and Other Essays in Art and Society. (Contains the original *To Hell with Culture, The Politics of the Unpolitical,* and other previously uncollected essays.) London, Routledge & Kegan Paul, 1963. New York, Schocken Books, 1963.

Truth is More Sacred. (A critical exchange between Edward Dahlberg and Herbert Read.) New York, Horizon Press, 1961. London, Routledge & Kegan Paul, 1961.

The True Voice of Feeling: Studies in English Romantic Poetry. London, Faber & Faber, 1953. New York, Pantheon Books, 1953.

Vocal Avowals. St. Gallen, Tschudy-Verlag, 1962.

Wordsworth. London, Jonathan Cape, 1930. New York, J. Cape & H. Smith, 1931.

A World Within a War. London, Faber & Faber, 1944. New York, Harcourt, Brace, 1945.

Youth and Leisure. Peterborough, Peterborough Education Board 1947.

2. BOOKS ABOUT HERBERT READ

Herbert Read: An Introduction to his Work by Various Hands. Edited by Henry Treece. London, Faber & Faber, 1944.

Francis Berry. *Herbert Read.* London, New York and Toronto, published for the British Council and the National Book League by Longmans Green, 1953.

Herbert Read: A Memorial Symposium. Edited by Robin Skelton. London, Methuen, 1970. New York, Barnes & Noble, 1970. (First issued as the January 1969 number of *The Malahat Review,* published by the University of Victoria; Victoria, British Columbia.)

PARTICIPATORY DEMOCRACY: Prospects for Democratizing Democracy

Dimitrios Roussopoulos, with C. George Benello

A completely revised edition of the classic and widely consulted 1970 version

First published as a testament to the legacy of the concept made popular by the New Left of the 1960s, and with the perspective of the intervening decades, this book opens up the way for re-examining just what is involved in democratizing democracy. With its emphasis on citizen participation, here, presented in one volume are the best arguments for participatory democracy written by some of the most relevant contributors to the debate, both in an historic, and in a contemporary, sense.

This wide-ranging collection probes the historical roots of participatory democracy in our political culture, analyzes its application to the problems of modern society, and explores the possible forms it might take on every level of society from the work place, to the community, to the nation at large. Part II, "The Politics of Participatory Democracy," covers Porto Alegre, Montreal, the new Urban ecology, and direct democracy.

Contains an essay by George Woodcock entitled "Democracy, Heretical and Radical."

> "The book is, by all odds, the most encompassing one so far in revealing the practical actual subversions that the New Left wishes to visit upon us."
> —*Washington Post*

Apart from the editors, contributors include: Murray Bookchin, Don Calhoun, Stewart Perry, Rosabeth Moss Kanter, James Gillespie, Gerry Hunnius, John McEwan, Arthur Chickering, Christian Bay, Martin Oppenheimer, Colin Ward, Sergio Baierle, Anne Latendresse, Bartha Rodin, and C.L.R. James.

DIMITRIOS ROUSSOPOULOS was a prominent New Left activist in the 1960s, locally and internationally. He continues to write and edit on major issues while being a committed activist testing theory with practice. He is the author and/or editor of some eighteen books, the most recent being *Faith in Faithlessness: An Anthology of Atheism* (2008).

2004: 380 pages
Paperback ISBN: 1-55164-224-7 $24.99
Hardcover ISBN: 1-55164-225-5 $53.99

ALSO by GEORGE WOODCOCK

DAWN AND THE DARKEST HOUR: A Study of Aldous Huxley

Dawn and the Darkest Hour explores the famously complex life and career of Aldous Huxley. A brilliant and satirical novelist of ideas; a popular journalist and essayist on scientific and political subjects; a prophet of the future; a pioneer of psychedelic experimentation: a man plagued by excessive intellectual curiosity and a withdrawn melancholic nature. In the dramatic range of his characters and the encyclopedic quality of his thought, Huxley expressed some of the most interesting and disturbing commentary about the condition of human beings and their relationship to society.

2006: 256 pages, paper 1-55164-284-0 $24.99 ✳cloth 1-55164-285-9 $53.99

CRYSTAL SPIRIT: A Study of George Orwell

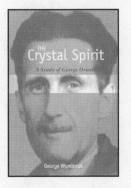

A close friend and colleague during the last decade of this remarkable writer's life, Woodcock was thereby uniquely qualified to delve into the complex personal history of George Orwell. Interwoven with his own memories, the letters which Orwell wrote to him, and the published and unpublished recollections of other people who knew him, all against the political and literary background of Orwell's work, this ground-breaking intellectual biography is a general critique that brilliantly traces the evolution of an original writer in his most productive years.

Like Orwell, Woodcock is fair-minded, warm-hearted and sensitive; the best criticism of Orwell's corpus that I have read. —*The Sunday Times*, London

2005: 366 pages, paper 1-55164-268-9 $24.99 ✳cloth 1-55164-269-7 $53.99

MARVELLOUS CENTURY: Archaic Man and the Awakening of Reason

The sixth century was an era of personalities and uprisings; it was the era of prose re-awakenings and the exploration of rational thought. George Woodcock's *The Marvellous Century*, brings the era and the personalities to life as he explores the literature, the philosophy, the politics, the sciences.

Filled with characters, events, romance, and intrigue, here is a fascinating journey that allows us to experience the beauty, savagery and all-encompassing impact of the 6th century B.C., a century characterized by a cluster of events that changed irrevocably the way humans looked upon the universe and even upon themselves.

2005: 256 pages, paper 1-55164-266-2 $24.99 ✳cloth 1-55164-267-0 $53.99

ALSO by GEORGE WOODCOCK

MALCOLM LOWRY: The Man And His Work

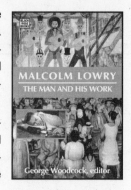

With compassion, honesty, and impressive research, George Woodcock presents Malcolm Lowry: the man and his works. This compelling collection of essays provides considerable insight into the challenge Lowry set for himself as an artist and the agonies he endured as he wrestled with the problems of integration in his work and life.

The first section of the book, *The Works*, considers all of Lowry's fiction and the evolution of his style as he struggled to find the form appropriate to a new approach to reality. The influences which shaped his world and gave form to his work are considered in the second section, *The Man and the Sources*. From Lowry's love of jazz and the cinema, to the books he read, Woodcock follows Lowry's life from London, to Paris, to New York, Mexico and Canada. Lowry's direct experiences had a profound effect on the structure and content of his writing. The essays on these facets of the man, together with his letters and poems, and the recollections of personal friends, reveal a great deal about the nature of Lowry's creativity.

Contributors include: Robert B. Heilman, Anthony R. Kilgallin, George Woodcock, Geoffrey Durrant, David Benham, Matthew Corrigan, Conrad Aiken, Hilda Thomas, Downif Kirk, W.H. New, Perle Epstein, William McConnell, and Maurice J. Carey.

2007: 224 pages, paper 978-1-55164-302-1 $19.99 ✱cloth 978-1-55164-303-8 $48.99

---

send for a free catalogue of all our titles

BLACK ROSE BOOKS

C.P. 1258, Succ. Place du Parc
Montréal, Québec
H2X 4A7 Canada

or visit our website at http://www.blackrosebooks.net

to order books

In Canada: (phone) 1-800-565-9523 (fax) 1-800-221-9985
email: utpbooks@utpress.utoronto.ca

In United States: (phone) 1-800-283-3572 (fax) 1-800-351-5073

In UK & Europe: (phone) London 44 (0)20 8986-4854 (fax) 44 (0)20 8533-5821
email: order@centralbooks.com

Printed by the workers of

MARQUIS IMPRIMEUR INC.

for Black Rose Books

Marquis Book Printing Inc.

Québec, Canada
2008